JUSTICE DIVIDED

A Judicial History of Sebastian County

JUDGE JIM SPEARS

Copyright © 2022 Jim Spears

All rights reserved. No part of this book may be reproduced or transmitted in any form or by any means, electronic or mechanical, including photocopying, or within any commercial information retrieval and storage system, without permission in writing from the author.

Library of Congress Control Number: 2022946190

ISBN: 978-0-9885891-4-8 (soft cover)

ISBN: 978-0-9885891-5-5 (hardcover)

Edited by David Ware

Cover Art by Joyce Faulkner

Printed in the United States.

Red Engine Press

Table of Contents

1. In the Beginning......1
2. Division, Destruction, and Rebirth......19
3. Toward a New State......24
4. Return of the Democrats......57
5. A Native Takes Over......75
6. A New Century—and a New Court......93
7. A New Courthouse and a New Era......141
8. The Winds of Change......175
9. New Faces, a New District, and a New Judicial Article......225
10. Conclusion......265
11. Sources......267

Introduction

This project has been underway for over forty years. It began with seeing pictures of the Chancery judges who served the tenth district in Judge Kimbrough's office when I was a brand-new attorney. There were no pictures of the circuit judges, and I had no idea who they might have been. Curious, I began research. It was not yet an obsession but over the years it became that. I wanted pictures of all the circuit judges as well. Who were they? I started to get serious about this after I was elected chancery judge in 1992. Hours in the library and running down family in attempts to find these men from the past. As I learned more the idea of doing a book crystallized. More work. Learning rumors about transgressions and long-ago political scandals made it fun. In the mid 1990s it came together in a manuscript. So what! No one was interested but my friends Tom Wing and Billy Higgins, both noted historians felt it had merit. There was an exhibit at the Fort Smith Museum of History with the photographs I had collected entitled *The Picture of Justice*. It had a good reception. But no one was interested in publishing a book by judge in Fort Smith.

Then I met Joyce and John Faulkner. They had retired to Fort Smith and had started a publishing company, Red Engine Press. This must have been in 2015. They first published my first book, *Yearning to be Free*, about my experience as the public defender for the Cuban refugees at Fort Chaffee in 1980-82. When we were working on *Justice Divided*, my friend David Ware, with whom I served on The Supreme Court Historical Society, volunteered to edit it for me. In short order he decided, and I agreed that this was an informal history and not an academic work. Hence no footnotes but a list of sources in the back. David is currently the Arkansas State Historian and director of the Arkansas State Archives. His input and assistance have been invaluable. It is David's wish that this could be a template for others to use and have a comprehensive history of the state's judiciary. Really a lot of the work for them has been done!

I hope the reader finds it educational and entertaining. Without the help and encouragement of Tom, Billy and many others and the help of David, Joyce and John and Red Engine Press this would never have been finished. I have attempted to tell the story of the men and women who have served Sebastian County in the judiciary along with the fascinating story of the one of the state's smallest counties and the battle over the location of the courthouse. From all of this we also learn of the history of this small state and its people through the prism of the judiciary. I hope the reader will enjoy reading as much as I have enjoyed, sometimes through blood, sweat and tears, bringing this story to you.

Judge Jim Spears
June 6, 2022

CHAPTER ONE

In the Beginning

Arkansas became a separate territory in 1819 and a state in 1836. With its lack of population, organization, and infrastructure, Arkansas was hardly ready for statehood. However, in the rush for new states to balance the U.S. Senate between free and slave states, Arkansas was paired with Michigan for statehood—ready or not.

The new state's Constitution provided for the judiciary in Article 6 of the document. The judicial power was vested in a Supreme Court. Trial courts known as circuit courts enjoyed jurisdiction over all criminal and civil trial court proceedings. Justices of the peace presided over inferior courts and the Constitution provided for—but did not mandate—the creation of corporation courts and separate courts of chancery. The Supreme Court consisted of three justices, one to be designated the chief justice. The Supreme Court enjoyed appellate statewide jurisdiction and superintending control over the inferior courts. It also held the power to issue the writs and orders necessary to carry out its duties. The Supreme Court, as well as circuit judges, were selected by a joint vote of both houses of the state legislature. A Supreme Court justice had to be thirty years of age and was selected for an eight-year term. Circuit judges were required to be at least twenty-five years old and were selected for a four-year terms.

The justice of the peace courts held jurisdiction over cases involving county taxes, the disbursement of monies for government purposes, local concerns and internal improvements. Each township elected its own justices of the peace, one for every fifty persons in a township, with at least two chosen from each township. Justices of the peace served two-year terms and had to be residents of their respective township. Originally, these justices had no criminal jurisdiction, but a constitutional amendment in 1848 specified that the legislature could bestow upon justices of the peace jurisdiction for assault and battery and other offenses less than felony and punishable by a fine only. The justice court could also act as an examining court to hold preliminary hearings in felony cases. They enjoyed the authority to discharge or bind over to circuit court. They could also issue process and peace bonds. The 1848 amendment granted the justice courts jurisdiction for contract cases up to $100 as well.

The popularly elected justices of the peace assembled constituted the county court. They elected from their members the county judge who presided and also functioned as the probate judge. The county judge following election, is commissioned by the governor. The county judge and justices of the peace served two-year terms. State's attorneys (later styled prosecuting attorney) for each county were selected by the joint vote of the two houses of the legislature. The state's attorney for Pulaski County served as the attorney for the state in cases before the Supreme Court as there was no state attorney general. The methods for selecting circuit judges, prosecuting attorneys (formerly styled 'state's attorney'), county and probate judges were changed by the constitutional amendment of Nov. 24, 1848 to one of popular election by the residents of the circuit or county. This democratic reform followed adoption of the Amendment of November 17, 1848, which provided that the Supreme Court would also be elected by the people.

Elected county sheriffs bore the main responsibility for law enforcement within the county. They shared this responsibility with constables, one elected by each township, who had concurrent jurisdiction with the township. Incorporated towns were permitted to elect a separate constable and town magistrate.

Early Arkansas, as both territory and state, consisted of large counties, whose boundaries sometimes followed geographical features and barriers and in other instances...did not. Ideally, a county's seat should be within a day's travel from the farthest reaches of the county territory but this was not easy to accomplish. There were no bridges across rivers and mountains proved difficult to cross. The only travel available was by foot, horse or, in some areas, water. As Arkansas developed and its population grew, it became necessary and practical to divide the early large counties into smaller ones, ones with accessible seats of justice and administration. The process also provided opportunities for profit, and in some instances led to long-running contention between locales.

Crawford County, from which Sebastian was mainly formed, stretched from the Washington County line to the northern boundary of Scott County and the Arkansas River bisected it. Sebastian County was created by an act of the legislature on January 6, 1851. It was named for United States Senator William K. Sebastian, who had previously served as an Associate Justice of the Arkansas Supreme Court and had been appointed to fill out the term of United States Senator Chester Ashley upon Ashley's death. He was later elected by the legislature to the Senate and served until the Civil War. *The Arkansas Gazette*, reported on January 17, 1851, in a story picked up from *The Fort Smith Herald*, that there had been much rejoicing in Fort Smith over the creation of the new

Act of 29 December 1848
Divided State into 6 Judicial Districts
The 4th Judicial Circuit consisted of Scott, Franklin, Johnson Newton, Crawford, Washington, Madison, Carroll, and Benton

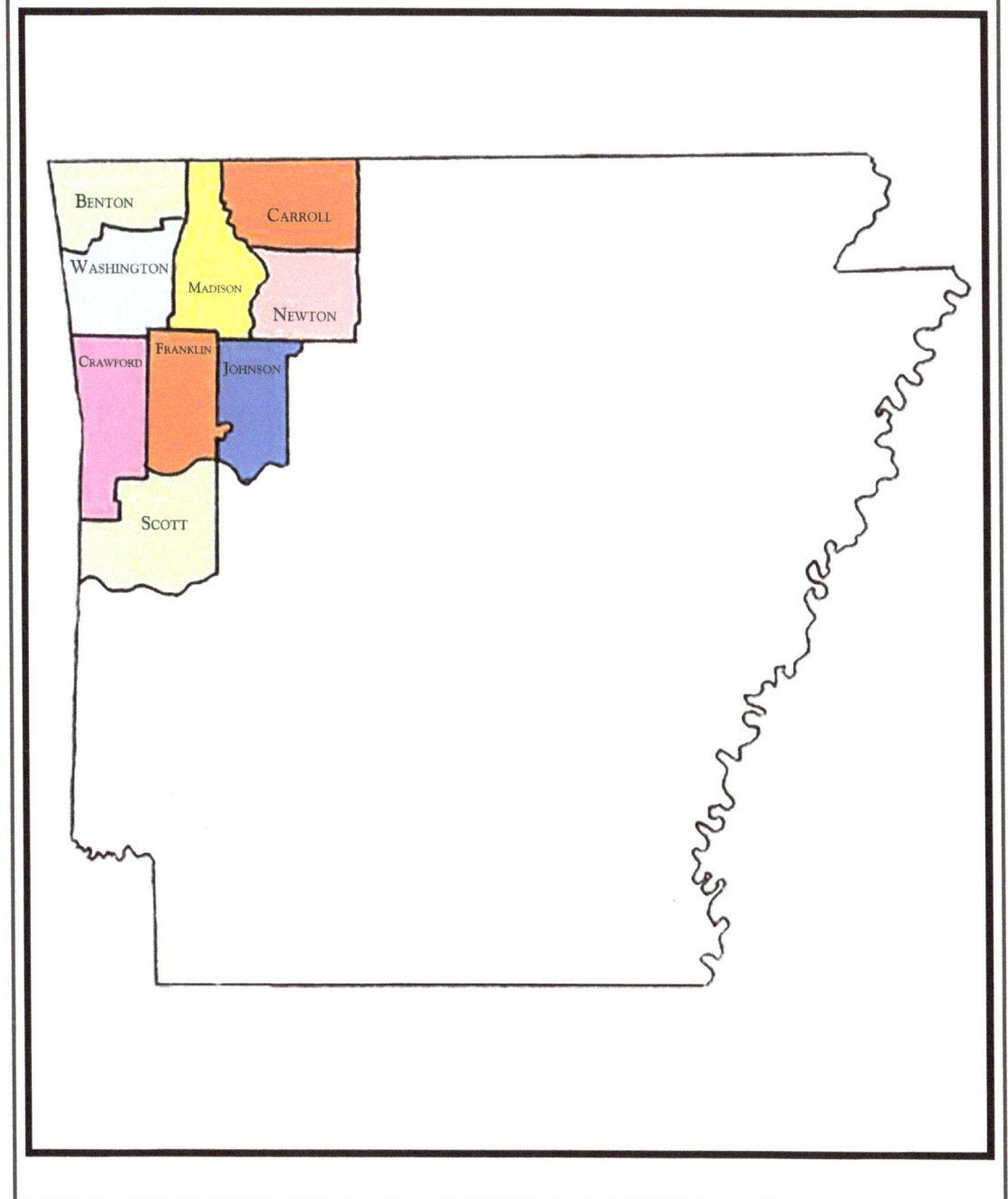

county, including the firing of 100 rounds of cannon fire. A premature discharge, however, shattered the arm of a Mr. Langham, formerly a member of the 7th Infantry who had passed unscathed through several battles in Mexico.

At its creation, Sebastian County lacked both courthouse and elected officials; records pertaining to the new county were lodged across the Arkansas River, at the Crawford County Courthouse in Van Buren. Fort Smith, adjacent to the old military post and an incorporated town since 1842, was the new county's only settlement of any size. In 1851 it was a bustling and thriving frontier post, an entry point to the Permanent Indian Territory and a jumping-off point for "Gold Rush" pioneers. As such, it may have seemed a logical choice for seat of county government but it was far from central. The original boundaries of the county extended south, taking in portions of what had been Scott County along the western boundary of the state and into Polk County. This was a great distance from Fort Smith. There was, however, also a small community at Jenny Lind, located nearer the center of the new county.

The act creating the county specified that its seat of justice would be temporarily in the home of Eaton Tatum in Jenny Lind until arrangements could be made for a permanent location, a site to be chosen by a representative commission. The commission was composed of one member from each existing township and two at-large commissioners. Tatum, who is sometimes styled "the father of Sebastian County," served on the commission charged with selecting a county seat and seat of justice, and it was his (unsurprising) desire that the permanent county seat be at Jenny Lind. Pride of place may have been a factor but possible gain may have also prompted his bid: Tatum owned land in the Jenny Lind district, the result of a land grant to him as a veteran of the Missouri Militia during the War of 1812, and its value could be expected to rise if Jenny Lind became the county's administrative center.

Eaton Tatum may well have been the "father of his county" but as such, he was quickly vexed by his virtual offspring. The county seat location selected by the commission, much to the disgust of Eaton Tatum (as well as the population of the northern portion of the county) was on forty acres on Vache Grasse Creek, also centrally located but some distance south from Jenny Lind, that had been donated for the purpose by settler Ruben Coker. No settlement existed at the site; it was undeveloped apart from the Coker farm. Nevertheless, the commission deemed it a suitable location at which circuit judge Alfred Greenwood might hold proceedings. Judge Greenwood signaled the birth of Sebastian County at 10 o'clock in the morning of March 10, 1851, when he banged his gavel down on Coker's split-log cook table and opened court at a location which Reuben Coker had named, in the judge's honor, Greenwood. The first building to be constructed at the new county seat was erected by James J. Baker and John Carnall.

ACT OF 10 JANUARY 1851
CREATED SEBASTIAN COUNTY FROM PORTIONS OF CRAWFORD, SCOTT AND POLK COUNTIES AND ASSIGNED THE NEW COUNTY TO THE 4TH CIRCUIT (IN WHICH THE PARENT COUNTIES HAD BEEN LOCATED)

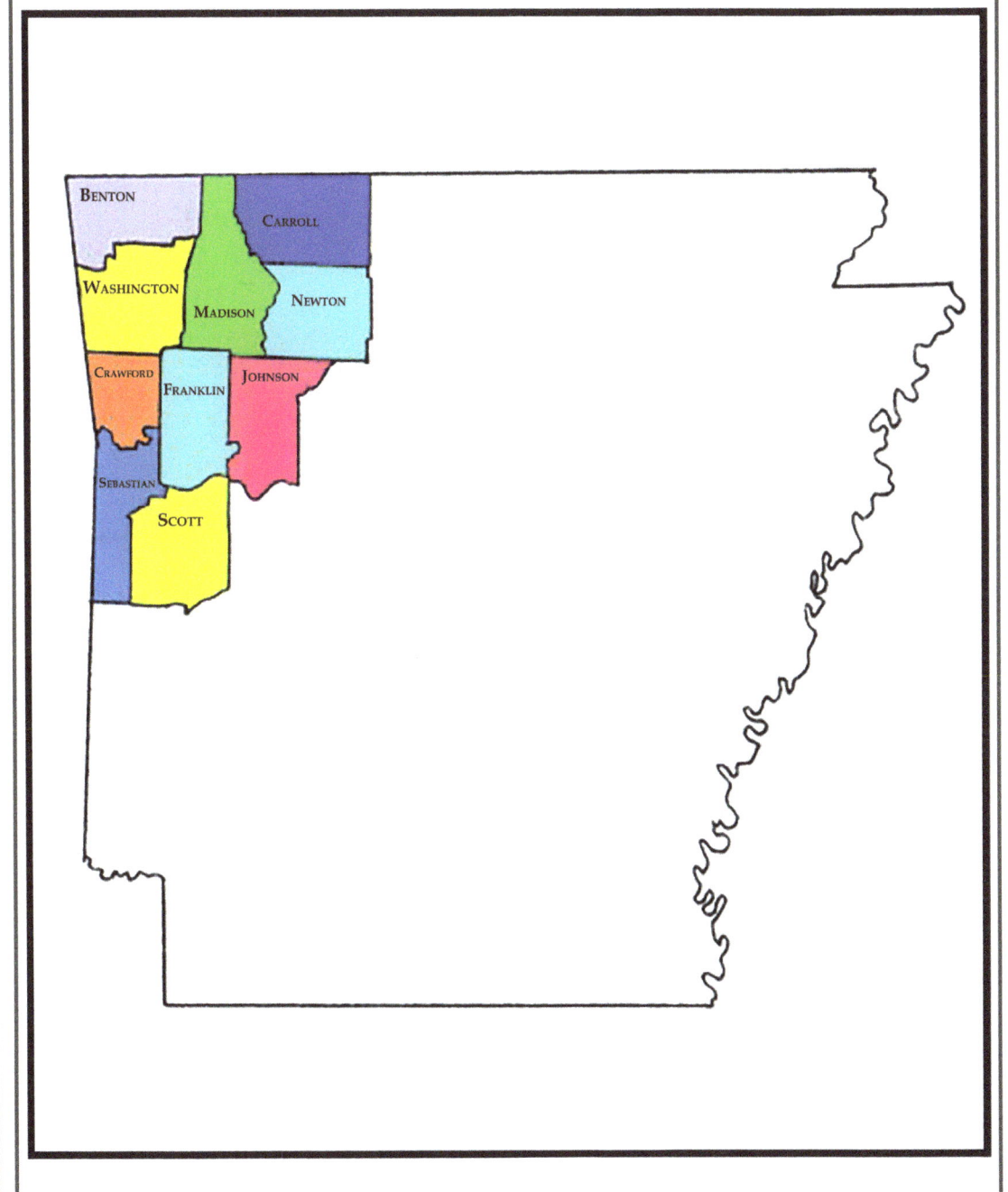

Carnall was the county clerk and former sheriff of Crawford County. It was a flat-hewn log cabin sixteen feet square, used for the office of the county clerk. A double-pen log house was built in 1852 on the corner of Center and Front Streets and served for some time as the courthouse as well as other private dwellings.

⁂

Alfred Greenwood was the judge of the Fourth Judicial Circuit and as such, his jurisdiction extended beyond the new county. Prior to 1851 the circuit included Scott, Franklin, Johnson, Newton, Crawford, Washington, Madison, Carroll and Benton. Sebastian County, largely created from Crawford, was duly included in it as well. Judge Greenwood remained circuit judge through 1852.

Alfred Burton Greenwood was born in Franklin County, Georgia, July 11, 1811. His parents were Hugh B. and Elizabeth Ingraham Greenwood. He attended school at Lawrenceville, Georgia and studied law under William Izzard. He was admitted to the bar in Georgia in 1832 and practiced in Decatur. He married Sarah A. Hilburn in 1833. They had 12 children. In 1837, he was commissioned to move 1,000 Cherokees from the Hiwassee River in Tennessee to the Indian Territory. The route, the so-called Northern route of the Trail of Tears, brought him through Bentonville, Arkansas and, apparently, he liked what he saw, because he moved to Bentonville with his family in 1838. At the time it was a community of 30 persons and he was the only lawyer. He served as state representative from Benton County from 1842 until 1844 and prosecuting attorney for the Fourth Judicial Circuit from 1845 through 1850. In that year he was elected circuit judge.

After serving for about two years, Judge Greenwood was elected to Congress in 1853. He served there into 1858. In that year, President James Buchanan offered him a position as Commissioner of Indian Affairs, a post Greenwood held until the spring of 1861. When he resigned from the Federal government in 1861, he became one of Arkansas's representatives to the Confederate and was commissioned by Confederate President Jefferson Davis as an emissary to the Choctaw and Cherokee Nations in order to enlist their aid in the cause of the Confederacy. He was successful in this. He also served the Confederacy as a tax collector in Arkansas and was responsible for raising some two million dollars. Following the war he practiced law in Bentonville. He died in October of 1889, at the age of seventy-eight.

There is a case in *Arkansas Reports* in which Judge Greenwood was involved first as the prosecutor seeking an indictment and then, during the trial, as judge: *Shropshire v. State*, 12 Ark. 190 (1851). The defendant was, understandably,

JUDGE ALFRED B. GREENWOOD
CIRCUIT JUDGE
1851-1852
PHOTO COURTESY OF SEBASTIAN COUNTY

a little upset that his prosecutor became his judge, but the eminences of the Arkansas Supreme Court seem not to have been impressed with this minor technicality. The sensational facts of this case, which originated in 1846, could be taken from the news accounts of today: Mr. Shropshire's daughter was married to a Mr. Williams who abused his wife and seems to have had a violent propensity. They had a child who was, the bill of particulars noted, breast-fed. According to the testimony of the mother, Williams was upset by the small child in some way and began beating it. The mother intervened and was in turn beaten and then turned out of the house without the baby. Mrs. Williams returned to the home of her father, Mr. Shropshire and on the next day the Shropshires, the father and his two daughters went to the Williams home There, Shropshire confronted Williams concerning the treatment of his daughter and grandchild. The response by Williams was that he could beat his child and wife if he chose to do so. The result was a confrontation that left Williams shot in the back and lying dead in the snow some 150 feet from the house.

The Shropshire defense was simple: self-defense. It was alleged that the deceased approached the defendant with two large rocks. The defendant also contended that he shot to frighten the deceased and not to hit him, but the bullet must have ricocheted. The jury did not accept this explanation and convicted Shropshire. Shropshire appealed the verdict and it reached the state Supreme Court and it let the guilty verdict stand. The defendant argued that he did not get a fair trial as the prosecutor at the time of indictment the indictment had also been the judge at the time of the trial: namely, Alfred B. Greenwood. Shropshire's attorney on appeal moved the court to take judicial notice that they were in fact one and the same person. The Supreme Court did not credit this since they deemed that no motion of objection had been timely made and, furthermore, that there was no proof presented to the Court that the prosecutor and judge had been one and the same.

Justice David Walker, speaking for the Court, wove the following semantic maze to avoid admitting the obvious:

> *We know at the time of the indictment was found, A. B. Greenwood was attorney for that circuit. (He had signed the indictment) This knowledge only extends to him as an officer. Whether he is an intimate acquaintance or an entire stranger in no respect changes the case. When he goes out of office we cease to take judicial notice of him, or to know anything of the changes of pursuit which may engage his time, and when as an incumbent of a different office, we recognize him as such; it is with no reference or connection with his former position, nor do the name add to or detract from such knowledge. This rule has its foundation in the necessity for its existence. Judicial notice of officers, and of their signatures, seals of office, &c., are all necessary*

starting points to be taken upon faith and credit due them, as connected with the administration of justice. As incumbents in public trust, they are known for the time being but in no other respect whatever.

This case is also notable for the verbose and overwrought Bill of Particulars, which certainly took more time to decipher and digest than had been required to dispatch Williams. A fraction of the document suffices to give the flavor of the whole:

... the said James Shropshire, with a certain rifle gun of the value of ten dollars then and there loaded, and charged with gunpowder and one leaden bullet, which rifle gun he, the said James Shropshire, in both his hands then and there had and held to, against and upon the said Lewis Williams, then and there feloniously, willfully, and of his malice aforethought, did shoot and discharge, and that the said James Shropshire, with the leaden bullet aforesaid, out of the rifle gun aforesaid, then and there, by force of the gunpowder, shot and sent forth as aforesaid, the said Lewis Williams, in and upon the left side of the backbone of him.

❧ ❧ ❧

In 1852, the struggle for the seat of Justice in Sebastian County began in earnest. The people of Fort Smith and the northwest portion of the county preferred Fort Smith to be the county seat rather than the upstart non-community on Coker's donated land. This move was accomplished by election in 1852. The *Arkansas Gazette* on May 28, 1852, reported that the seat of government for Sebastian County had been permanently established by the commissioners at Fort Smith. Capt. John Rogers, the proprietor of the town, had donated a block of lots as a site for the public buildings and about $3,500 had been contributed by the citizens for their construction. The county offices and court was located in a building at the corner of Walnut (North A) and Second Street in Fort Smith. There it remained until 1854.

The next judge to serve the Fourth Judicial Circuit was Felix I. Batson. A resident of Johnson County, he served from 1853 through 1858. Judge Batson's letters, provided by his descendant Liz Powers, illuminates both his court work and life as a circuit judge often separated from family and sometimes far from a major population center. On February 12, 1854, he wrote:

...[I] will not be able to see home until after Scott Court. I have got through with near three hundred cases(and have but a few more to try but they are important and will occupy the entire week, a murder case comes up in the morning which I suppose will take three days. I have not been about town much

but think times here are pretty dull, all the stores are empty or nearly so. I have inquired in all the stores I have been in for Emma? Books, but can't find any. I have been to a show two nights quite a good affair of the kind. There is also a theater in operation here but I have not been to it.... I will try to get something for Emma and yourself and send it down by Dummy. [Dummy refers to John Wesley Woodard who was born deaf. A native Virginian he was educated in France and arrived in Arkansas in the 1840's. He was Batson's court clerk. He was also a tutor and a journalist.]

Judge Batson was selected to serve on the Arkansas Supreme Court in 1858 and served one year, 1859. He also served as a member of the State Secession Convention in 1861, and as a Confederate congressman for two terms. He passed away in 1871.

A case decided by Judge Batson in Sebastian County and appealed to the Arkansas Supreme Court, concerned the donation of the land for the courthouse in Fort Smith and touched on the ongoing contention between Greenwood and Fort Smith for influence. John Rogers, considered the "Father of Fort Smith", had been the grantor of certain land for a courthouse. *Rogers vs. Sebastian County*, 21 Ark. 440 (1860), dealt with Rogers' efforts to recover the land when the county seat was relocated again to Greenwood. The opinion of Justice Fairchild relates that before May 6, 1852, commissioners Mitchell Sparks, Felix G. Ake and Zachariah Hemby had located the seat of justice in Fort Smith. They planned to place a courthouse on a certain part of block 32 of the new addition to Fort Smith, owned by John Rogers. Rogers and his wife deeded the land to the county with the expectation that Fort Smith would remain the county seat. The deed, filed May 10, 1852, made no mention of any conditions.

Another deed to satisfy objections by the county to the form of the original deed was executed and filed on May 2, 1854. The commissioners, acting on behalf of the county, had agreed with Rogers that, should a courthouse not be built on the property or if the property were to be used for any other purpose, the land would revert to Rogers. This "gentlemen's agreement" was not put into writing or attached to the deeds. After the first deed and before the second deed, the commissioners, with the consent of the county court, contracted for the building. The courthouse was under construction. when the second deed was executed. Soon after the second deed the work on the courthouse stopped and the construction contract was rescinded. In 1855, new commissioners were elected and the county seat relocated eighteen miles from Fort Smith to Greenwood once again.

Rogers then filed suit seeking to regain his property because the courthouse had not been built and it had been agreed orally that should the construction not occur the property would be returned. The county disagreed. The Supreme

Court ruled for the county, affirming Judge Batson. The Court cited a law to the effect that counties could not accept real estate with restrictions on the title. This was established law and Rogers was presumed to know that. He also knew, according to the court, that the county could not be bound to maintain Fort Smith as the county seat and certainly not because of a land donation from Rogers. The county thus retained the land and the incomplete courthouse because the deeds did not contain a reverter clause or condition. If they had, the conveyance would have been illegal. As there was no restriction in the deed, the county held the land in fee simple. Pursuant to a plat filed in 1824 on file in the Sebastian Co. Clerk's office the land in question now contains the Bonneville House at 318 North 7th Street. This is the house owned by the widow of Gen. Benjamin Bonneville for whom the Bonneville salt-flats and the Bonneville Dam is named. It is on the historical register.

The system of divided justice continued to stir the electorate and inflame political passions. After the move in 1855, the citizenry of Greenwood decided that it was time to have a real courthouse. The court met in private residences for a time. As there was no security that the county seat would remain in one particular place the reluctance to invest in a building seems reasonable. In 1856, however, Peter K. Beam began building a courthouse located on the square in Greenwood. It was a two-story frame structure, fifty feet square, with offices on the first floor and the court on the second.

Construction moved along slowly. An article in the *Gazette* on April 17, 1858 related a story from the *Fort Smith Herald* that a Mr. McKinney, who had come in from Greenwood, reported that the frame of the courthouse under construction was blown down and very seriously broken by a storm the previous night. The story also said that the contractor would lose several hundred dollars. The story had an editorial comment that rang true:

> *"We believe the chances are against this county as it appears difficult to have a court house erected."*

A report in the *Gazette* on May 15, 1858, stated that there were complaints that the courthouse would not have blown down had inferior materials not been used. The *Gazette* noted that this was a valid complaint since all Sebastian County's internal improvement funds had been squandered on public buildings. They insisted that the commissioners and the county court should be held responsible and the citizens be shown what had become of their money. The county judge refused to accept the inferior work but the county court overruled him and ordered payment to the contractor. It was reported that the sills for the windows had been constructed of sweet gum. Through this adversity, however, the work progressed and the completion of this courthouse, the seat of justice

JUDGE FELIX I. BATSON
CIRCUIT JUDGE
1853-1858
PHOTO COURTESY OF BENTON COUNTY

in Sebastian County seemed to be securely placed in Greenwood. It is in this courthouse that first Judge Batson, and then Judge John M. Wilson held court according to the dates.

Judge Wilson became judge in 1859, when Judge Batson took a seat on the Arkansas Supreme Court. He held office a little more than a year. Little is known of Judge Wilson, at least of a personal nature. He had previously served as county surveyor of Washington County.

Arkansas Territory on March 2, 1829, and as Washington County Judge from 1832 until 1833. He may also have been the John Wilson who practiced law with his brother A.M. Wilson in Carrollton. Judge Wilson first held court at Huntsville in Madison County, on April 11, 1859.

A case decided by Judge Wilson out of Sebastian County that ended up in the Arkansas Supreme Court was *Tucker vs. Bond*, 23 Ark. 268 (1861). This case points out the important role played by justices of the peace and constables in the judicial process of antebellum Arkansas.

The plaintiff, Tucker, had purchased twenty-three hogs from Moore. The main defendant was Bond, the Constable of Sugar Creek Township. Constable Bond took possession of the hogs pursuant to an execution on a judgment against Moore, who had sold the hogs to Tucker. Tucker sued Bond and the other defendants in the local justice of the peace court and lost. He then appealed to the Circuit court. Judge Wilson decided the case without a jury. Again, Tucker lost. He then appealed to the Arkansas Supreme Court.

The case turned on the facts and the prior knowledge of Tucker. Tucker purchased the hogs on October 10, 1856. At the time he purchased the hogs there were three judgments against Moore, the seller, from the justice of the peace court in Sugar Creek Township. Tucker knew this.

Prior to the purchase in October, one Gardenhire, the previous Constable, had served the executions on Moore and levied against the hogs. This was on July 12, 1856. Gardenhire did not take possession of the hogs or sell them although he had advertised the sale. This was because Bond succeeded him as Constable and he was without authority to act. Moore then drove the hogs to Tucker's farm and sold them. When Constable Bond got involved, he called a jury to determine the ownership of the hogs. This was authorized by statute in order to create a defense for an officer taking possession of disputed property. Evidently this was a jury presided over by the Constable (which indicates the Constable had a fact-finding quasi-judicial function). The jury determined that the hogs were subject to the execution as levied by Constable Gardenhire and that a lien existed on the hogs in favor of the judgment creditor.

JUDGE JOHN M. WILSON
CIRCUIT JUDGE
1859-1860

PHOTO COURTESY OF BENTON COUNTY

The case was determined on possession of the hogs and the validity of the service of the executions on Moore by Constable Gardenhire. Gardenhire testified that he served the executions on Moore and his property, the hogs. His endorsement on the document was sufficient for this. Taking possession of the hogs was left by Constable Gardenhire to Moore. Precedent held that in instances where personal property was levied upon at the direction of the plaintiff and the sheriff permits it to remain in possession of the defendant without sale, the levy does not continue as a lien against an intervening person such as a bona fide purchaser. In this case the property was not left at the direction of the plaintiff but due to the constable's belief that he no longer had authority to act. The ruling precedent went on to say that to leave the property with the defendant for too long a period would open the officer to liability to any bona fide purchaser or judgment lien holder with less priority. The court then ruled that Tucker was not a bona fide purchaser in any event since he had actual knowledge of the executions. The system worked and ultimately thwarted a scheme by Moore and Tucker to defeat the judgment creditors.

The next person to serve as circuit judge in the Fourth Circuit served for a very short period and a very tumultuous one. Joseph J. Green defeated Judge Wilson and took office in 1860. He died in office in 1862. Green hailed from Crawford County. He served as a state senator from Crawford and Sebastian counties in the years 1854 through 1855 and prior to that as a state representative. He was a law partner to William Walker in Crawford County prior to becoming judge. Mr. Walker himself would be circuit judge in the post war era.

A case decided by Judge Green that made its way to the Arkansas Supreme Court arose in Franklin County. *Omey vs. State*, 23 Ark. 281 (1861), concerned a criminal indictment of one Omey who was charged with selling ardent spirits to a slave, Charles, a Negro belonging to Thomas Aldridge.

A statute provided that no person shall sell, or cause to be sold, to any Negro or mulatto slave, ardent spirits in any quantity, without permission of the master, mistress, overseer, or person having charge of said Negro or mulatto slave, and any white person offending against the provision of this act shall be guilty of a misdemeanor. A motion to quash the indictment was filed by the defendant and overruled by the trial court. The defendant was convicted and, on appeal, the verdict was reversed. The Supreme Court said the motion to quash should have been granted as there was no allegation in the indictment that the sale was without the consent of all the persons listed in the statute that could have given permission; i.e. master, mistress, overseer, or person having charge of the slave. Of the three indictments in the case, one named the owner alone; the other two named no one. Talk about letting someone off on a technicality! This case was selected to highlight antebellum slave culture and the dehumanizing of the black

JUDGE JOSEPH J. GREEN
CIRCUIT JUDGE
1860-1861
PHOTO COURTESY OF BENTON COUNTY

Act 107 of 1861
9th Judicial Circuit
Consisting of Scott, Polk, Pike, Montgomery, Sebastian, Clark, and Sevier Counties

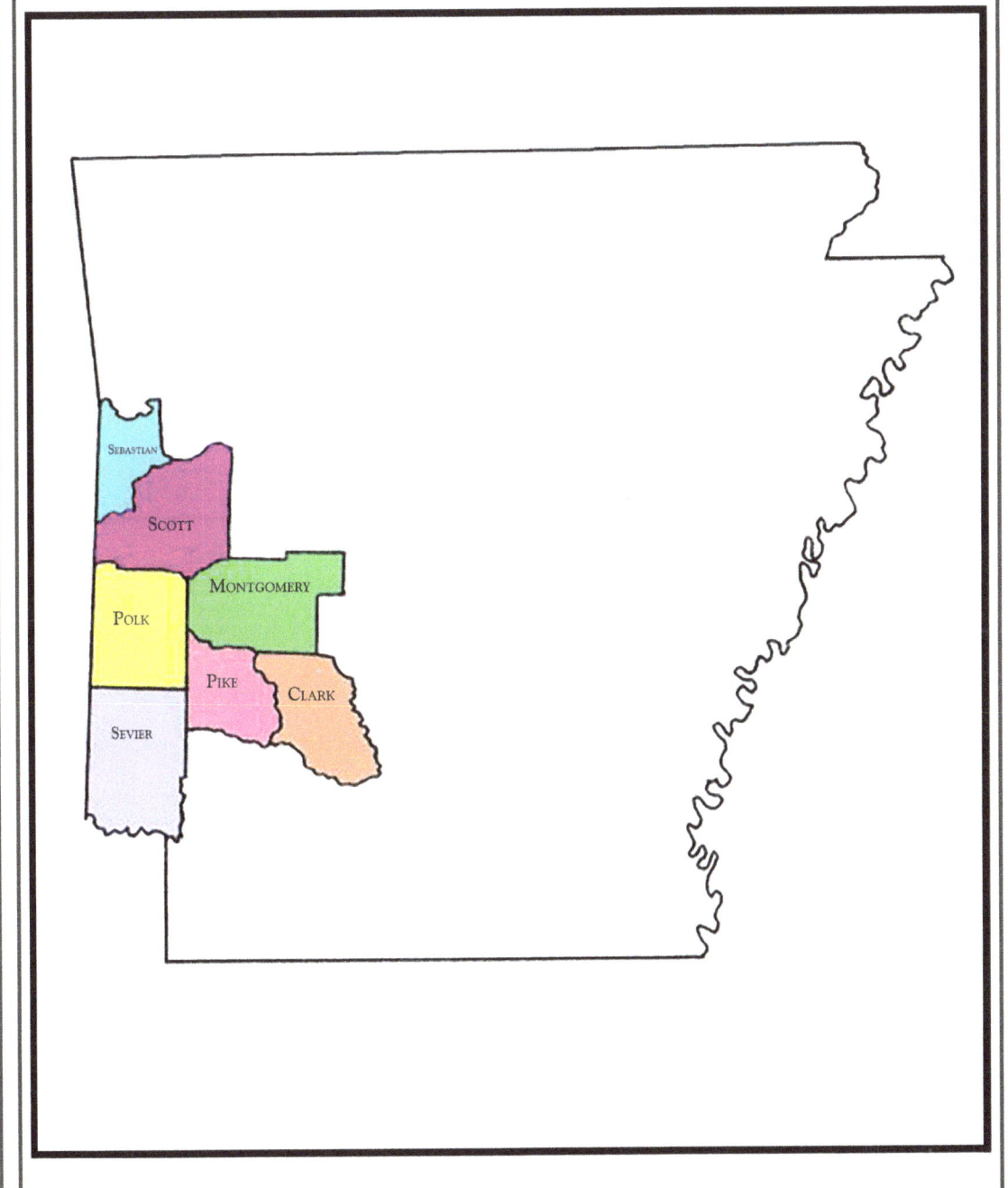

man who could not take a drink without his owner's permission as well as the strict rules of pleading which could mean instant death to litigation not consistent with form.

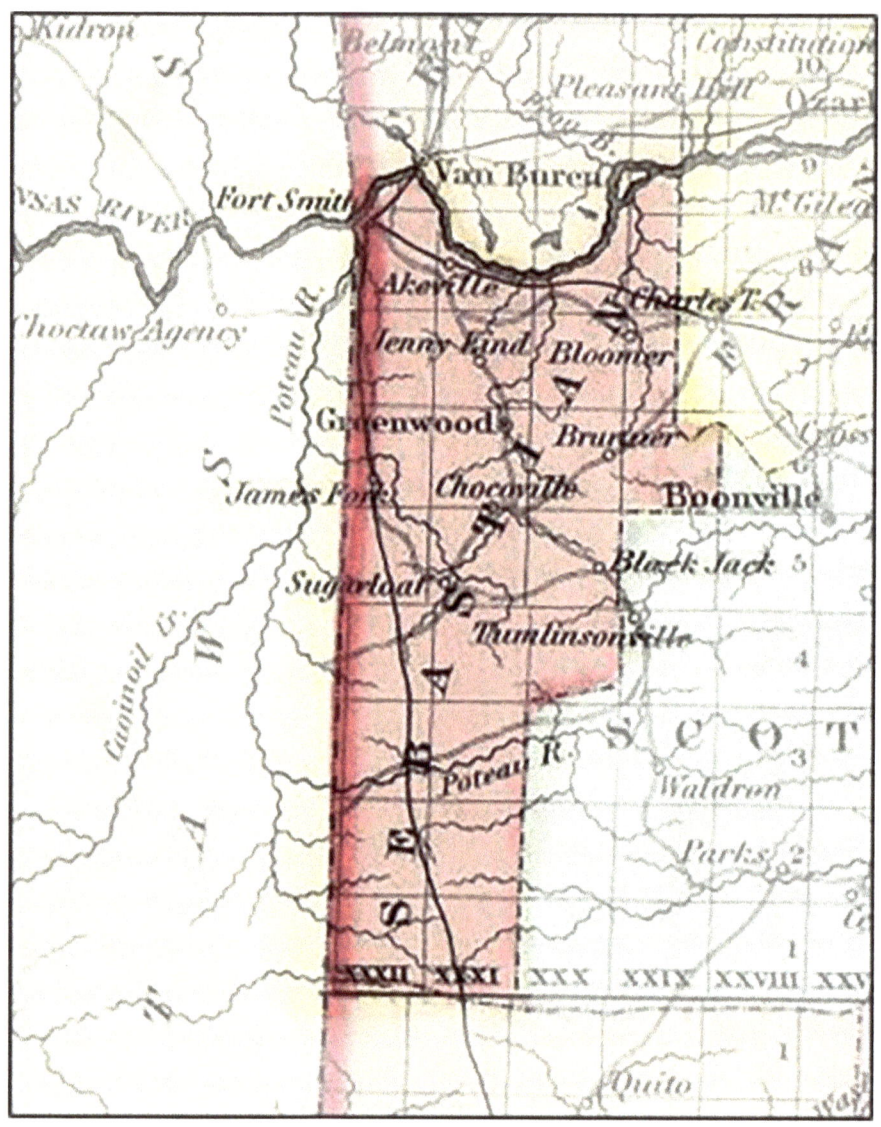

Sebastian County
and surrounding area
from
Colton's Atlas of The World, Illustrating Physical and Political Geography. New York: J.H. Colton And Company, 1856.

Courtesy of Arkansas
Secretary of State's office.

CHAPTER TWO

DIVISION, DESTRUCTION, AND REBIRTH

THE YEAR 1861 BEGAN A time of upheaval and conflict. Arkansas joined other Southern states in seceding from the Union and the adoption of a new constitution. The secession constitution made few changes in the makeup of the judiciary. The senior justice on the Supreme Court was designated the chief justice and the justices were now nominated by the governor and confirmed by the state senate. The officials holding office under the old constitution would continue in office until the legislature next met. The only difference concerning circuit judges was a provision to allow the selection of a special judge in the absence of the regular official. The special chancery court previously established for Pulaski County was reaffirmed as well. The terms for Supreme Court justices remained eight years long, with circuit judges' terms remaining at four years. Justice of the peace courts now held jurisdiction to hear bastardy cases and negligence cases involving $100 or less. Each township merited at least two justices of the peace; those with populations over 200 qualified for additional justices, one per 100 voters (instead of the fifty voters stipulated in the Constitution of 1836). There remained no attorney general and the prosecuting attorney for Pulaski County retained the job of representing the state before the Supreme Court.

All court records from that time have been destroyed from both the Fort Smith and Greenwood Districts. The records from Washington County, which have been preserved, politely state: "Court in Vacation." In reality the courts ceased to function. Even in Confederate-held portions of the state, most trial courts were "In Vacation". *The Washington Telegraph* noted in an editorial on August 6, 1862:

> *We were never in such a political condition before. Everything pertaining to the administration of justice and the regulation of business intercourse and the protection of civil rights is in a state of disorganization.*

This condition of disorganization was effectively recognized and even encouraged by the Arkansas Supreme Court. In its June 1863 term, the Court ruled that an act of the legislature continuing all court proceedings for the duration of the war was unconstitutional.

Two developments from the secession-era Legislature affected Sebastian County: the legislature once again established two county seats, Fort Smith and Greenwood, and placed the county into a different judicial circuit. Act 107 of 1861 placed the county into the Ninth Judicial Circuit that included Sebastian, Scott, Polk, Montgomery, Sevier, Pike and Clark Counties. The reasoning behind this change can only be speculation. It may have had to do with the stronger Union sentiment in the more northern counties. In any event the new district was not the product of clear logic or geographical expediency: it stretched from Arkadelphia in south central Arkansas to Fort Smith on the western border. With this change also came a new circuit judge, Henry Bolling Stuart, who took office in November 1862. Clark County records preserved at Ouachita Baptist University indicate that he did hold court in that county, at least, but there is in fact no evidence that Bolling Stuart actually held court sessions in Sebastian County.

Judge Henry Bolling Stuart was born on February 26, 1826, in Athens, Georgia. In 1848, at the age of 22, he moved to Clark County, Arkansas, read law and was admitted to the bar in 1849. In 1858 he was elected to the legislature representing Clark County. After election as Circuit Judge in 1862, he served until replaced, at least in the Union-occupied counties, in 1864. Following the war, in 1876, he was an unsuccessful candidate for Congress, losing to Jordan E. Cravens. In 1878, he was once again elected judge in the Eighth Judicial Circuit when Sebastian was no longer in the same circuit as Clark County. Following his time on the bench, he practiced law with his son in Arkadelphia until his death at age 64 on March 19, 1890.

Fort Smith reverted to Union control on September 1, 1863, after its recapture by Federal forces under the command of General James Blunt, who promised protection to residents who stopped fighting the United States and to begin restoring a civil government loyal to the Union. Lt. Colonel Elhanan John Searle was named Provost Marshal. The Provost Marshal was the judicial officer for the post and, in fact, for the Fort Smith area, as there existed no civil authority. Fort Smith and the rest of the area were desolate. During the preceding years of Confederate occupation, the people had been called upon to sacrifice to provide supplies necessary for that army. The economy had basically stopped functioning and those left at home were barely able to sustain life. Complicating this situation of privation were the numbers of so-called "Mountain Feds"—these included both native unionists who had previously fled into the mountains to avoid conscription into the Rebel army and deserters from that army who had been forcibly drafted—who took refuge in Fort Smith. Managing affairs both civil and military presented profound challenges to the Union forces.

Shortly after the reoccupation of Fort Smith, moves toward restoring civil authority began. With General Blunt's approval, a meeting was held in Fort Smith on October 20. This, the "Cradle of the First Southern Free State" meeting, attracted Unionists from some twenty Arkansas counties. Valentine Dell, a German immigrant and staunch unionist, published a newspaper called *The New Era* which was printed on a press abandoned by J. F. Wheeler, a secessionist, when the Federals took over Fort Smith. Dell reported:

> *For two years, thousands of Union families of the border slave states have been driven from their homes. Friends were murdered and thousands more were dragged from their homes and compelled to fight for a cause they did not agree with.*

The meeting resolved to support a state convention in Little Rock to reorganize state government into one made up of unionists which would explicitly abolish slavery in Arkansas. Other meetings in several counties followed the precedent of Fort Smith. In December, mass meetings held in Benton, Dardanelle and again in Fort Smith pressed for the return of civil government and law to the Union occupied portion of the state.

The Reconstruction State Convention convened in Little Rock on January 4, 1864. Harsh weather conditions kept delegates from northwestern Arkansas close to home but fifty-seven counties had been represented. Order and civil government were, possibly, returning. The convention drafted a new constitution to be presented to the voters on March 14, 1864. The new constitution was very much like the 1836 constitution, albeit with changes reflecting changed times: it declared the act of secession null and void and also prohibited slavery. All actions of the Secession Convention or the Confederate state government—including debts incurred that were incompatible with Federal laws—were declared invalid. The convention established a provisional government to serve until the voters could decide the successors. Isaac Murphy of Madison County, the only delegate to the 1861 Secession Convention not to support secession, was unanimously elected provisional governor.

The Constitution of 1864 contained few changes in the judiciary. The Supreme Court was once again elected with one of the three members designated chief justice. The senior member was no longer automatically named chief justice. Judicial circuits were once again to contain not less than five or more than seven counties and the circuit court was given superintending control over the inferior courts. Jurisdiction for the justice of the peace courts was raised to $200 for cases in contract with the circuit court having concurrent jurisdiction of cases valued between $100 and $200. The county judge was designated as the presiding judge of the county court. Perhaps the most significant judicial innovation of the 1864 constitution was the creation of the office of state attorney general. The requirements for the post were not onerous: they specified that he be learned in the law and at least thirty years of age. His duties were to represent the state and give opinions to the governor and other state officers.

ଈ   ଈ   ଈ

While Fort Smith and other parts of Union-occupied Arkansas feverishly prepared for the March 14 election, the parts of Arkansas primarily south of the Arkansas River and still under the control of the Confederacy continued to function under that system of civil and military government the best it could. The Confederate state capitol had twice moved, first to Hot Springs in 1862 and then to Washington in southeast Arkansas following the Federal occupation of Little Rock on September 10, 1863. After the organization of the Reconstruction provisional government the state actually had two functioning state governments: the Confederate in Washington and the Unionist in Little Rock. There were, in fact, two circuit judges for the Ninth Judicial Circuit. Augustus N. Hargrove was named on March 14, 1864, to hold that office in the Reconstruction government that controlled just Sebastian and, more loosely, Scott Counties in the district, while Henry Bolling Stuart in Clark County held the office for the Confederate government. Little has been found concerning the life or service of Judge Hargrove. *The New Era* published advertisements for him as an attorney; some appeared after his election and indicated that he would or could appear both before the Provost Marshal and in federal courts. These suggest that his position as Circuit Judge must not have prevented his private law practice before the federal courts.

In Arkansas, the March 1864 election gave approval to the Reconstruction Constitution by more than the required 10% of the vote cast in the 1860 Presidential election and selected a whole slate of local and state officials as well as a delegation to Congress. The situation for the people did not change. Civilians continued to flee the area. On August 8, a wagon train of 1,500 left their home state, heading to safety in the north. Things continued to deteriorate in Fort Smith through autumn and into winter as resupply was a problem due to the persistent Rebel activity. At one point in early December, Fort Smith was ordered abandoned. This brought protests and appeals from Fort Smith citizens. Ultimately, President Lincoln and General Grant countermanded the abandonment and ordered supplies shipped upriver to Fort Smith.

By mid-January 1865, Fort Smith was in a sad shape. Fences, fruit trees and shrubbery had been destroyed or torn down. Much of the damage was done by families coming in from the country for protection at the garrison and staying in houses vacated by the owners. On the 15th, however, four steamboats bearing supplies and provisions reached town. Soon telegraph service was restored and supplies started arriving more regularly as the river became navigable. An order was issued by the military imposing a one cent sales tax to help pay the cost of the Provost Marshal's office and the policing of the city including the removal of animals from the streets. Dead cows, horses, dogs, hogs, etc. were lying on streets and in alleyways and were a health problem.

The war was now only weeks from finality. On March 4, 1865, a rally was held in Fort Smith to celebrate Lincoln's inauguration. There were flags, martial music and speeches. The last speaker was Lt. Col. Searle, the former Provost Marshal. He spoke of the war but also of the coming peace and the bright future in store for Arkansas. Prophetically, Valentine Dell noted that although Searle was from Illinois, he would no doubt, settle in Arkansas when this cruel war is over.

By the spring, Fort Smith was beginning to stir. People were farming, confident of protection. Citizens were holding up their heads, at least those who remained. Some danger remained, as Secessionist partisans or bushwhackers remained at large in the countryside, killing and plundering but in truth, there was not much left to plunder. The tax assessor began taking assessments again in March for those who had anything to assess. Editor Dell warned that not many could pay any taxes as the people were destitute.

The war and the rebellion officially ended with Lee's surrender at Appomattox, April 9, 1865. E. J. Searle's old law mentor Abraham Lincoln was assassinated on April 14. In Arkansas, the hostilities lumbered on a while longer: Kirby Smith, the Confederate commander for the region which included Arkansas did not surrender until June, one of the last Confederate commanders to do so. The state's Confederate government, including the courts, ceased to exist. The last entry in the judgment book of the Confederate Arkansas Supreme Court was dated January 6, 1865; the court's last published opinion appeared in *The Washington Telegraph* of Hempstead County, the only newspaper still in circulation in Confederate Arkansas, on April 19, 1865, ten days after Lee's surrender.

On April 24, the local members of the Arkansas General Assembly returned to Fort Smith from a special session called to ratify the thirteenth amendment to the United States Constitution that abolished slavery. The legislature, however, refused to pass bills granting blacks the right to testify in court or honoring marriage contracts between blacks. This undoubtedly delayed Arkansas' readmission to the Union. It was important that blacks be allowed to testify in court against their former masters, who, in some cases, were cruel and would make no attempt to free them. Dell was outraged. He stated: "The people of Arkansas have been cruelly wronged by the Copperheads in the Legislature who showed their true colors." Copperheads were "Peace Democrats" in the north and the reference was incorrect. Dell merely used it as a pejorative.

Congress still refused to seat the delegation from Arkansas. Hard-line Unionists who did not forgive old grudges easily believed that the loyalty oath requirement prescribed by the President was too lenient and allowed former Rebels such as Augustus Garland of Hempstead County (elected to the U.S. Senate by the Arkansas Legislature in 1864 but rejected by the Senate when he came to Washington to take up his duties) too easy access to high office. Congress did, however, accept the vote of the state legislature in ratifying the Thirteenth Amendment as they needed Arkansas' vote in favor of ratification in order to reach the required three quarters of the states. Thus, while not quite officially a state, Arkansas made steps toward resuming its place in the federal Union while the state government that had been elected in March 1864, including the courts, functioned on a limited basis, reclaiming authority from the military. Arkansas and Sebastian County limped along into the period called Reconstruction.

CHAPTER THREE

Toward a New State

President Lincoln's assassination ended the prospects for his plans for Reconstruction. Under his plan, Arkansas had acted to restore the functions of state government loyal to the Union but the Congress refused to accept its delegates, as earlier discussed, or to credit its electoral votes in the Presidential election of 1864. There was a general feeling among Northern Congressmen that the Lincoln-envisioned process of reentry into the Union was too easy; a fear persisted of unrepentant Southerners walking the halls of Congress. In contrast with Lincoln's goal of reconciliation, many Northerners harbored feelings of hostility and hatred for Southerners and felt that there must be a genuine repentance and something like meaningful punishment before any pardon that would restore their right to vote was granted. Many, though not all, also wanted to assure freedom and safety for freed former slaves, for reasons humane, practical and political. Ironically, though, there also existed a parallel sentiment that now liberated but ill-educated blacks should have limited voting rights. Senator John Sherman of Ohio, brother to General William T. Sherman, expressed his doubts about the new Black voters and indeed, many Southern voters generally:

> *"I admit the Negroes are not intelligent enough to vote, but how much more ignorant are those slaves than the uneducated white people down South?"*

Within Congress, a core group of Radical Reconstructors wanted to confiscate the property of rich rebels and redistribute it to formerly enslaved workers, usually styled "freedmen." Not many wished to go this far but most in Congress did insist that the former Confederate states be kept out of the Union until, it was felt, their populations showed a proper spirit of repentance. Into this climate the new President, Andrew Johnson, was cast. A former congressman from Tennessee, Johnson had been a stout Unionist but postwar, found himself totally out of step with the spirit of the Radical Reconstructionists. He was instead a constitutional conservative, a strict constructionist who had for instance opposed the Smithsonian Institution on the grounds that there was no specific constitutional authority for it, no matter its desirability. For similar reasons, he opposed Republican plans to help ex-slaves and to reform and stimulate the economy. He thus set himself on a collision course with Congress that would result in his impeachment in 1868 and the failure of his conviction by a single vote.

In the summer of 1865, Johnson brought out his own plan for readmission. He first accepted Arkansas, Tennessee, and Louisiana back into the union as they had acted in good faith on Lincoln's plan. He added to this Virginia as it had a Unionist governor. For the rest he granted amnesty to former Confederates in exchange for a loyalty oath, excepting those who had held high civil or military positions in the Confederate or state governments and those whose worth exceeded $20,000.00. Those newly re-enfranchised voters had to then call state conventions that would adopt new state constitutions that nullified the ordinance of secession, abolished slavery, and repudiated the Confederate and state war debt.

The 39th Congress was in recess when Abraham Lincoln was assassinated; when they reconvened in early December 1865 they found delegates seeking admission that were former Confederates. For hard-core Unionists this was intolerable: the former Confederates (and others) were not recognized by Congress, which in December created The Joint Committee on Reconstruction, formed of members who strongly disagreed with Andrew Johnson's policy of quick readmission, which would ultimately set the terms of the former Confederate states' reentry into the Union.

In the meantime, Southern legislatures and conservative political leaders, including those of Arkansas, sought to maintain their traditional positions of authority in their respective states' political and social systems Legislatures enacted restrictive measures, known generally as "Black Codes," which discouraged Blacks from serving on juries, owning weapons, and having mass meetings. The legislatures also set up systems of segregated schools. This fueled the anger of the Radicals who feared that a new system of forced peonage and second-class, incomplete citizenship would replace slavery. In response, the Republican-led Congress passed the Civil Rights Act of 1866 for the purpose of invalidating the Black Codes.

The Congress also proposed the 14th Amendment to the Constitution as a means for a seceded state to regain admission. It defined a citizen of the United States as being a person who was born in the country or one who was naturalized by law. It required that no state could abridge the rights of a citizen or deprive any person of life, liberty or property without due process of law. It also disqualified any person from state or national office that had previously taken an oath to uphold the Constitution of the United States and had subsequently taken part in or supported the Rebellion. In order for one to gain a pardon and thus re-qualify for office he must first be pardoned by the Congress by a two-thirds vote of each chamber. It also required the states to validate the United States' war debt and repudiate the Confederate debt. The amendment also contained a provision that would reduce a state's representation by the proportion of eligible voters in that state excluded from this right, thus reducing the discriminating states' representation in the U.S. House of Representatives. After the House and Senate both voted on the amendment in June 1866, it was submitted to the states for ratification.

President Johnson made clear his opposition to the 14th Amendment as it made its way through the ratification process, but Congressional elections in late 1866 gave Republicans veto-proof majorities in both the House and Senate, so the president was forced to accep5t this challenge to his will.

Southern states also resisted, but Congress required them to ratify the 13th and 14th Amendments as a condition of regaining representation in Congress; the ongoing presence of the occupying Federal Army in the former Confederate states ensured their compliance. Tennessee was the first southern state to ratify, followed by Arkansas in the spring of 1868. On July 9, 1868, Louisiana and South Carolina voted to ratify the 14th Amendment, the last two approvals needed for ratification.

※ ※ ※

In the midst of this constitutional wrangling Arkansas's court system managed to function. In Sebastian County Augustus N. Hargrove, who had been named circuit judge under presidential Reconstruction in 1864, advertised in *The New Era* as an attorney on May 5, 1865. His advertisement did not mention state court where he, of course, was the judge. Elijah D. Ham, later circuit judge and then U. S. Attorney, advised that he would be available to represent persons as an attorney "except where U. S. is a party." Another advertisement for Ham reported that his office was in front of the Provost Marshal's office and that he would handle debt collection and real estate. Legal notices also were appearing, a sign of activity among the judges and advocates: on August 5, 1865, a notice was published regarding the appointment of Hannah Sparks as administratrix of the estate of Mitchell Sparks and for constructive service on Decatur Mumford on a bill of divorce filed by his wife Mary Ellen Mumford. Meanwhile, Judge Hargrove held court on a regular basis. Former Judge and Confederate Congressman Felix Batson wrote, in a letter dated March 24, 1867, "I understand that Judge Hargrove intends to hold court at Ft. Smith this spring. If he does, I shall try to attend...."

A case heard by Judge Hargrove that made its way to the Arkansas Supreme Court during this period was *Harper v. State*, 25 Ark. 83 (1867). This was a criminal case that was reversed and remanded for a new trial due to an improper oath given the jury. The reasoning of the High Court suggests the "straining at gnats" quality of much legal wrangling of those days. The official record of the trial flatly stated that the members of the jury were sworn, impaneled and took their seats in the jury box. There was, however, a fatal flaw in this record: the court reporter failed to explicitly affirm that a "proper" oath had been asked of the jurors. The court cited precedent to the effect that had the record had stated that the proper oath had been administered to the jury, it would have presumed that it had been proper. The court record did not, however, explicitly state that an oath by which each juror swore to give a true verdict according to the law and evidence (as required by law) had been administered. In all probability such an oath had been administered, but the court reporter, working in pen and ink, trying to keep up with courtroom proceedings, had taken a shortcut to save a little time and a few lines of scrivening—and this was judged mispractice enough to have the verdict reversed and a new trial ordered

Times were still hard in Sebastian County. On May 7, 1867, *The Arkansas Gazette* reported from *The Fort Smith Herald*:

> *In the upper portion of the county there is considerable destitution...many without bread or meat and no money to buy food. Corn is very scarce...none to sell at any price....those who can should assist those in want...We hope our people may be enabled to get along without being compelled to call for assistance from abroad...(the situation) is caused by late spring and bad weather.*

While a semblance of business as usual returned to Arkansas's legal community, the state itself continued to be in limbo: no longer in rebellion but, like most of the rest of the former Confederacy, not fully a member of the Union once more. In 1867, Congress set out a road map to recovered statehood, in the form of its Reconstruction Acts of that year. The Acts applied to all of the once-seceded states excepting Tennessee, which had ratified the 14th Amendment in the previous year, precociously winning its readmission. Under their terms, the old Confederacy was divided into five military districts. Arkansas was placed in the 4th Military District. All state governments set up under Presidential Reconstruction were declared void and an army general was placed in control of each district. General E.O.C. Ord was the commander of the 4th Military District. Governor Isaac Murphy was allowed to stay in office but the legislature was barred from meeting. The Arkansas Supreme Court was allowed to function but all cases involving Blacks and whites were placed under the jurisdiction of a military tribunal.

As a part of this revised and more restrictive Reconstruction, new circuit judges were named. For Arkansas's Ninth Circuit, a familiar name replaced that of Judge Hargrove: Lieutenant-Colonel Elhanan J. Searle, the former provost marshal at Fort Smith, was named Judge for the Ninth Judicial Circuit on February 25, 1867.

Elhanan John Searle was born on January 18, 1835, at Royalton, Fairfield County, Illinois. He was the eldest son of James and Elizabeth Quinn Searle. In 1855, he entered Rock River Seminary at Mount Morris, Illinois, where he prepared for college. He entered Northwestern University at Evanston, Illinois, in 1856. He completed the course in three years graduating in 1859, with a BA. He later received an AM degree from the same school. While at Northwestern he began the study of law under General John L. Beveridge of Chicago who later became the governor of Illinois. When he completed this course he went to Springfield, Illinois, where he entered the practice of law in the firm of Abraham Lincoln and William Herndon in November 1859. Searle had a close relationship with Lincoln which continued after his mentor put aside the law and took up the splendid burden of the presidency; the two corresponded until Lincoln's death. Searle was admitted to the Illinois bar in 1861. He then entered the Union army as a private in Company B of the Tenth 10th Illinois Volunteer Cavalry. During the war he rose to the rank of Lieutenant Colonel, taking part in the battles of Cane Hill, Prairie Grove, and Fayetteville, Arkansas, as well as Perryville, Indian Territory, and Jenkins Ferry and Camden, Arkansas. He served as Provost Marshal at Fort Smith and organized the First Arkansas Volunteer Cavalry. He mustered out of the service on August 10, 1865, at Fort Smith where he decided to make his home. His wife had already joined him and a son, Charles J. Searle, had been born there on May 16, 1865.

On February 19, 1866, Searle was commissioned Prosecuting Attorney for the Ninth Judicial Circuit and also served as United States Commissioner and Assistant United States Attorney for the district and circuit court in the Western District of Arkansas. When he was named circuit judge he relocated to Arkadelphia in Clark County, the easternmost county in the Ninth Circuit and probably the most populous and least affected by the desolation of the war. While in Arkadelphia, Searle was a target of the violence that had erupted over

JUDGE ELHANAN J. SEARLE
CIRCUIT JUDGE
1867-1868
PHOTO COURTESY OF ILLINOIS HISTORICAL SOCIETY

Reconstruction: the desperado Cullen Baker, who was responsible for 27 murders, reportedly attempted to assassinate Searle.

King v. Carnall (26 Ark. 36 1870), a Sebastian County case originally decided by Judge Searle, made its way on appeal to the Arkansas Supreme Court in 1870. The defendant (and appellee on appeal) was John Carnall, the former county clerk of Sebastian County, who had erected the first government building in Greenwood. He had signed a promissory note in 1862 for one thousand dollars, payable in Confederate money. Judge Searle, sitting without a jury, sustained Carnall's demurrer (that is, a riposte or objection, without disputing the facts in the case) to the plea in that Carnall admitted he signed the note but that it was unenforceable in light of the fact that the chosen "consideration," Confederate money, was in fact not legal tender, thus ineligible as consideration for the contract. Thus, King, the holder of the note, was left high and dry—unable to collect, even in now-discredited secessionist money. The Supreme Court affirmed Judge Searle, stating they had already decided the issue in the prior case of *Clark v. Latham* reported in 25 *Arkansas Reports*.

Under the Reconstruction acts all adult males were to be registered to vote and that included African Americans. Often, more Blacks than whites were registered. This caused a decided political shift of power to the south and east parts of the state due to those areas' greater population of newly enfranchised Blacks. Following registration, an election would be held to choose delegates for a constitutional convention. This convention would draft a new fundamental document for state government including a provision for black suffrage. This constitution would then be submitted to voters in a referendum and after approval, an election for new state officers and legislators would be held. Finally, the newly elected legislature would ratify the 14th Amendment to the U.S. Constitution. When all these provisions were met, the state would be fully readmitted to the Union.

The registration was completed and delegates elected to the Constitutional Convention of 1868. They first met on January 7, 1868, in Little Rock. The convention was dominated by Unionists due to the registration rules. These included "Carpetbaggers" (Northerners who came south after the war to profit), "Scalawags" (southern whites loyal to the Union), and "Black Republicans" (former slaves now politically active). One of the leaders in the convention was Rev. Joseph Brooks, a former Methodist preacher from Iowa who was said to have a voice like a "brindletail bull." This characterization would later be used to describe his partisans as "The Brindle Tails" in the Brooks-Baxter War of 1873-74.

The drafted constitution satisfied Congressional requirements or expectations: it declared racial discrimination illegal, provided support for public education and for a university, and fixed legislative apportionments to favor counties with large African-American populations and opened the franchise to adult male African Americans. This constitution also greatly enhanced the power of the state government, especially that of the governor. Four-year terms for constitutional officers were restored, and the governor was given broad power to appoint officials, including judges. The judicial article of The Constitution of 1868 was, for many, particularly troubling: the ultimate judicial power of the state now effectively resided in the state Senate, sitting as a court of impeachment. The Supreme Court, circuit courts and inferior courts all obtained their authority through the state Senate, rather than existing as a body independent of political pressure. The doctrine of separation of powers was thus turned on its head in this time of "reform." Impeachment of officials was initialed in the House of Representatives and the Senate was body that conducted the trial. Conviction required a two-thirds vote. The chief justice of the state Supreme Court would preside and the Secretary of State served as clerk of the court. Any officer facing impeachment and subsequent trial was to be replaced by temporary appointment made by the governor. Grounds for impeachment included any misconduct or maladministration in office. Punishment was removal from office and a disqualification from subsequently holding any office of public trust. A person so convicted could still be criminally prosecuted.

The Supreme Court in this constitution consisted of a chief justice appointed by the governor and confirmed by the Senate. He served an eight-year term. There were four associate justices making the total court consist of five justices. The associate justices were elected and served staggered terms of eight years. The constitution also provided that the Supreme Court was a court of record and that its decisions must be in writing and signed by the concurring justices. Dissenting opinions must also be in writing and all opinions and dissents must be published and filed and kept by the clerk. Circuit judges were appointed by the governor to a six-year term with the advice and consent of the Senate.

Apparently judges who were not politically acceptable were liable to be impeached (example: Hargrove) and replaced by governor's appointment (example: Searle). Other changes included requirements that judges not comment on the facts at trial and that jury instructions be in writing. In a trial to the court without a jury, all findings and conclusions were required to be set out in writing, along with a statement of applicable law. All inferior (trial) courts were designated as courts of record. The justice of the peace courts had their jurisdictional limit raised to $200 and enjoyed exclusive jurisdiction in cases of contract and replevin and concurrent with circuit in cases up to $500.

The drafters of this document were seemingly more interested in impeachment than representative or elected governance. Article 15 provided that in all cases not provided for in the constitution, the general assembly might determine the mode of filling all vacancies in all offices and of choosing all necessary officers, and should define their respective powers and duties, plus provide suitable compensation.

A statewide election was held in March 1868, seeking approval of the document. The slogan of the opposition—consisting mainly of the self-styled "Conservatives," mainly former secessionist Democrats, was "A white man's government in a white man's country." But in this hope, the Conservatives were sorely frustrated. Voter fraud was claimed in the election and no less a figure than attorney, former Confederate Congressman, Senator and future U.S. Attorney General Augustus H. Garland opined that by an honest count the new constitution would have been rejected by 20,000 votes.

On June 22, 1868, Arkansas was readmitted to the Union. Onetime Union General Powell Clayton was elected governor and there was but one Democrat in each of the two chambers of the legislature. From this point the violence and bitterness escalated. The promise of "presidential" Reconstruction had been pulled back and the former Confederates were even more bitter than before. In their view, political power had been taken from them by intimidation, corruption and fraud. One the other side of the political fence, Unionists in both Arkansas and Washington were not about to allow the old ways to return to Arkansas or to the rest of the South. The agricultural economy based on slave labor was a shambles, but the old Rebels were not going to take any attempts to restructure the region's society along northern ideals lying down. Some of this mood was reflected in a letter written by former Judge Felix Batson in March of 1867 concerning a former slave:

> *I fear that our "freedman" is not destined long to stay. He feels all the importance of his position in society, has frequently thrown out hints that he wanted pay, and yesterday told your Ma that he wanted to make a contract for a year, and told of several offers he had. One of which was for 10$ a month, he has been here three weeks, done but little, and we have given him clothing to double the amount of his services. I think by the time he gets a new wardrobe he will leave. It is astonishing to find out the persons both black and white that will try to persuade off a Negro. And it appears to be more particularly the case with one who is with the former owner.*

The mood of rebellion was even more evident in an editorial, probably composed by William Woodruff, Jr., in *The Arkansas Gazette*:

"In the present political struggle we believe that the end we seek will justify the use of ANY means. We will not "play honest" with utter scoundrelism but will use any and every weapon with which Providence has gifted us to fight it."

The means turned out to be violence and intimidation.

❧ ❧ ❧

The year 1868 brought change to the judiciary in Sebastian County. The legislature reconfigured the judicial circuits and Sebastian was placed in the Fifth Judicial Circuit along with Benton, Washington, Crawford and Scott Counties by Act 7 of 1868. After brief service in the circuit, Judge Searle was appointed by Governor Clayton to the Arkansas Supreme Court on July 22, 1868. He was elected to a term in that office in 1872 and continued to serve the state until the end of Reconstruction in 1874.

His departure for the High Court was probably not mourned by all: the author of *Clark County, Past and Present* relates a tale in which Judge Searle held an Arkadelphia editor in contempt of court, and jailed him, after the editor printed an editorial criticizing the judge for dissolving a grand jury called to investigate an election where more votes were cast than there were registered voters. Upon release the editor did not conceal his contempt for Searle and the other Reconstructionists and in an editorial referred to him as "His Jackass-ship"

The new judge of the Fifth Judicial Circuit, appointed July 23, 1868, was Elijah D. Ham. He was born in Talledega County, Alabama, probably in 1839 or 40, to parents James T. and Elizabeth Whaley Ham. His father was a native of Petersburg, Virginia and his mother from Walker County, Georgia. They moved when he was a child first to Bedford County, Tennessee and, when Elijah was fifteen, to Washington County, Arkansas. Young Elijah Ham received his education in Tennessee and later at Arkansas College in Fayetteville. He studied law, was admitted to the bar and was practicing law in Huntsville, Arkansas when the war broke out. Ham, along with the rest of his family, was a Unionist; he fled to the mountains to avoid conscription into the Confederate service or hanging as a Union sympathizer. By early 1862 he escaped into Missouri and joined Bowen's Battalion attached to the headquarters of General Samuel Curtis. Ham was detailed as a scout due to his knowledge of the territory. He showed ability and soon was made chief of scouts with the rank (and pay) of Captain. Ham's two brothers also served in Federal units. Ham's father went into hiding

Act 7 of 1868
5th Judicial Circuit
Consisting of Sebastian, Scott, Crawford, Washington, and Benton Counties

to avoid arrest by Confederate authorities and would die due to exposure during the winter of 1863.

In February 1863, Elijah Ham was commissioned Major of the First Arkansas Volunteer Infantry and served in that capacity until close to the end of the war. He participated in all the battles in Southwest Missouri and Northwest Arkansas including Pea Ridge, Cotton Plant, Prairie Grove, and Fayetteville. In 1864, while still in the service, he was elected state senator under Presidential Reconstruction representing Benton and Washington Counties. He served on the state's Judiciary Committee. President Lincoln also appointed him as the United States Attorney for the Western District of Arkansas, which included eleven counties in western Arkansas and all of the Indian Territory. In 1868, he was appointed by Governor Clayton as circuit judge for the newly constituted Fifth Judicial Circuit.

The old dispute concerning the location of the county seat in Sebastian was the subject of an election in December 1868. the *Arkansas Gazette* reported from *The New Era* on January 9, 1869:

> *"The election held last Saturday as to where the county seat is to be permanently located resulted as was to be expected, in the choice of this city (Ft. Smith). This is as it should be and even those who voted against this place, will, in a brief period, discover that it is in the interest of the people of the whole country to have the county seat at Fort Smith. Some few persons will doubtless be disappointed, but they must remember that their interest must give way to the interest of the great majority." The vote was 523 for Fort Smith and 393 for Greenwood.*

Four hundred and sixty-seven votes came from Upper Township (Fort Smith). In the rest of the county, only 56 votes were cast for Fort Smith.

On January 26, 1869, the *Gazette* reported that the county court refused to acknowledge the election of December 24. It was claimed by the majority that there had not been adequate notice of the election, despite articles in the paper and handbills, and that the measure had not passed by a majority of the qualified voters as the legislative enactment required. The article proclaimed that there must be something done and suggested taking it to a higher court. The legislature, not to be denied, passed an act amending the previous act to the effect of requiring only a majority of the votes actually cast to authorize a move of the county seat. They also made it retroactive so as not to require another election.

JUDGE ELIJAH D. HAM
CIRCUIT JUDGE
1868-1874
PHOTO COURTESY OF HAM FAMILY

On January 25, 1870, the *Arkansas Gazette*, reprinting a *New Era* story, reported:

> *Last Friday, Col. Lockhart, deputy county clerk, proceeded to Greenwood with the necessary conveyance and help and brought away the records of the county to this city (Ft. Smith) in accordance with the recent order of The County Court. We learn that the board of commissioners appointed by the County Clerk to determine where within the city limits the new court house is to be built will most probably accept the donation of our liberal minded former fellow townsman, Col. Samuel L. Griffith, at present in business in Little Rock, of that splendid block of town lots, known formerly as Fort No. 4, overlooking the valley of the Arkansas and a vast space of country in every direction.*

On May 26, 1870, the *Arkansas Gazette* reported:

> *Dr. E.R. DuVal of Fort Smith has been appointed by the County Court, commissioner of county buildings for Sebastian County, Arkansas, and will receive until the first of July,1870, plans and specifications for a courthouse and county jail. The building must be of hewn stone or brick, three stories high, 60 x 70 feet. All architects are invited to present plans and specifications and the approved plan will be liberally paid for by the county.*

On July 17, the *Gazette* again quoted *The New Era*:

> *The County Court met on the 11th inst. Dr. E.R. DuVal, chairman of the commissioners to procure and submit plans and specifications for the new court house, reported two plans. The commissioners decided in favor of the one submitted by Messrs. Green and Edwards of Little Rock. The building to be erected according to this plan will be one that will be an honor to the county. It is to contain two large court rooms, for federal and state courts; clerk's office fire proof vaults etc. The county jail will be under the same roof, arranged in such a manner to ensure both the comfort and perfect safe keeping of all the prisoners. An eye was also had to the architectural beauty of the building, and standing upon the most commanding site within the city limits. It will present from all sides, especially the river, a grand appearance. The estimated cost is between $40.000-$50,000.*

The plans for a Fort Smith courthouse were a bit premature. The battle shifted to the legislature once again. State Representative C.B. Neal of Greenwood, an attorney and mentor to several law students who would become circuit judges, introduced a bill to allow for two places to hold court in Sebastian County. *The Arkansas Gazette* reported that it passed the House on March 4, 1871, and on March 15 stated:

> *The county seat question in this county has been a source of bitter trouble for a number of years. As Representative (J.B.) Stevens said, ' This question*

> *had well nigh ruined both political parties of the county'. The bill of Mr. Neal which passed the house the other day to create separate courts in that county has stirred up the blood of the Fort Smith District. Says the **Herald** of recent date; 'We learn that a remonstrance against the folly and madness of Mr. [C.B.] Neal of Greenwood, in trying to divide this county, has been forwarded to the legislature, this should have been done long ago and he who abates that Neal bill as a compromise between Greenwood and Fort Smith, should be made to swallow that lie. If the senator from this district (Valentine Dell, the editor of the competing 'New Era') has any influence and wishes to benefit this county, we trust he will use it in this matter.*

The *Gazette* went on to state that it wanted it "...strictly understood that we take no side in this dispute, it would be like interfering between a man and his wife." The bill passed the Senate as well and became law. On March 25, the *Arkansas Gazette* reported:

> *The House bill to divide the county of Sebastian into two county courts districts (Neal's bill) was passed (by the senate). All the Radicals except (Valentine) Dell and White voting for, and all the Democrats voting against the bill. After passage of the bill, under the whip and spur of the radical leaders, a buzz went through the Senate chamber, "Neal's reward."*

For what was Neal being rewarded by the Radicals? It doesn't say.

The matter made its way to the Arkansas Supreme Court in. *Patterson v. Temple*, 27 Ark. 202 (1871). On April 17, 1871, Newton J. Temple, the Prosecuting Attorney, filed in circuit court an application for a writ of mandamus directed to William Patterson, as clerk of the various courts, to not remove any of the books, records, papers, etc., to Greenwood as he was required to do pursuant to an Act of the General Assembly, approved March 28, 1871. The act in question was the "dual districts" bill championed by Rep. C. B. Neal of Greenwood. Temple alleged that the act was void as it violated the United States Constitution and that Fort Smith was the only county seat of Sebastian County, thus the only legal place in the county to hold court. The answer denied that Fort Smith was ever the county seat, asserted the validity of the act of the General Assembly and rehearsed the history of the matter. Judge Ham of the Circuit Court had ruled in favor of Fort Smith and the defendant appealed.

On appeal the matter was reversed and remanded by the Supreme Court. Associate Justice John E. Bennett's lengthy opinion reviewed the history of the divided judicial arrangement; he opined that that the legislative act which required that the assessor keep separate the assessments and collections of the two districts destroyed the integrity of Sebastian as a county in the state and was, hence, therefore, unconstitutional. Having decided that the act of the General

Assembly allowing the move of the county seat was unconstitutional, the High Court then turned to the question of the true location of the county seat of Sebastian. The court ruled that the county seat of Sebastian was Greenwood and that there were two places that court might be held: Fort Smith and Greenwood, pursuant to the Act of 1861.

Interestingly, the court stated that it could have very easily tossed the appeal on the grounds that the prosecuting attorney did not have standing to bring an action on behalf of the state. The court ruled that this was not done as it was a question of great public interest in Sebastian County and that the court would have been guilty of a dereliction of duty had they avoided an adjudication of it upon the technical question of practice as to who may have been the proper parties to bring suit. In this day of voluminous rules of practice, would such common sense prevail?

In Fort Smith, the county owned no facility for its court. Prior to 1872 the offices of Sebastian County in Fort Smith had been located in rooms in a building at the corner of Walnut (the present North "A" Street) and Second Street. This building burned in that year. As previously reported, during the preceding year there had been plans to build a courthouse in Fort Smith, reflecting that town's confidence that it would be named the county seat, and in fact work had begun on the building's foundation. *The New Era*, on April 7, 1871, asserted that the payment for the foundation work on the courthouse was paid in scrip, the nature of which was not explained, and not currency. The contract, however, had called for payment in currency. Editor Dell urged the Fort Smith officials to pay up and finish the courthouse. He stated that it had been promised that if the county seat were to be placed in Fort Smith and that if the Federal Court were removed to Fort Smith, a new courthouse would be built to house them. The Federal Court was moved from Van Buren to Fort Smith in 1871 and located in the old barracks building of the fort.

Even though the status of Fort Smith as county seat was in doubt, Dell wrote, "Do not let it be said we entered upon an undertaking and gave it up, that we wished to build but could not see how to do it or that we have bought an elephant (foundation) and have no use for him. If it is possible to complete the courthouse, let's do it." In spite of Dell's brave exhortation, the courthouse project was abandoned but it left a legacy: it would be the subject of litigation in the years to come.

The court's offices, following the 1872 fire, were moved to a building at the corner Garrison Avenue and First Street. This site is today located under the approach to the Garrison Avenue bridge near Harry Kelley Park. In 1875, both the court and its records were moved to a building in the Kannady Block of

Garrison Avenue near The Leflore Hotel. This building was next to Adelaide Hall, the site of the present Bricktown Brewery.

From this internecine tempest in a teapot named Sebastian County, we turn once again to the boiling cauldron of Arkansas as whole and the brewing rebellion against the Radical Republicans in charge. In 1867 and 1868, Conservative opposition to the reforms and innovations surfaced: disenfranchised former Confederates who had been unwilling to swear an oath of allegiance and were hence left politically excluded and powerless began terrorizing the state's freedmen and their supporters, as they did in other Southern states. In April of 1868, ominous flyers issued by the Ku Klux Klan's local affiliates appeared on the street corners of Little Rock, and the Klan's presence quickly spread across the state, intimidating, terrorizing and killing. In a two-year period, 385 Republicans were killed, mainly Blacks.

This statewide racial and political conflict often involved personal quarrels as well. Valentine Dell, editor of *The New Era* and Republican state senator, found that he had his own battles to fight, literally. He reported in the September 8, 1871, edition of *The New Era* that T.H. Scott, Sebastian County Sheriff and Collector, had accosted him. If this were the case, Dell could hardly deny that Scott might have had a few grievances to work out: Dell had accused him in print of collecting taxes in currency and paying bills in scrip; he also denounced Scott as a drunkard, belittled dismissed Scott's report to the *Arkansas Gazette* that there was a reign of terror and disorder in Sebastian County, accused Scott of trying to intimidate *The New Era* and stated that it could not be done. In another article, Dell accused the sheriff of being a Klan member and alleged that Scott had assaulted a Black man, then voluntarily paid the fine for having done so. Dell's accusations attracted notice: a commission was convened to dispel the stories of discord in Sebastian County that had been spread by Scott. It found, perhaps unsurprisingly, that the county was a peaceful place.

The Klan movement had started in Tennessee and spread to the rest of the old South. Night riders, dressed as the shades of dead Confederate soldiers in shrouds of black and white, would swoop down on their victims and inflict their damage: threats and intimidation, property damage, violence and, too often, death. This racial and political terrorism was embraced by disenfranchised former Confederates who were, they felt, otherwise powerless. The KKK's activities reached their zenith in advance of the November 1868 general election. The Klan sought, effectively, to prevent voter registration and to intimidate prospective Republican voters. In the three months before the election, the governor's office recorded more than 200 murders; one of these was Congressman James Hinds, shot in the back in late October.

In the wake of the election, Powell Clayton took action: On November 24, Clayton told the Arkansas General Assembly that the present "reign of terror" would carry Arkansas toward "anarchy and destruction." Clayton declared martial law in ten counties that he deemed to be in revolt. To enforce this, he sent militia forces organized months before. Only voters might serve in the militia hence it was mainly made up of loyal Republican, and incidentally, African American—troops and white officers.

Soon, Clayton's counterattack on the Klan proved effective. The militia fought hard and won battles; hundreds of Klan members fled to Tennessee and other surrounding states. Because of this quick success, by February 6, 1869, martial law was lifted in nine of the ten counties. Nathan Bedford Forrest, the onetime slave trader turned Confederate general and alleged leader of the Klan, is said to have ordered the Klan to disband. This stranded thousands of secret supporters who were allegedly ready to march on Little Rock. On March 13, 1869, the General Assembly adopted a law declaring the Ku Klux Klan illegal. The legislature, however, recognized that there was danger in making outlaws of so many: an olive branch was proffered on April 6, 1869. The General Amnesty Act of that date granted amnesty for any acts committed by the Klan or the militia. All persons who had property confiscated by the militia could file claims with the state. Thus some peace was bought, at the price of letting criminals walk free, but the state's troubles were not yet over by any means. The stage was now set for what has come to be known as the Brooks-Baxter War, Arkansas's very own civil war.

At this remove of nearly fifteen decades The Brooks-Baxter War seems confusing, in part because it was not a contest between Federals and Confederates, or between Republicans and Democrats; instead, it pitted factions of the state's Republican party against one another, with conservative ex-Confederate Democrats enjoying the spectacle from the sidelines. To make sense of it, it must be understood that the Republican coalition in Arkansas was never a united front or party in the modern understanding. It was composed of the old Unionist men from Northwest Arkansas, who resented being passed over in favor of recently arrived "Carpetbaggers" for government appointments and good business deals, and the Carpetbaggers themselves. In the middle of this mix was the Rev. Joseph Brooks, who was largely responsible for turning out the black vote and obtaining passage of the 1868 Constitution.

The Ohio-born Brooks, though technically a Carpetbagger, was a maverick with a social and racial reformist element in his personality, which set him apart from other pragmatic opportunist Republican acolytes of Powell Clayton. In the wake of the 1868 election, Brooks was denied any major office and was dissatisfied; he began to break with the Clayton faction and criticized the government as being too expensive, with too many wasteful practices. He also claimed that there was corruption in refunding state debts and financing railroads with bond money. Idealism might have been tolerated but violating what would become known as Ronald Reagan's Eleventh Commandment—thou shalt not speak ill of any fellow Republican—broke the bounds of acceptability: by early 1869, *The Daily Republican* was demanding that he be purged from the party. Lieutenant Governor James Johnson was likewise no friend of Clayton's: he accused Clayton corruption in handling railroad bonds and of abusing his powers in suppression of the violence following the 1868 election. Johnson's backers, mostly from northwestern Arkansas, also claimed the mantle of reformers and style themselves "Liberal Republicans." In the summer of 1869, the Brooks faction encouraged Johnson to actively assume the governorship while Clayton traveled out of state. This possible coup attempt was foiled by Clayton's rushing back to Little Rock.

Thus, the state's young Republican party fell into factional conflict. Clayton's faction was known as "Minstrels" after the former occupation of the editor of *The Daily Republican*, J. G. Price. Brooks supporters were dubbed "Brindletails," inspired by a description of Brooks, an experienced Methodist preacher, as having a "voice like a brindletail bull." Facing opposition from Johnson and other disgruntled native "Liberals" Clayton recognized the "handwriting on the wall": he tried to co-opt parts of the reformist agenda of the Brooks faction of the Republican "combine" in calling for economy in government, cutting taxes and extending the franchise to ex-Confederates.

In the legislative election of 1870, however, Governor Clayton started to see the power he had enjoyed wane. He was able to keep control of the legislature, despite an active attempt (supported by Lieutenant Governor Johnson) to have him impeached, but Clayton seemed to understand that his political fortunes could best be pursued away from Little Rock. He was elected to the U.S. Senate in January 1871 by the Arkansas General Assembly. However, he did not immediately accept this honor: if he were to take the seat, Lieutenant Governor Johnson would assume the office of governor, which Clayton could not countenance. Clayton therefore delayed until a deal was struck: Johnson would resign and be appointed to the office of secretary of state, which had become vacant. With the office of lieutenant governor vacant, the succession to the governor's seat would fall to Clayton's ally and Arkansas Senate president *pro tempore* Ozro Hadley. In March 1871 the deal was consummated and Clayton ascended to the U.S. Senate, from which he would still be active in the affairs of Arkansas' Republicans.

In May of 1871, Joseph Brooks, who had tried unsuccessfully to enter the state Senate, began his campaign for governor. In 1872, his "Brindletail" Republicans held a state convention and nominated him as their candidate for governor. They organized as the Reform Republican Party, aligning with the reformist national Liberal Republican movement. Brooks state platform seemed straightforward enough: "universal suffrage, universal amnesty and honest men in office." This appealed to ex-Confederates and conservatives. Most freedmen went with Brooks as well.

The state's regular Republicans (who, confusingly, sometimes styled themselves "Liberal" Republicans) nominated circuit judge Elisha Baxter, a "scalawag" who relied on the Clayton-erected Republican machine in his campaign. The election of November 5, 1872, was marred by violence, fraud, intimidation and multiple voting. No returns were received from four counties at all. Baxter won the vote by 2,919 votes. The "Minstrels" aligned with Baxter and, by implication, Clayton, retained control of the legislature and Arkansas' electoral votes went to Grant. There were, however, challenges to the state's Members of Congress as well and one "Brindletail," Thomas Gunter, was seated over the objections of Senators Clayton and Dorsey.

Brooks' only recourse for his complaints of election irregularity was to appeal to the "Minstrel" dominated legislature from which he could expect little sympathy. Elisha Baxter was confirmed and sworn into office by Chief Justice John McClure on January 6, 1873. All seemed to have worked out well for the Regular Republicans, but once in office, Baxter made mis-steps: he made overtures to former Confederate leaders (including the naming of a prominent ex-Confederate officer as head of the state militia), advanced the re-enfranchisement of former Confederates, thus allowing them to serve in the legislature, and then broke with party leaders over railroad legislation. Baxter's Minstrel supporters began to suspect that they had backed the wrong man: one such was Chief Justice McClure. McClure instigated the filing of *quo warranto* proceedings to have Baxter removed from office; this was rejected by the Supreme Court itself, but more trouble lay in store for Baxter. His fall from Minstrel grace was assured on March 16, 1874, when he declined a funding request from a railroad backed by Senator Stephen Dorsey and also questioned the legality of other previously approved railroad bond issues This threatened the basis of funding for the reconstruction of Arkansas; Clayton, Dorsey and, perhaps, McClure came up with a plan to replace Baxter with Brooks.

The pretext was a long-stalled lawsuit filed by Brooks in 1872, contesting the election results. *Brooks v. Baxter* still lay, unresolved, in the circuit court in Pulaski County. In May of 1874, Judge Whytock ruled on it in favor of Brooks without any notice to Baxter or his lawyers. Brooks was speedily sworn into office by Chief Justice McClure; he then, with a force of about 20 armed men, proceeded to the state Capitol and removed Baxter. Baxter set up headquarters in the Anthony House hotel, located a few blocks down Markham Street, and the Brooks-Baxter War was on.

Brooks lost support from the old guard Republicans, Democrats and conservatives because he was now supported by Clayton's "Minstrels." Little Rock became an armed camp and battle ground. Both sides had a militia. The Brooks forces were led by ex-Confederate Brigadier General James Fagan and the Baxter forces were led by ex-Confederate Colonel Robert Newton. The mayor of Little Rock called for Federal troops. About 200 people, mainly African Americans, were killed in the hostilities across the state. On May 3, 1874, General Fagan of the Baxter forces led a group of armed black recruits and successfully kidnapped Justice Elhanan Searle and Justice John E. Bennett of the Arkansas Supreme Court, since Baxter feared that they would set up court and declare that Brooks was the legal governor.

President Grant, mystified and misinformed, hesitated to act: he was dissatisfied with Baxter because of Baxter's embrace of ex-Confederates, to the detriment of his former Republican supporters. On the other hand, Brooks had promoted a bloody family feud, threatening Republican prospects in the state. Grant sought to strike a peacemaker's position: he suggested that each "governor" jointly call a session of the legislature. Brooks rejected this, but Baxter complied. The legislature met, duly reconfirmed Baxter and set a date for an election on calling a constitutional convention. Grant and Clayton realized the support for this and opted to cut their losses, ultimately throwing their support behind Baxter. To ease the sting, Grant appointed Brooks as postmaster of Little Rock and the Brooks-Baxter "war" was history.

During this time Sebastian County also had its own political war; like the party conflict that rocked the central part of the state, it too featured a character named McClure. It may in fact have been an outgrowth of the larger conflict and did gain some statewide notoriety due to a report by Sebastian County Sheriff John H. McClure (not to be confused with State Supreme Court Chief Justice John McClure) that was noted in a response in *The Fort Smith Herald*, then reprinted as an exchange in the *Little Rock Daily Republican*. The report had to do with the bond required of the elected sheriff, McClure, in order for him to act in his *ex officio* position of tax collector.

McClure was required to present the bond to the Board of Supervisors, a creation of the Reconstruction legislature under Article 15 and made up of three justices of the peace: Howard, McKibben and Ferguson.

The bond was presented to the chairman, Mr. Howard, on November 27, 1873, and was approved "in vacation," pending approval of the whole board. It was so presented on December 2, 1873, and, after examination, it was rejected. The pretext was that the bond must be "to the satisfaction of the board." And, the county board claimed, McClure's sureties were insufficient. The bond was withdrawn by McClure's lawyer. McClure, in a later petition for a writ of *mandamus* to the Arkansas Supreme Court, contended that the board excluded him and all others from the room and then "secretly and fraudulently" rejected the bond. This accusation was, however, disproved in the responding filings before the court. After the rejection, according to the report of the mandamus proceedings in the *Fort Smith Herald* on February 21, 1874,

> *McClure threatened to make the board eat the bond, put on his pistols and came into the courtroom and as Supervisor McKibben got into his buggy to go home spit at him, and afterwards boasted that he had spit in his face; and several times threatened his life if he attempted to hold court at Greenwood.*
>
> *On the 11th day of January, 1874, the regular session of the board commenced. McKibben was elected president and McClure's bond was to be again acted on, he having, after its first rejection and withdrawal, procured other signatures and the approval of Howard in vacation. On that day McClure, his deputies and others hangers-on assembled at Greenwood, fired off anvils and tied black strips around their legs, which they stated was 'mourning for hedgehogs' as they derisively termed Supervisors McKibben and Ferguson. They were frequently seen in court during the day, acting in a rude manner. McClure repeatedly stated that he 'was ready to die' and if his bond was rejected "he would get even, etc." The horses of himself and two more deputies were brought near the court-house door and held by a negro, and the conduct of his party was so threatening that the board was advised that it would be at the risk of their lives to act on the bond. Under these circumstances they adjourned court until Thursday January 8.*
>
> *McClure's threats on McKibben's life were openly repeated and communicated to McKibben. He took out a warrant for the arrest of McClure, to hold him to security to keep the peace; and Ferguson also filed an affidavit before Justice of the Peace C.P. Swift, charging McClure and his deputies with intimidating the court, riot, etc."*

The writs were placed in the hand of Constable Duff of the Upper Township for execution. His report, published in the January 30, 1874, *Herald*, in response to a report in *The Daily Republican* in Little Rock signed by "Republican," tells us what transpired when the warrants were executed:

> *"On the sixth day of January, 1874, I received from C.P. Swift, Justice of the Peace, a warrant of arrest for J.H. McClure, Sheriff of Sebastian County, on a charge of threatening 'to kill and murder David A. McKibben' President of the Board of Supervisors of Sebastian County.*
>
> *On the 7th of January 1874, I received four other warrants from said Justice of the Peace for the arrest of J. H. McClure, R. W. McClure, John Patterson, and Horace H. Fellows, charged with intimidating the Board of Supervisors of Sebastian County on the 5th of January 1874.*
>
> *It was currently reported here at that time that one of McClure's Deputies who had been in town on the 6th, that if we intended to arrest John McClure, we had better bring men enough to do it. D. A. McKibben, President of the Board of Supervisors, directed me to summons a sufficient number of men, as a posse to aid me in making the arrest, and to remain and protect the Supervisor's Court during its session, from interruption or intimidation.*
>
> *I summoned a number of men, and with about thirty good men, including my Deputies, summoned without regard to political party, I went to Greenwood. I had been informed that McClure had about twenty or thirty armed men concealed in his store and in the Court-house at Greenwood, determined to resist the execution of process which I had, and to prevent the court from sitting if his bond was not approved.*
>
> *Upon this information, I determined to make a night march of it, and enter Greenwood at an early hour in the morning, which I did and with my posse surrounded both the Court house and McClure's Store. McClure was in the upper room of his store, myself and William Falconer (later County and Probate Judge and Chancery Judge for the 10th Chancery Circuit) one of my Deputies, Henry Williams, another Deputy, and Dr. Frayser went up the side steps, to where there were two doors, Falconer went to one door and I went to the other and knocked. I had previously knocked at the lower front door and received no answer. Some person opened the door which Falconer had knocked at, we inquired for Mr. McClure stating we had a warrant for his arrest. Some one opened the door and saw Falconer standing there; he then slammed the door shut to, and at that time a shot was fired within the room where the person had been, and when Falconer opened the door again some person was going down the inside stairs.*
>
> *We found in this room, one of McClure's brothers-in-law, Mr. Morris, whom we asked if it was McClure that went down the stairs, to which he made an*

evasive answer, and said, 'If there is going to be trouble here, for God's sake let me out.' I told him that I had a writ for McClure and that if he would surrender there would be no trouble. I then called and said, 'McClure, if you are down there, come up and surrender, there shall be no harm done to you'. Falconer then said, 'come up, we intend you no harm, and will protect you at the risk of my life as Duff and myself are both your friends, we will see that you are not harmed.' Falconer offered to help him up the stairs-McClure came up, and I shook hands with him and McClure laid his pistols on the table, and surrendered. During this time there were some three or four shots fired on the outside of the house.

I was about to read the warrants to McClure but he said 'if you have them it is all right', and about that time Dr. Bennett came up the stairs and I had the writs in my hand, and he asked me to let him see them. I gave them to him and he read them aloud and McClure said 'that is quite satisfactory.' I then asked McClure where Fellows and Patterson were, that I had a writ for them also. He told me and asked me not to take too much of a crowd with me. I took my deputies Rounds, Joe Swift, Henry Williams and Constable Morris of Centre Township with me and I arrested Jno. Patterson and Horace Fellows. They said when arrested that they expected to be arrested for what they had done but not at so early an hour that if we had come at a late hour in the day, we could have seen some fun. When they saw the force I had, they said it was well that I had brought so many men, that at a late hour no ten or fifteen men could or would have taken them, that they would have given us a little fun. After this I arrested W. R. McClure, J.P; brother of John H. McClure, and his family being sick, I took his recognizance to appear before C. P. Swift, J.P. on the 10th of January to answer.

I told McClure, Patterson and Fellows, that I should send them to Fort Smith, and they could choose from my posse the men they wished to go with them, which they did and came to town. After they had gone I heard that some persons were intending to follow the prisoners and to kill them, and I immediately sent some of my posse to aid these who had the prisoners, in defending them and it was the party who 'the man in the <u>Republican</u>' said tried to assassinate McClure and his deputies.

After McClure and his deputies left for Fort Smith, with their guard, quite and additional number of my posse being business men, were sent home.

During the day (Jan.8,74), I heard that quite a number of McClure's friends were gathering to attack my party, now reduced to myself, D. A. McKibben and Mr. Ferguson, Supervisors, and three Deputies, Swift, Rounds and Williams, and five posse, and believing that the report was true, fifteen or twenty men, who had come from different parts of the county came to me and volunteered to aid us in protecting ourselves and the court. I accepted their aid and took the necessary precautions to prevent the anticipated attack, which was done in a gentlemanly and quiet manner.

William Falconer left Greenwood before McClure did, and went to his home, and was not there during my stay at Greenwood. As to the men in my party being drunk, I pronounce it to be an unmitigated lie. There was not one man in our party that showed any evidence of being under the influence of liquor, and I afterwards learned that he obtained it from a person who attempted to get through my pickets, (during my night march to Greenwood) to apprize McClure of our approach, but was stopped by the pickets and kept until we moved on, and he went with us. This man and another who went with us-who were McClure's friends, were the only persons that I saw <u>drunk.</u>

William Falconer, who went with me, was one of my deputies, and behaved himself in a courteous and gentlemanly manner. I have been an officer in this county for the past six years, and have always found not only Wm. Falconer but his Brothers, also the 'Wheeler Boys'- <u>John and Bill</u>-and the others like them, have been called <u>Bushwhackers</u> and <u>Rebels</u>, ready and willing to aid and assist me or any other officer in enforcing the laws-a compliment by the way, which I cannot pay to some of my <u>so-called</u> Republican friends-who are now persecuting me and other Republicans, for doing our sworn duty on this occasion, as will appear from the following notice from McClure, which I am satisfied was dictated by one of his <u>tall friends.</u>

Sheriff's Office
Sebastian County Ark. Jan. 10, 1874
C.Duff, Deputy Sheriff:

Sir—Your appointment as deputy sheriff under me is hereby revoked from and after this date, for conduct unbecoming an officer, gentleman, and Republican.

J. H. McClure, Sheriff

I desire it now distinctly understood that although I am a Republican, elected by Republican votes to the position of township constable, I am not constable for the Republican Party alone, but for the whole people; and that if warrants

or other process are put in my hands to serve, be it against Republican or Democrat, I will serve them, without fear, affection or 'partiality' regardless of the terrific roars of the 'Bull of Bashan'.

In conclusion I desire to extend my sincere thanks to the men who went with me and aided me in this affair for their gentlemanly and courteous conduct while with me, and that I am ready at all times to bear testimony to the cheerful and prompt aid extended to me.

C. Duff, Constable
Upper Township

What happened to McClure? The case was to be heard before Elijah Ham but, as a letter in *The Fort Smith Herald* on January 20, 1874 related,

"Judge Ham got scared again and did not come." He must have heard about the arrest of McClure and the fuss about it. The friends of McClure elected his attorney, Neal, as special judge (the same Neal that was the champion of Greenwood as the county seat) and so no case against McClure could be tried. This episode also may explain why in later writings C.B. Neal of Greenwood is referred to as "Judge Neal."

Sebastian County's own Brooks-Baxter-ish "war" came to an end with Sheriff McClure leaving office upon the adoption of the new constitution. It is remarkable, however, that McClure later served the county as circuit clerk from 1874-78. Evidently his power base was Greenwood, where he owned a retail store.

While the Republican family feud simmered and seethed in mid-state, Fort Smith saw a steady increase in sentiment for the location of the county seat in that town exclusively. An editorial in *The Fort Smith Herald* on January 31, 1874, expressed it well:

In all the transactions of life, when anything fails to answer the purpose assigned it, it is changed and one more suitable put in its stead.

The location of the county seat of Sebastian County has long been a vexed question, and year after year it has been moved, until it may well be termed a court on stilts.

It has been tried at Jenny Lynde, (sic) at Fort Smith and Greenwood; and time after time does each place, after its removal, seek to have it back.

At Jenny Lynde (sic) it was a failure, at Greenwood it has proved to be worse than a failure, and at Fort Smith is the only place, where all the necessary appliances, conveniences and protection can be had, so a court can hold a full term in peace and quiet and without molestation.

We have ever advocated Fort Smith as the most suitable place in the county for the county seat; not so much from local bias, nor because we live here; as that it is the place offering the most advantages, where nearly every man in the county visits at least four times a year; where all who attend court can be cared for and feel safe in his person; where now having a foundation for a new courthouse at an expense of over $10,000—money can be saved to the county, and where instead of supporting two districts at an increased expense, one, properly managed, can do all the business of the county; and where accommodations and protection can be afforded for all. And when Fort Smith, as 'tis said is built up by the court; as it advances in wealth, so in proportion does every point in the county..."

On June 30, 1874, the election for the calling of the statewide constitutional convention was held and approved overwhelmingly. The main issue was the restoration of the vote to the disenfranchised ex-Confederates. The new constitution, under which Arkansas still operates, was approved on October 13, 1874. A slate of new statewide officers, including judges, was elected at the same time. Reconstruction in Arkansas was now officially over. Augustus H. Garland of Washington (Hempstead County) was elected governor and many of the old scalawags and carpetbaggers that had held office left the state. This included Judges Searle and Ham. Regarding the Republicans' legacy, Professor Michael Dougan maintains that the Republicans during Reconstruction made and tried to make many needed reforms in the face of a defeated and defiant people. However, the methods used—raw force, corruption, and fraud—only caused resentment that resulted in many good things being abandoned in the ensuing years.

Judge Elhanan Searle left Arkansas after having been removed from office with the adoption of the new constitution and returned to Illinois. It is a shame that we lost such an erudite gentleman to political squabbles. He contributed much to Arkansas while here. In addition to his service on the bench he served on the state board of education and was one of the original trustees for the Arkansas Industrial University in 1871. This institution later became the University of Arkansas. In 1875, he returned to Illinois and practiced law in Chicago and St. Louis. Later he moved to Pana, Illinois, where he owned a large tract of land and served two terms as city attorney. In 1887, he returned to Rock Island, Illinois, where he retired. He was said to have had a very retentive mind and was a student of the times and "a living encyclopedia" of information, particularly on social and political questions. He died August 18, 1906.

Judge Elijah D. Ham also was forced by circumstances to leave the area although he was a longtime resident. He had, in fact, not been holding court for some time due to the ill feelings. The courageous young officer of scouts seems to have become a visibly cautious jurist; as reported in *The Fort Smith Herald* of January 20, 1874, "Judge Ham got scared again and did not come..." He moved to Santa Rosa, California, and practiced law there until 1879, when he moved to Portland, Oregon, for one year. He then moved to Napa, California. In 1890, he was elected as a Republican to the office of Superior Court Judge of Napa County. Judge Ham first married in Arkansas in 1857. His wife's health was poor and he moved her to Denver, Colorado, where they remained until her death nine months later. He then married Miss Julia Conn. There were three children, including two from his first marriage. Rosa was married to W.W. Wright, cashier of a bank in Hot Springs, Arkansas, and Lucie was married to L.W. Gregg, an attorney in Fayetteville, Arkansas, and son of Justice Lafayette Gregg of the Arkansas Supreme Court. His daughter Kate was the product of his second marriage to Miss Conn. Ham served eighteen years on the Superior Court and later retired to Santa Rosa. *The San Francisco Call* of December 17, 1905, reported that Ham was near death, after having suffered an attack of paralysis two months earlier.

Act 53 of 1873 altered the Fifth Judicial Circuit by removing Benton and Scott Counties. The new circuit consisted of Washington, Crawford and Sebastian. The next judge to serve the circuit was Benton Brown. He served only one month in office: October 1874. This term followed the removal of Judge Ham and was prior to the election of W.W. Mansfield who would take office with the institution of the new constitution.

Benton Brown was born in Dickson County, Tennessee, on February 19, 1836. He was the 14th child of John B. and Sarah Houston Brown. In the latter part of 1836 the family moved to Johnson County, Arkansas. At age 20 he attended Cane Hill College in Washington County, teaching school to pay his expenses.

He studied law under General S. H. Hempstead in Little Rock in 1858 and completed his studies in the offices of Walker and Green in Van Buren. (These were Judge Joseph J. Green and Judge William Walker.) He was admitted to the bar in 1860 and also married in that year Miss Margaret Rothrock of Van Buren. He joined the Confederate army in 1861 as quartermaster with the rank of captain. He served mainly in Dardanelle, Lewisville and in northwest Arkansas. He was elected prosecuting attorney for the Fourth Judicial Circuit in 1862, under the Confederate government. In 1872 Brown was elected state senator under the Reconstruction government and in October 1874 he was appointed circuit judge for the Fifth Judicial Circuit. He later served as a presidential elector in

Act 53 of 1873
5th Judicial Circuit
Consisting of Sebastian, Crawford, and Washingon Counties

JUDGE BENTON BROWN
CIRCUIT JUDGE
1874
PHOTO COURTESY OF CITIZENS BANK

1876, pledged to Samuel Tilden and his running mate Hendricks. He founded the Citizen's Bank in Van Buren in 1876 and successfully farmed, as well. The Browns had three children: Lillian (Mrs. T. C.) Finney, Eula Kate Brown and Harold Rothrock Brown. Benton Jackson Brown died in New Jersey in 1910.

Arkansas Constitution of 1874
5th Judicial Circuit
Consisting of Sebastian, Crawford, Franklin, Johnson, Pope, Yell, and Sarber (Logan) Counties

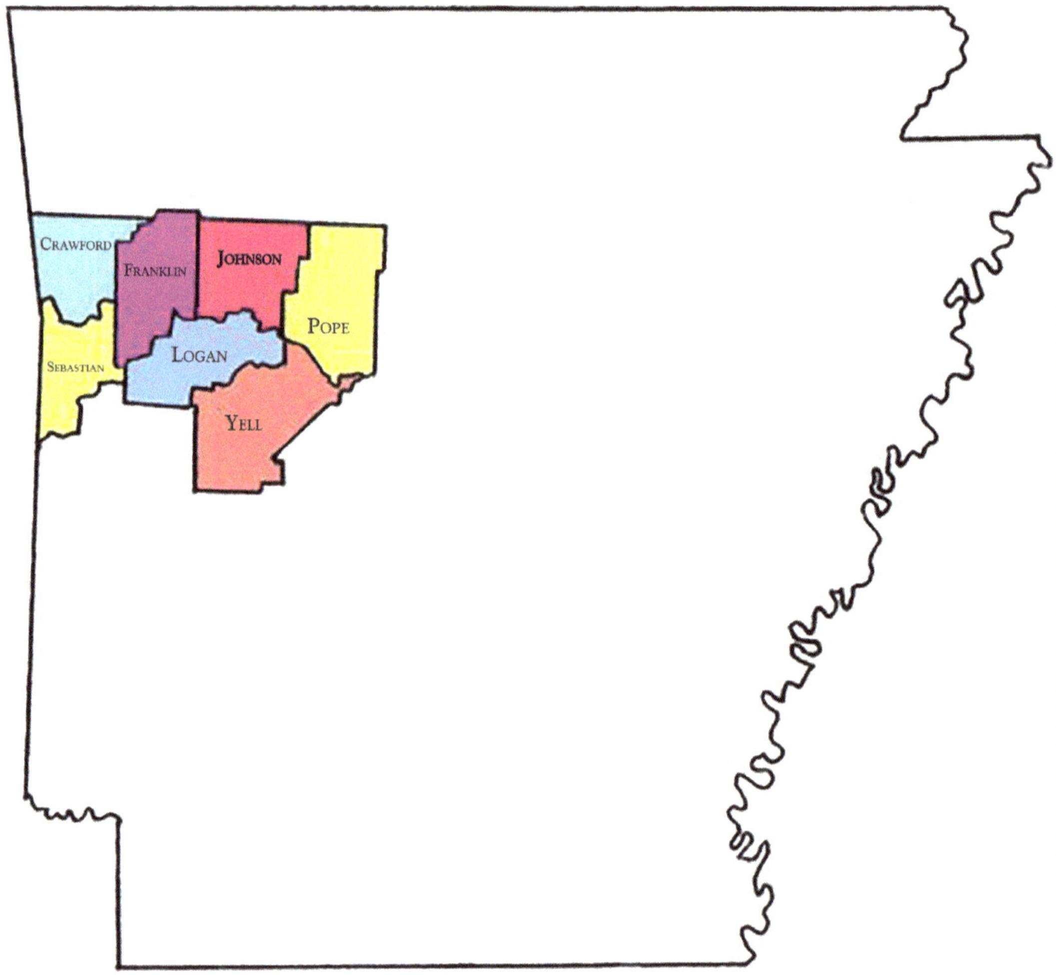

CHAPTER FOUR

Return of the Democrats

The ratification of the Constitution of 1874 began the process of reinstitution of much of the prewar agrarian mindset, as it applied to governance and justice. The Democratic party was once more in near-total control of state government and the carpetbaggers—opportunists and reformers alike—were on the run or soon would be. Justice Searle and Judge Ham were among those seeking their fortunes elsewhere. The new constitution established the framework, as amended, of the judiciary that remained intact until the year 2000 when Amendment 80 to that document was adopted.

The new constitution returned judicial power to the courts and provided for a supreme court, circuit courts, county courts, probate courts and justice of the peace courts. The legislature was empowered to create municipal courts, courts of common pleas and separate courts of chancery. The Supreme Court was made up of three justices, reduced from the previous five. One of the justices was designated chief justice and was elected as such. All three justices were elected statewide: a justice was required to be 30 years of age, of good moral character, learned in the law, a U.S. citizen and a two-year resident of Arkansas. He was also required to have been in the practice of law or a judgeship for at least eight previous years. It required but two justices to constitute a quorum and decisions were by a majority vote. The legislature was empowered to increase the number of justices to five when the state's population reached one million. The powers of the court remained the same as in the previous constitutions.

The circuit court enjoyed jurisdiction as per the previous constitutions and held superintending control and appellate jurisdiction over the county, probate, common pleas, corporation and justice of the peace courts. The circuit court also exercised equity jurisdiction until such a time as separate courts of chancery might be created. A circuit judge was required to be a U.S. citizen, 28 years of age, of good moral character, "learned in the law" and have six years' law practice or a previous judgeship. Circuit judges were elected from the circuit in which they would serve and enjoyed a 4-year term. It was also provided that a judge could not hold any other office, either state or federal, during his term. This seems to have been a provision put in as a reaction to abuses during Reconstruction.

The Constitution of 1874 expanded the responsibilities of the state's county judges. They were now empowered, in the absence of the circuit judge, to issue injunctions returnable to the circuit court and to hear habeas corpus motions. This power was, however, qualified: such orders could be vacated by the circuit court. The county judge was also designated the probate judge. The quorum court for each county consisted of that county's justices of the peace. Its mission was to assist the county judge in levying taxes and making apportionments. These were to be decided by the county judge and a majority of the quorum court's JPs. In the absence of the county judge, one of the justices could be selected to preside over the quorum court.

A court of common pleas was authorized (though not required) by the constitution and could be established by the legislature. Such a court could serve one or more counties. It met quarterly and was a court of record dealing with civil matters not involving real estate. No record was found of a court of common pleas ever serving Sebastian County.

Justice of the peace courts enjoyed jurisdiction in contracts up to $100, in replevin up to $300 and property damage cases up to $100. They had original criminal jurisdiction for misdemeanors and acted as examining courts returnable to circuit for felonies (preliminary hearings). They could also issue peace bonds and necessary process. Cities and towns were authorized to create corporation courts which had the same jurisdiction as the justice of the peace courts. Separate criminal courts, which appear to have been the creation of the Reconstruction-era legislature, were abolished.

The Constitution of 1874 placed Sebastian in the reconstituted Fifth Judicial Circuit along with Crawford, Franklin, Johnson, Pope, Yell and Sarber. Sarber was named for John Sarber and then changed to Logan after a long-time resident. The new constitution also addressed the long-time feud between Fort Smith and Greenwood over the location of the county seat. Article 13, section 5 provided that "Sebastian County **may** (emphasis added) have two districts and two county seats, at which county, probate and circuit courts shall be held as may be provided by law, each district paying its own expenses." Sebastian County thus was—and remains—is the only county specifically authorized <u>by the Constitution</u> to have two county seats. It is not the only county to have two districts and two county seats but these are statutory, while Sebastian County has its permissive language embedded in the Constitution. It is noted that the constitution did and does not specify the county seats or the boundaries of the districts. That was, apparently, was to be dealt with by statute.

The issue was addressed by the Arkansas General Assembly in January, 1875. The act, as amended, provided that Sebastian County would be divided into two districts, to be called the Greenwood and Fort Smith districts, and that the boundaries of the districts would remain as they had previously been until the whole county court met and set the new boundaries at the April term of court in Greenwood. After that time the jurisdiction of said County court, comprised of the County Judge and the Justices of the Peace from both districts, would cease and the jurisdiction would be transferred to the twin District County courts, each of which would be comprised of the County Judge and the respective Justices of the Peace from that district. The exception to this separation of jurisdictions was that any pre-existing debt of the entire county required the county courts of <u>both</u> districts to meet—in Greenwood—and pass levies to satisfy that pre-existing debt from properties in the entire county. After the county-wide debt was satisfied the districts would be independent of each other financially. They were each responsible for "all expenses of holding courts, opening and repairing of highways, building bridges, providing for paupers, erecting public buildings, and all other County expenses accruing (sic) within and on account of their respective districts, as if separate and distinct counties."

Circuit, Chancery, County and Probate courts would be held in the respective districts with the same number of sessions equally in each district. The amended act provided that the courts would sit at both the Fort Smith and Greenwood courthouses. The jurisdiction of the courts would consist of the territory of that district, the same if they were separate counties. The style of the cases was to be, as it is today, "The Circuit (or Probate, Chancery or County) Court of Sebastian County, Greenwood or Fort Smith District". The districts were, for all purposes, separate and distinct counties except that process from the court in one district was valid in the entire county. The act provided for a change of venue from one district to the other, the same as any other county in the judicial circuit. Judgments were only liens on real estate in the district in which the judgment was rendered since the judgment was not of record in the courthouse in the other district. Executions in the hand of the sheriff, however, would have lien force throughout the entire county. Execution sales would be at the courthouse in the district in which the property was located. Juries could be summoned only from the district in which the court sat.

The County Judge of Sebastian County was the County Judge for both districts; the Clerk, Sheriff, Treasurer and Collector also enjoyed this concurrent jurisdictional status. This great honor, of course, came with strings: the treasurer was to keep separate accounts and make settlement of the accounts with the County courts of each district. The treasurer's liability extended, naturally, to each district. The Clerk was to keep separate deed filing records and a seal for each district in the respective clerk's offices as if the districts were separate counties. Provision was also made for the Assessor and Collector to each keep totally separate records as if they had two separate counties and the Sheriff and Clerk were authorized to appoint deputies to serve and to reside in the district in which the elected official did not reside. In essence, Sebastian was now two counties that shared a name and elected officials but parallel court jurisdictions (with the exception that processes issued by the court in one had effect in the other, except for judgment liens on real property in the other district). This arrangement was unique. Other counties had dual county seats but only Sebastian's two districts were authorized in the Constitution and were totally independent of each other financially. This would continue until the passage of Amendment 55 to the Constitution of Arkansas in 1974.

The first circuit judge to serve Sebastian County in its new configuration and new judicial circuit was William Walker Mansfield.

He served from November 1874 through 1876. The son of George W. and Frances N. Mansfield, he was born in Scottsville, Kansas on January 16, 1830. Mansfield was admitted to the bar in Kansas in 1852. In February 1853, he moved to Arkansas, settling at Ozark. Beginning soon after his relocation, he served as justice of the peace. In 1856 he was elected a state representative and in 1861 he was a member of the State Secession Convention. Later that year he served as a presidential elector from Arkansas for the election of the Confederate president. A delegate to the Constitutional Convention of 1874, Mansfield was elected in the first election under that document as circuit judge for The Fifth Judicial Circuit. Act 41 of 1877 created the Twelfth Judicial District consisting of Crawford, Sebastian, Sarber (later renamed Logan) and Scott Counties. At this time, Judge Mansfield ceased serving as the circuit judge serving Sebastian County as this county was no longer in the circuit he served.

In 1883, Judge Mansfield was appointed by Governor James H. Berry to digest (that is, to compile in complete form) the statutes of Arkansas, a work which appeared in 1884 and is known popularly as *Mansfield's Digest*. In 1887 he was appointed as the reporter for the decisions of the Arkansas Supreme Court. He became an associate justice on the court in 1891 following the death of Justice Mont Sandels in November of 1890. He served until resigning in 1894. He married Miss Sallie Shores, the daughter of Alfred and Elizabeth Shores of Franklin County, in 1859. There were six children; Mary, John H., William W. Jr., Sallie Adelaide, and Asher C. Mansfield.

No transcripts of cases decided by Judge Mansfield have been found in the court reports from Sebastian County, but indications of some of his decisions may be found in appellate court records. A case decided by Judge Mansfield, then appealed to the Arkansas Supreme Court, was

Judge William Walker Mansfield
Circuit Judge
1874-1876

Photo courtesy of Arkansas State Historical Commision

Barlow vs. Lowder, 35 Ark. 492 (May 1880). This was a case originating in Pope County. This was a suit for damages for trespass *vi et armis* alleging that the defendant did bodily damage to the plaintiff by assaulting and beating him with a stick and a knife. He sought damages of $1,000. The jury returned a verdict for the plaintiff for $180. It was appealed alleging incorrect instructions to the jury. The judgment was affirmed. The facts are that Mr. Barlow was upset at the plaintiff Lowder because Lowder had abused some of Barlow's livestock outside the Barlow enclosure. Barlow, along with his stepson, a certain Mr. Woodworth, then assaulted Lowder. Barlow struck Lowder with a large stick "clinched" him as he fell, cutting him in the side with a knife and called on Woodworth to help. Woodworth then beat Lowder with a stick. The court instructed inter alia, that if the jury found that the animals were abused by Lowder then that could be considered in mitigation (lowering the award) of money damages. They decided the assault was worth $180. The Arkansas Supreme Court affirmed Judge Mansfield.

As earlier noted, the legislature placed Sebastian County in the Twelfth Judicial Circuit in 1877. This placement had been sought for some time and was the subject of an article in the *Fort Smith Herald* on November 6, 1875. The proposal at that time was to create a district from Sebastian, Scott, Sarber (later renamed Logan in honor of a long-time resident) and Yell. Crawford county, rather than Yell, would eventually be included in the new district. The article is revealing in terms of the concerns expressed. It was felt that a new district was desirable due to the work load and distances involved in the former district. The article noted that with Yell, as well as Sebastian, being split into two districts, the four counties proposed would have six courthouses among them. The *Herald* stated, "We are not particular as to the plan which may be adopted beyond the adoption of someone by which the business in the courts may be disposed of." Addressing some of the objections to the formation of a new district, erudite editor James H. Sparks opined,

> *Some we are informed, in a spirit of demagoguery or consummate stupidity, oppose the project because they say Judge Mansfield is required to hold courts only thirty-two weeks in the year while the farmer has to work fifty-two weeks. If the labors of the judge ceased with the completion of his round of courts, or when court adjourned in the evening to meet the next day, then there might be some reason in this objection. The farmer wearied from the toil of his daily labor, seeks and finds repose at night.- The Judge, after holding court all day, must often burn the mid-night lamp in the reading of authorities to aid him in the nervous system so wrought up that he woos in vain nature's sweet restorer.- And then his short vacation is taken up in the consideration of cases 'taken under advisement' to say nothing of applications for injunctions, mandamus and other duties requiring patient hearing and laborious investigation. This*

Act 41 of 1877
Created 12th Judicial Circuit
Consisting of Crawford, Sebastian, Logan, and Scott Counties

> *brain labor is much more exhausting than the hardest physical work and hence we say the objection alluded to is either sheer demagoguery or worse.....We insist that unless we find relief in this manner, the cases on the docket will accumulate until counties will be ruined and a suit in court will last through generations.....Whatever is done let it be done quickly."*

It is unlikely that our present-day judiciary would find such a sympathetic voice in the press!

The next judge to serve Sebastian County (and the first to serve as part of the Twelfth Judicial Circuit) was John H. Rogers. He was a native of Bertie, South Carolina, and was born October 9, 1845. He was a veteran of the Civil War, having enlisted at the age of 16 and serving in the 9th Mississippi Volunteers regiment of Infantry. During the conflict he rose to the rank of 1st Lieutenant. In 1868, he graduated from the University of Mississippi and was admitted to the bar in 1869. Following his relocation to Sebastian County, Arkansas, he was elected circuit judge in 1877, to the newly created 12th Judicial Circuit. In 1882 he resigned from the bench to become a candidate for Congress. He was elected and served from 1883 until 1890. In 1892, he was a delegate to the Democratic National Convention. While in Congress, he was a vocal critic of United States District Judge Isaac C. Parker and the court in Fort Smith; it was largely through his efforts that an appeals process to the United States Supreme Court from Parker's court was instituted. Ironically, upon Parker's death, it was Judge Rogers who was appointed to succeed him on the Federal bench by President Cleveland! Judge Rogers was awarded an honorary LLD degree from Center College in Danville, Kentucky. He died in Little Rock while staying at the Capital Hotel. He was in Little Rock to hear cases for Judge Trieber, the United States Judge for the Eastern District, at the time.

A case decided by Judge Rogers and appealed to the Arkansas Supreme Court was *Hicks vs. Brown*, 38 Ark. 469 (May 1882). This was a civil case involving the statute of limitations from the Greenwood District of Sebastian County. On August 23, 1880, Hicks sued Brown on a judgment Hicks had recovered against him before a justice of the peace court on August 24, 1870, for $200. Hicks did not bother to try and collect the judgment for nine years and three hundred and sixty-four days. The case's initial determination turned on the fact that the usual five-year statute of limitations had expired before the institution of Hick's action. Judge Rogers ruled for the defendant and assessed costs against the plaintiff.

There was a conflict in the statutes. Sec. 3791 of *Gantt's Digest* provides that no execution shall issue after five years. It was therefore inappropriate to merely issue a writ of execution. Sec. 4128 of Gantt's Digest said that actions on all judgments and decrees shall be commenced within ten years after the cause of action shall accrue, and not afterwards. The court ruled that there was no relation

JUDGE JOHN H. ROGERS
CIRCUIT JUDGE
1877-1882
PHOTO COURTESY OF UNITED STATES DISTRICT COURT

between the two sections. It was clear that an action on a judgment is allowable for ten years. The plaintiff made it by one day. Judge Rogers was reversed.

In 1881, the last year of Judge Rogers' tenure, the courthouse in Greenwood burned. This was the building constructed on the town square in 1856-7, a two-story frame structure that measured fifty feet on a side. The Fort Smith *New Era* reported on March 2, 1881:

> *"Last Wednesday night the courthouse at Greenwood, the county seat of Sebastian County, for there are two county seats, was burned to the ground with all its records. The house itself was but a mere shell of wood and of little value, though[it] cost the people enough to have in its stead a far more substantial and safe building. But the destruction of all the county records is a most serious loss and calamity to the people of the whole county. To the shame of this county it must be said, that, though one of the most populous and prosperous in the whole state its care of the public records and the means of holding its courts are the most shabby of any county in the state. This is owing to the wretched wrangling about the county seat, in the interest of a few persons who would sacrifice the public good to their own private advantage. Sebastian County ought to have but one county seat, and one fireproof building ever. The Greenwood District will have to go the expense of building another courthouse and as experience is the best teacher, the next courthouse will probably be built on a different plan. The Fort Smith District will meet with a like catastrophe sooner or later, unless the people of Fort Smith have a better place for the records of the district, which is now over a saloon. When the damage is done it will be too late to wish it were otherwise. As well said a few weeks since, when the question was agitated here, it is simply a criminal neglect and wretched parsimony not to have a solid, substantial, fireproof building for the preservation of our records and the holding of our courts.*

The remaining Greenwood records were removed to a mercantile building nearby which also burned the following year. Many, if not all, of the district's records were lost.

Greenwood citizens and the county pitched in $2,500.00 to build a replacement courthouse at the total cost of $5,555.00. The builder was George Holt of Alma. The *Arkansas Gazette* reported on August 4, 1881, "Deputy Sheriff Burton of Greenwood informs us that the foundation of the new courthouse has been laid and that large quantities of brick and other material have been delivered on the ground." It was a two-story brick building set on a rock foundation, measuring measured 50X54 feet. The first story contained a county offices and the second story held the courtroom and the judge's chambers. On February 2, 1882, the *Arkansas Gazette* quoted *The Greenwood World* of January 26th of that year:

"The pride of our people is the new brick courthouse. It is provided with fireproof vaults and a tin roof and presents such a splendid appearance."

On March 1, 1883, *The New Era* reported:

"We are to have a fireproof vault for the county records and papers.(in Fort Smith) It will cost the sum of $500.00, which is small considering the importance of the action and the necessity for it. Commissioners have been appointed to attend to the construction. It will be erected in the rear of the clerk's office and will have burglar proof doors. The lease of the present court rooms has been extended five years."(19)

This new vault was obviously intended to be a response to the fires in Greenwood. Anticipation might have been preferable.

THE GREENWOOD COURTHOUSE, DEDICATED 1882

On June 20, 1883, the *Arkansas Gazette* ran a story from a "special correspondent" concerning his trip through western Arkansas including Greenwood. It related:

> *Late in the afternoon Greenwood was reached, and the travelers alighted at the door of R. L. Cowne's hotel and walked about the town. The courthouse of brick as usual occupied the center of the town, surrounded by the stores, of which there are twelve or fifteen. There are about four or five hundred inhabitants, two churches, Baptist and Methodist, one good newspaper, The Greenwood Times of which Reese and Embrey are the proprietors, and J. F. B. Embrey the editor, and a fair public school.*

The article went on to identify the various shop owners. Each mentioned was apparently exemplary in his field of endeavor: singled out for praise were, among others, M. S. Gaines, T. Little, J. B. Robertson, G. N. Spradling, Baker and Neal and J. L. Yates. The article described the region as a "land of milk and honey" with deposits of coal and iron.

When Judge Rogers resigned to run for Congress, the person appointed by Governor Thomas J. Churchill to fill out his unexpired term was William Walker. Judge Walker came to Crawford County around 1842. His tombstone in Oak Cemetery relates that he was born in 1812, making him thirty years old when he arrived in the district. He had been a law partner of Judge Joseph J. Green prior to Green becoming judge in 1860. Goodspeed's *Biographical and Historical Memoirs of Northwest Arkansas*, issued in 1889, described him as:

> *"a fine lawyer of a highly analytical mind, and is a genius as a special pleader; no flaw in legal papers can escape his microscopic vision, and his own papers are faultless. He is an effective speaker of intense earnestness and feeling and has many other strong characteristics. He is a fair writer and an aggressive worker."*

He was also a partner in Fort Smith with Sam A. Miller in 1882. At the time he was appointed as circuit judge he was 70 years old. He had been practicing law in the area for forty years, since 1842. According to Fadjo Cravens he was married to a Mary Rector and they had a daughter Maggie who never married and a son William Jr., known familiarly as "Willie." Willie was, apparently, an inebriate who, perhaps inspired by the young American adventurer of the same name, may have dabbled in South American intrigues.

A case heard by Judge Walker that was appealed to the Arkansas Supreme Court is *State of Arkansas vs. Parker*, 39 Ark. 174 (1882). This is a criminal case involving assault with a pistol with intent to inflict bodily injury. Parker, the assailant, moved to quash the indictment against him on the grounds that Elisha L. Cobb, the party whom he was charged with assaulting, did not sign the indictment as the prosecutor required and that, furthermore, Cobb had not entered into any obligation to pay or secure the costs of the prosecution. Judge Walker sustained the motion and the state appealed. The Supreme Court reversed Judge Walker, stating that

> *"By section 98, chapter 52, of* **Gould's Digest***, taken from the Revised Statutes, no indictment for any trespass on the person or property of another could be preferred, unless the name of the prosecutor was endorsed thereon, except when the same was preferred on the information or knowledge of one or more of the grand jury, or on the information the testimony of some witness other that the party injured, in which case, a statement of the fact was required to be made at the end of the indictment, and of some public officer, in the necessary discharge of his duty, or signed by the attorney for the state. .... But the criminal code , which prescribes the substance of indictments, and what shall be endorsed upon them, contains no such provision, and the above statute was treated as repealed by it, and not carried into Gantt's Digest, Criminal Procedure, taken from the criminal code. The statute requiring the prosecutor, or some person for him, to give bond for costs, in prosecutions for misdemeanors applies to prosecutions before Justices of the Peace, and other inferior courts, and not to prosecutions by indictment in the Circuit Courts."*

This affords a fine example of legal practice during "The Gilded Age." Loopholes and contradictions could be found within the pages of Arkansas's code, and courtroom fortune favored those who could find them and put them to work.

A new circuit judge was elected and took office in 1883: Robert Beall Rutherford. Judge Rutherford, unlike his predecessors, was a native of the state: he had been born February 20, 1833, in Little Rock, the son of Samuel M. and Eloise Marie Rutherford. His parents had been married in 1822 in the home of Territorial Governor Pope, who was a cousin to the bride. He grew up in Pulaski and Sebastian Counties and, in 1854, graduated from Arkansas College in Fayetteville. He practiced law in Lafayette County from 1857 until 1867. He interrupted his law practice to serve in Company F, 6th Arkansas Infantry (Confederate) during the Civil War. He then returned to Fort Smith to practice law. He was elected justice of the peace in 1874 and served two terms as county and probate judge from 1878 through 1882. He served as circuit judge from his election in 1882 for one term ending in 1886.

A case decided by Judge Rutherford that was later appealed to the Arkansas Supreme Court dealt with the old question of a courthouse in Fort Smith to serve Sebastian County: *Griffith and another vs. Sebastian County*, 49 Ark. 24, 3 S.W. 886 (1887). The county had undertaken the building of a courthouse in Fort Smith following the election in 1868 held for the purpose of removing the county seat from Greenwood to Fort Smith. The discussion in the case reveals that the quorum court disputed the initial determination that the question had

JUDGE ROBERT BEALL RUTHERFORD
CIRCUIT JUDGE
1883-1886
PHOTO COURTESY OF FADJO CRAVENS JR

not passed by the requisite majority and declared the proposition to have been approved. The quorum court appointed commissioners to select a site for a new courthouse in Fort Smith. The commissioners contacted Mrs. Griffith who owned the property and her husband, (who, at that time in history, had to act on behalf of his wife in legal matters) and induced them to donate one block of property on Knox Street for this purpose.

The old plats of the city of Fort Smith reveal that Knox Street is the present 6th Street upon which the present Sebastian County Courthouse for the Fort Smith District is located. The case does not reveal exactly where on Knox Street this particular property lies. On March 5, 1870, the Griffiths conveyed the property by deed, citing a nominal consideration of a single dollar... which was never paid.

The Griffiths were assured that the county seat move was legal and they believed that the construction of the new courthouse would greatly enhance the value of their other property in close proximity. The county began construction on the courthouse and the foundation was laid prior to the Arkansas Supreme Court ruling in *Patterson vs. Temple*, supra, that the removal of the county seat had, in fact, been illegal. The Griffiths maintained in their petition to Judge Rutherford (sitting as Chancellor as there were no separate courts of chancery at that time) that because the election to remove the county seat was illegal, the deed was null and void. They contended the property should be returned to them.

The suit was brought in chancery (equity) as there was no adequate remedy at law. The Griffiths sought an equitable remedy and they were prohibited otherwise by sovereign immunity from bringing suit against a county. They further pleaded that the 1874 Constitution, which had specified that Sebastian Cou8nty would have two county seats, did not change the fact that the inducement to them to donate the property to the county was based on a falsity, that being that their donated property would be the sole seat of county government.

Bringing the issue to the forefront was the fact that County Judge B. J. H. Gaines advertised the property for sale at public auction to be held on the first Monday in September 1885. The Griffiths, to keep their property from being sold, began legal proceedings. The county demurred *inter alia* (that is, "among other things") that the Griffiths had failed to state a cause of action. Judge Rutherford agreed and dismissed their petition. They appealed. The Supreme Court reversed Judge Rutherford. The court ruled that the chancery court did have jurisdiction and, since it was a suit brought by a married woman through the agency of her husband for the recovery of lands, the statute of limitations did not apply. They also dismissed any allegation of fraud on the part of the commissioners and stated that all parties had acted in good faith on the erroneous assumption that the county seat had been legally removed to Fort Smith from Greenwood. That was a mutual mistake not realized until the Arkansas Supreme Court ruled in *Patterson vs. Temple*. The result was the same as if the condition of building the courthouse had been written into the deed of conveyance. This mutual mistake of fact was such as to exclude real consent to the conveyance. The court sent the case back for trial with instructions that the county be reimbursed for any lost taxes for the time it held title under the conveyance and that the county also be compensated for any increase in value to the property because of any improvement done to the property.

A similar case, *Rogers vs. Sebastian County*, supra., was cited in the court's opinion. In that case, John Rogers, often referred to as the "Father of Fort Smith", also conveyed land in Fort Smith for the construction of a courthouse for Sebastian County but, this time, the county kept the land. In the matter of *Rogers vs. Sebastian County*, the county had first voted to remove the county seat to Fort Smith from Greenwood. Rogers then donated the land in Fort Smith for the courthouse. The county then held another election and voted to remove the county seat from Fort Smith to Greenwood. The question of a Fort Smith courthouse therefore became moot. Both elections were valid. There was no mistake on the part of anyone and there was no condition or reverter in the deed. There appeared to be an oral agreement to that effect but it wasn't worth the paper it was written on. Very close facts but different results in these two cases. The Griffiths got their property back, but the "Father of Fort Smith" did not.

It was reported in *The New Era* on October 2, 1884 that the Secretary of the Treasury had approved the request that the whole of Block 514 of the abandoned Fort Smith military reservation be reserved for public buildings. This was the start of a new push for a courthouse in Fort Smith. *The Fort Smith Elevator* reported on July 30, 1886, "The county and city are also soon to erect a fine court house near the government building: probable cost $55,000." This report followed an earlier one on July 16, stating that the Quorum Court, at the request of County Judge B. J. H. Gaines, had appropriated $10,000 toward the new building. It is interesting to note that this was a year before Judge Gaines advertised to sell the Griffith property.

The Federal court was also getting a new building, located across the street from the new city/county building. On February 19, 1886, The *Fort Smith Elevator* reported that a Congressional committee had approved an appropriation for the construction of a new post office and court building in Fort Smith and the construction of a new jail and offices from the existing structure. On

March 5, *The Elevator* related that the appropriation in the amount of $125,000 had been passed by Congress and awaited presidential approval. This was reassurance that the federal court would remain in Fort Smith:

> *As citizens of Fort Smith we wish to thank our senators and representatives for the interest they have manifested in this matter. Our own member, Hon. John H. Rogers deserves the kind appreciations of our people.* **The Elevator,** *always willing to give credit where it is due, on behalf of ourselves and other citizens, congratulate him on his efforts in thus contributing to the elevation and importance to which our city aspires."*

Justice in Fort Smith was getting a new face and the area was undergoing a boom in population growth. Some of it was due to the location of the Federal Court in 1871 and in the establishment of the Fort Smith District county seat. On New Year's Day 1885 the *Elevator* reported on this growth:

> *"Our population in 1880 was only a little over 3000, in 1883 it was over 6000, and now, say January 1st, it is at the lowest calculation 10,000, and if the city continues to increase in the same ratio as in the past five years, we will in five years have a population of 30,000 to 40,000, and indications are that it will grow as rapidly as ever."*

The article went on to talk of the soon-to-be-completed railroad bridge into Indian Territory and the availability of coal and timber in the area for industrial use. The entire county was experiencing vigorous growth due to the development of coal fields and the *Elevator*, repeating a story from *The Greenwood Times*, stated that the Greenwood jail must go. The county judge had ordered the old county jail at Greenwood to be torn down.

> *"This is hailed with pleasure by every lover of progress in this district of the county. The old jail was about as valuable as a pig pen would have been for the purpose of confining criminals and was about as hard to keep clean. The Quorum Court that meets here in July must devise us a means to build a new jail...."*

Fort Smith and Sebastian County were growing faster than any other place in the state and the needs of the legal community were advancing as well.

Judge John Sebastian Little
Circuit Judge
1887-1890
photo courtesy of Mary Vertrees

CHAPTER FIVE

A Native Takes Over 1887-1914

The year 1887 bought a new judge and a new courthouse under construction in Fort Smith. Judge Rutherford had not been selected by the Democratic committees of the counties comprising the judicial district to be the Democratic nominee for circuit judge (The Democratic Party did not require primary elections for local officials in all counties until 1898), therefore was not on the ballot. He was instead slated to leave office at the end of the year; John Sebastian Little was to be his successor. An article in *The Fort Smith Elevator* on November 26, 1886, titled *"Banquet of the Bar. Judge R. B. Rutherford—Judge J. S. Little,"* gives a good sense of the tone of Fort Smith's comfortable Victorian-era professional circle:

> *On Thursday evening of last week the members of the Fort Smith bar banqueted the retiring judge of the circuit court, Robt. B. Rutherford and his recently elected successor, J. Sebastian Little. There was good attendance at Mivelaz's dining hall at the Le Grande, where the large banquet was held....All went well—plenty to eat and enough wine to brighten their minds. Col. Wm. M. Fishback, who presided, announced the first toast, 'The Retiring Judge', response by W.H.H. Clayton, who paid just and good compliments to Judge Rutherford. Judge R. thereupon responded and in a few words express[ed] his gratification in knowing that the members of the bar were pleased with his career as judge. 'The Incoming Judge' by M. H. Sandels ... spoke of Bass Little's many excellent accomplishments and claimed him to be both a philosopher and a poet. Judge Little in response said he knew how the lawyers on the losing side always went for the judge, but hoped all criticism might be poetic. 'The Bench' response by Hon. I. C. Parker, 'The Bar' response by Col. B. T. Duval, 'The Officers of the Law' response by Col. Thomas Marcum. 'Early Times in Arkansas' response by Col. E. C. Boudinot, 'Our State,' response by Hon.(Hugh) Thomason of Van Buren, 'Our City' response by C. M. Cooke, 'The Future of Our Profession,' by Col. J. H. Clendening. The roasts were closed by a few remarks by Col. Wm. Walker on the suggestion of a toast to the oldest member of the bar....*

This banquet was a veritable "who's who" of Arkansas and Sebastian County history. Present at the feast were two future governors, a congressman, the famous Judge Parker of the Western District of Arkansas, his prosecuting attorney, a justice on the Arkansas Supreme Court and at least three circuit judges... as well as both of the honorees.

Circuit Judge John Sebastian Little was the first person born in Sebastian County to hold that position. In fact, he was the first person born in Sebastian County following its establishment and his name honored that fact. He was born in a log cabin in Jenny Lind on March 15, 1851, the grandson of Eaton Tatum who has been dubbed the "Father of Sebastian County." For some reason, the future Judge Little was popularly known in his home district as "Bass Little." A present day township in the county also bears that name. Judge Little's father was Jesse Little, a North Carolinian who married Eaton Tatum's daughter Mary Elizabeth.

John Little worked as town marshal for the town of Greenwood when still a young man and saved his money, in order to attend Cane Hill College in Washington County. When he returned to Greenwood, he read law under the Hon. C. B. Neal. He was admitted to the bar in 1872 and in 1874 moved to Paris in Logan County due to the discovery of coal and the increase in legal business that accompanied the mining boom. He served in the state legislature, became a respected attorney and served three terms as prosecuting attorney in the newly formed 12th Judicial Circuit beginning in 1877.

He and his wife had five children; Paul, Jess Edward, Monte Olivia, Lizzie Lou, and Thomas Eugene. In 1882 he moved back to Greenwood and within a few years began to exhibit political ambition. He served as circuit judge from 1887 until 1890. He resigned the judgeship to seek a congressional seat but was defeated in the nominating convention. His prospects, however, would soon improve. In June 1893, he served as chairman of the state Judicial Convention. In 1894, Clifton R. Breckinridge of Pine Bluff, Congressman for District 2, was named Minister to Russia by President Cleveland; Judge Little was nominated by convention to run for Breckinridge's former post. He was elected and won subsequent elections, serving in Congress until 1907. In 1906, Little ran for governor against Governor Jeff Davis' political enemy, Attorney General Robert Rogers. Davis supported Little, although this support was not fully appreciated: Little spent much time and effort in the primary campaign trying to prove his independence from Davis. He carried all but three counties in the primary and won handily in the general election against the Republican John Worthington. Victory had its price, however: Little's health had been generally poor even before the campaign and his exertions, probably coupled with the prospects of the work in store, led to his mental and physical collapse within days of his inauguration. He never fully recovered and died Sept. 8, 1916, in Little Rock.

A case decided by Judge Little that was appealed to the Arkansas Supreme Court was *Echols vs. Tate*, 53 Ark. 12, 13 S. W. 253 (1890). It was from the Fort Smith District of Sebastian County and had to be one of the first tried in the new courthouse. It involved an attachment by Echols on the property of Tate. Echols was a wholesale merchant at Fort Smith. Tate was, in 1887, a citizen of the United States, licensed to trade with the Choctaw at "James Ferrill's old place" in the Choctaw Nation. The debt owed to Echols was for $435.25. Tate sold out his business without notice to Echols and left the area at which he was licensed to trade; he apparently took a good deal of what had been business assets, including wagons, cattle etc., with him. He headed further west, stopping for a while at one McAllister's ranch.

Echols learned of this and went before the U. S. Indian agent at Muskogee. Upon Echols's application and the posting of a bond, the agent had the Indian police remove Tate and the property to Arkansas for the action of the courts there. The agent advised Tate that the agency could not be used as an asylum for the concealment of persons or property as against creditors. When the property was relocated into Arkansas, Echols had the property attached. Echols answered the suit in Arkansas alleging that Tate was illegally brought into the jurisdiction.

At trial, the prominent Cherokee attorney E. C. Boudinot testified that no courts existed in the Indian Territory in which any but citizens of the Indian Nations could seek redress. There was no process for the collection of debts between citizens of the United States in the Territory. D. M. Wisdom, the chief clerk at the Union Indian Agency which served the Five Civilized Tribes, testified that it was the practice of that agency to cause removals of this nature by use of the U. S. Indian Police. These actions were based on orders of the Secretary of the Interior and the Commissioner of Indian Affairs.

This was a case of first impression. If the removal was legal, the Echols's attachment of the goods taken by Tate was legal also. Judge Little ruled for Tate, but the Arkansas Supreme Court reversed. They held that no white person enjoyed the right to go into the Indian Territory unless authorized by law. The President of the United States was charged with maintaining treaty stipulations, and precedent existed for persons illegally in the Territory to be removed. The court held that a licensed trader was is protected by the law; but if he were to sell out and abandon his post, he would be considered, except while in the process of leaving the Territory, a white man in the Indian Territory without license, thus improperly there. Therefore the removal of Tate was not an unauthorized removal, and, given that he and his property having been legally ousted from the Indian Territory, the attachment of the plaintiff was not based on fraud and

Justice Divided

The Fort Smith Courthouse, Dedicated 1887

the motion to quash the levy should have been overruled. This is an interesting insight to doing business in the Indian Territory before Oklahoma statehood in 1907.

The county had erected no buildings in Fort Smith previous to 1887 although there had been two attempts, both of which were abandoned due to the county seat being relocated to Greenwood. The Fort Smith courts had instead been located in rented space. Before 1872, the offices of the district were in a building at the corner of Walnut and Second Streets that burned in that year. They were then moved to a building on the corner of First Street and Garrison Avenue where they remained until moved into a building in the Kannady Block on the south side of Garrison Avenue next to the present Varsity Grill.

With the closing in 1871 of Fort Smith as an Army post, the military reservation and the buildings on it were disposed of. Much of the land was ceded to the city of Fort Smith for public purposes including the construction of new government buildings. On Block 515, part of the onetime military reservation, the city of Fort Smith and Sebastian County constructed a court house worthy of the name. Architects Nier and Byram designed the four-story building that would house both county and municipal offices. A grand Romanesque structure with a tall clock tower, it would stand and serve for half a century.

The walls of the new courthouse's basement were made of stone quarried near Eureka Springs. The faces of the brick walls were built of St. Louis brick, while the hidden structural brick was sourced locally. The building's "footprint" was a generous 84 X 102 feet and the tower extended 148 feet above the ground. In the tower, 100 feet above the ground, was a clock with four dials, each measuring four feet in diameter. The clock featured a massive bell which now rests in The Fort Smith Museum of History along with at least one of the clock faces. There were ten rooms on the floor above the basement and eight in the second. The offices of the city were on the first floor, as were spaces occupied by the county treasurer and recorder. County government, including the judge and court, occupied the balance of the building. The new courthouse, a point of pride for both municipal and county governments, cost $55,000 to erect. This building remained in use until demolished and replaced by the present structure in 1937.

The boom times in Fort Smith continued with a great deal of construction including the new state and federal courthouses. A special section in *The Fort Smith Elevator* on January 22, 1888 related:

Act 31 of 1889
Twelfth Judicial Circuit
Consisting of Sebastian and Scott Counties

We walk the streets from week to week, as one improvement following another slowly progresses....Our population has increased; our trade has increased; we have established many manufactories....The beginning of last year found us with a population of 11,000 or 12,000, the beginning of the present with 15,000 or 16,000. During the year 1886 the influx of population was so rapid that our people were crowded in their homes and cramped in their business operations for the want of space and suitable buildings....Beginning at the intersection of Fifth Street we see the new Grand Opera House, costing $80,000, than which no city in the Union of the same size as ours, can claim a handsomer....the new county courthouse, involving an expense of $55,000 or $60,000 is nearly half completed, while across on the opposite corner the United States courthouse to cost $125,000 is progressing...

This was the greatest period of growth the town ever witnessed.

In 1881, the Legislature once again fiddled with the boundaries of western jurisdictions: Act 31 reconfigured the 12th Judicial Circuit. Franklin, Johnson, Pope, Logan and Yell Counties were removed and placed in the newly formed 15th Judicial Circuit. The 12th Circuit now consisted of only Sebastian and Scott Counties (Scott had not been in the 12th prior to that time). This rearrangement "stuck"; the district's configuration would not change until 1967.

The next judge to serve Sebastian County and the 12th Judicial Circuit was T. C. Humphrey. He was the son of Charles Humphrey and was born in what is now Logan County, Arkansas, on December 20, 1846. He had a limited education in early life. Humphrey enlisted in Confederate service at age 17 and served for two years. He was discharged several months before the surrender due to disability. He then settled at Galla Rock in Pope County and apparently expended a great deal of energy trying to get an education. He apparently succeeded; he later became a teacher in order to pay his way through a course of studies at the Missouri Medical College (a forerunner of today's Medical Department of Washington University in St. Louis). He graduated in 1869 and practiced medicine for three years before abandoning it due to his dislike for the work. Some good came, however, from his time in the medical field: he married Annie McLeod of Quitman in 1871, a marriage which would produce six children.

In 1874, Dr. Humphrey was elected to the Arkansas House of Representatives from White County. He performed good service, including successfully sponsoring a law taxing railroad land in the state. This law was challenged all the way to the United States Supreme Court where it was held to be constitutional. He often presided over the Arkansas House as Speaker *pro tem* and showed marked

JUDGE T. C. HUMPHREY
CIRCUIT JUDGE
1890
PHOTO COURTESY OF UALR SPECIAL COLLECTIONS

ability. He also decided on a new professional path: he read law for two years and was admitted to the Arkansas Bar. He was not satisfied with this level of training, however, so entered the University of Louisville for a post graduate law course. He finished in one year and received a Bachelor of Laws degree. He was admitted to practice before the Supreme Court of the state.

In 1879 he was appointed to fill an unexpired term as County and Probate Judge of Logan County; in 1880 he was elected to the position on the Democratic ticket. By 1882 he owned and edited the *Paris Express* newspaper, published "in the interest of democracy and the people." In the fall of 1886, however, he removed to Fort Smith. He practiced law there until Judge John Little resigned his post in 1890 to seek a congressional seat; Humphrey was appointed to the vacancy on March 3, 1890. He did not, however, hold it in a regular capacity for long: on September 1, 1890 Judge Edgar E. Bryant was elected to a regular term in that position. Judge Bryant claimed the seat on October 30, 1890 and Judge Humphrey vacated in his favor. Humphrey did not, however, disappear from the bench: Judge Bryant recused from all the cases in which he had an interest and Judge Humphrey was elected special judge by the lawyers to hear those cases, and was noted for his flashes of eloquence. When not sitting in judgement, he was a partner in the firm of Humphrey and Warner and was a well-known Mason, serving as Grand Master of the State of Arkansas.

A case heard by Judge Humphrey and later appealed to the Arkansas Supreme Court was *Railway Co. vs. State*, 55 Ark. 200 (1891), originating in the Greenwood District of Sebastian County. It was brought by the prosecuting attorney for the benefit of Sebastian County and turned on the interpretation of a statute. The measure in question bore on railway safety, providing:

> *[That] A bell of at least thirty pounds weight, or a steam whistle, shall be placed on each locomotive or engine, and shall be rung or whistled at the distance of at least eighty rods from the place where said road shall cross any other road or street, and shall be kept ringing or whistling until it shall have crossed said road or street under a penalty of $200 for every neglect, to be paid by the corporation owing the railroad, one half thereof to go to the informer, and the other half to go to the county; and the corporation shall also be liable for any damages which shall be sustained by any person by reason of such neglect.*

The penalty provided for was clearly meant to be a civil penalty. The Sebastian County prosecutor, however, brought the action by way of criminal indictment issued by the grand jury against the railroad. The act had been passed when the Constitution of 1868 was in force. This constitution provided that civil penalties should all go to the school fund. The prosecutor, evidently, did not want the money to go to the school fund. Instead, he wanted it either to be paid

JUDGE EDGAR E. BRYANT
CIRCUIT JUDGE
1890-1898
PHOTO COURTESY OF FORT SMITH MUSEUM OF HISTORY

to his office as feed based on a criminal penalty, or into the general fund. The judgment was for the state, and the railroad company appealed on both on constitutional and jurisdictional grounds: the company alleged that the statute was unconstitutional and that even if it were not unconstitutional, the state had no authority to bring a criminal action on a civil penalty.

The judgment was affirmed, in spite of the technical correctness of the railroad's complaint. The Supreme Court once again engaged in common sense—possibly encouraged by the railroad not being held in high regard by most Arkansans. In regard to the defect in bringing the case by criminal indictment the Court, through exhaustive legalese penned by Justice Hemingway, opined:

> *If he (the prosecutor) had prepared the same pleading, and filed it without a return in court by the grand jury or an endorsement by the foreman, and thereafter prosecuted the case, it would have been a suit by him for the penalty, although the complaint might have been subject to technical criticism; if such pleading, without the return of a grand jury or the endorsement of its foreman, would have been sufficient as the basis for a suit by the prosecuting attorney, could it have been insufficient with them.*

The Court observed that had the prosecuting attorney filed a civil suit instead of a criminal indictment, the plaintiff would have been the prosecuting attorney of Sebastian County, rather than the state. This would have been the only difference and—the difference wasn't enough to make a difference. It would simply be a suit for a civil penalty. The pleadings were, otherwise, just fine. The Supreme Court ruled the criminal indictment to have been superfluous but the pleading sufficient. The other main issue was the constitutionality of the act because of the distribution of the penalty being contrary to the state Constitution in effect at the time of the enactment of the statute. On this they ruled that the act was not void for this reason and that the division of the penalty would merely be done as per the proper constitutional provisions. In fine, the railroad company had to pay, and the School Board got its money. The prosecutor won his case but lost his money; justice was served.

The next judge to preside over the 12th was, as previously noted, Edgar E. Bryant. He served from 1890 through 1898. Bryant was born at Paris, Mississippi on December 9, 1861, the son of A. A. and Margaret Stein Bryant. His father was a physician. Bryant attended the common schools of Coffeeville, Mississippi, until age 15, then entered the University of Mississippi as a sophomore. Judge Bryant graduated in 1880 at the head of his class and with the highest honors ever achieved to that date. He was also a graduate of Vanderbilt University School of Law. He accomplished the completion of the two-year course of study in only one year and again graduated with honors. He then attended the Columbian Law University in Washington, D. C. and again completed the two-year course in one yea, graduating in 1883.

In the winter of that year he began practice in Columbus, Mississippi, then removed to Fort Smith in 1884 and began the practice of law with T. P. Winchester in the firm of Bryant and Winchester. He practiced for nearly six years before being elected Circuit Judge on September 12, 1890. Bryant enjoyed a reputation as a fine orator and had his eye on higher office: he was a candidate for Governor of Arkansas in the 1900 Democratic primary. In that race there were four candidates. Due to fierce personal attacks by the eventual winner, legendary fire-brand populist Jeff Davis, both Bryant and fellow candidate John Gould Fletcher withdrew from the race. Davis won the election, was re-elected twice and in 1907 was elected by the Arkansas Senate to represent the state in the U.S. Senate.

A case heard and decided by Judge Bryant that was appealed to the Arkansas Supreme Court was *Wallace vs. Bernheim*, 63 Ark. 108 (1896). Originating in the Greenwood district, this was an interesting case involving fraud and collusion to defraud creditors. A certain Mr. Aitken was engaged in the saloon business in Hartford, Arkansas. He was indebted to Mr. Wallace who sold whiskey wholesale from Fort Smith. Aitken was also indebted to Bernheim Brothers, Kentucky distillers, for wholesale whiskey and other items.

Aitken was in financial trouble. On May 8, 1893, Wallace sold to Aitken five barrels of whiskey on credit for $500. Aitken already owed Wallace $700. Wallace then discovered that Aitken was trying to sell all his stock and filed an attachment on all of Aitken's goods to secure payment. This attachment included all of Aitken's stock of goods, including the barrels of whiskey not yet delivered to him and the whiskey supplied by the Bernheim firm. Bernheim Brothers in fact learned of the lawsuit and filed an intervention in the suit seeking an attachment as well. Wallace's attachment totaled $1550, which was more than was owed him. With Aitken's assent, Wallace procured an order from the judge in vacation (meaning court was not in session) to sell the goods, as being of a perishable nature and thus likely to greatly deteriorate if kept on hand. Chief Justice Bunn, in his dissent found this to be highly unlikely as the goods in question consisted entirely of whiskey which, he understood, gained value with age! The court's order required the goods attached to be sold on five days' notice. The intervenor's attachment was filed on the very day of the sale. They were not local and had little time. Wallace bought the goods at the sale for $1550, the amount of the debt to him. He then immediately resold the goods to Aitken for $2000 and took a deed of trust and note from Aitken.

This action gave Wallace a security interest in the property to the exclusion of the other creditors. Wallace set Aitken up in business again. From this transaction came this litigation. At trial the Bernheim Brothers were successful in setting aside both the sale and Wallace's appeals. There were some evidentiary rulings in the appeal but the crux of the matter was an instruction given by Judge Bryant that resulted in the case being reversed and remanded. In essence, Judge Bryant instructed the jury that if Wallace, at the time he sold any portion of the goods charged in the account on which he brought suit, had intended to attach for such debt, then his debt was fraudulent, and the finding should be in favor of the intervenors.

The Supreme Court ruled otherwise. A creditor, it noted, enjoys the right to bring suit on a debt when it becomes due and a suit on a bona fide debt cannot be said as a matter of law to be fraudulent. The judge in the case had, without being asked to do so, instructed the jury that it would be fraudulent to sell goods on credit with, at the same time, an intent to attach the goods and destroy the debtor's business. There was no such allegation and the substance of the appellant's position was that the conspiracy was in order for the business to be preserved to the detriment of the Bernheim Brothers. The Court held that it was confusing and wrong to so instruct the jury. The question presented by the pleadings was whether Wallace, by collusion with Aitken, brought suit and attached for more than was due him, with the intent to aid Aitken in putting his property beyond the reach of his creditors. That was not in the instructions and the case was reversed. It is interesting to note that the attorneys for Wallace were John S. Little, the former circuit judge and soon to be congressman and governor, and John H. Rogers, a former circuit judge, present congressman and future federal district judge.

The next judge to serve Sebastian County and the 12th Judicial Circuit was Styles T. Rowe, who presided from 1899 until 1906. Rowe was born in Troy, Alabama, on May 28, 1861, the son of Daniel and Margaret Taylor Rowe. His mother was a descendent of President Zachary Taylor and a relative of Alexander H. Stephens, who served as the vice president of the Confederacy, while his father was a Baptist preacher. The Rowes moved to Sebastian County in 1872 when Styles was eleven years old. He was schooled at home by his parents, both of whom were well educated. At age 19 he became a school teacher and taught for three terms. He also worked as a clerk in Thomas McCord's store. He read law under Judge C. B. Neal of Greenwood and was admitted to the bar on October 22, 1882. He practiced with his brother Robert A. Rowe in the firm of Rowe and Rowe in Greenwood until he was elected judge on October

JUDGE STYLES T. ROWE
CIRCUIT JUDGE
1899-1906
PHOTO COURTESY OF STYLES ROWE FAMILY

31, 1898. He left the judgeship in 1906 and joined his son Prentiss in the Rowe, Little & Rowe law firm in Fort Smith. In 1912 he was narrowly defeated in the Democratic primary for Attorney General of Arkansas. He was married in 1884, to Miss Emma Patton. The marriage produced four children: Prentiss, who attended the University of Arkansas and served as state representative in the legislature as well as deputy prosecuting attorney; Emma, who lived in Fayetteville and was the wife of Alcuin Eason; Styles Jr.; and Rupert H. Rowe, a veteran of World War I. Styles T. Rowe was a 32nd degree Mason who served on the board of the Masonic Orphans Home at Batesville, Arkansas. In 1894 and 1895 he served as grand master of the Masonic Grand Lodge of Arkansas. It was said of Judge Rowe in the *Centennial History of Arkansas*,

> *"His course was characterized by a masterful grasp of every problem presented for solution and by the utmost fidelity to the cause of justice and right. He was the ablest circuit judge the district ever had and was reversed less by the supreme court than any other circuit judge."*

Judge Rowe met an unfortunate and untimely death on June 2, 1913. As reported in *The Southwest American* on June 3, 1913, he died as the result of an assault in front of the Kansas City Southern depot which stood on the site of the present Holiday Inn, across 7th street from the court house in Fort Smith. The person who assaulted Judge Rowe was one Alonzo E. Willett. At about 4 in the afternoon, Willett came up to Judge Rowe and asked his identity. Willett then struck Judge Rowe in the jaw with such force as to send him headlong into the pavement. His head struck the curb fracturing his skull. Willet also kicked him as he fell. Willet was immediately subdued by bystanders; police then arrived and took him to the police station. Putman's ambulance transported the unconscious Rowe to St. Edward's Infirmary. Three of the city's leading physicians were summoned but they could do nothing: Judge Rowe died later that evening without regaining consciousness, his wife and three sons at his side.

What had provoked the deadly assault? Rowe's attacker, carpenter Alonzo Willett, worked for the freight department of the Kansas City Southern railroad and lived with his family at 622 So. 9th Street. Evidently Judge Rowe had been at the Willett home to interview Mrs. Jessie Willett, a decade younger than her husband, concerning a criminal case that Rowe was handling. Alonzo Willett was upset and was coming to the court to get a warrant for Judge Rowe's arrest when he encountered him. According to Rowe's law partner, prosecuting attorney (and later, circuit judge) Paul Little, Judge Rowe had been the attorney for the wife of Willett's brother in a divorce case. In police court the morning of the assault, a neighbor of the Willetts, as well as a couple who were found in her home, were convicted and fined on a morals charge arising from a family disturbance. Mr. and Mrs. Willett had been witnesses against the woman. Judge Rowe subsequently visited Mrs. Willett, presumably on a fact-finding errand; whatever upset Mr. Willett occurred during or issued from that interview. Notably, Willett himself was unsure of Rowe's identity, suggesting that Rowe had not been involved in the police court proceedings.

The Southwest American reported on June 7th that the grand jury was hearing the Willett matter. They interviewed many of the residents of the 700 block of South 9th. Judge Daniel Hon, presiding, instructed them in the case of a person making a physical assault upon another resulting in death when the intended result was a beating. The grand jury adjourned for the weekend and it was anticipated that Willett would be indicted for involuntary manslaughter. The disposal of this case is not known, but Alonzo Willett appears in the census for 1920 as a free man, living with his wife and four children.

A case decided in Judge Rowe's court, later appealed to the Arkansas Supreme Court was *Kansas & Texas Coal Company vs. Gabsky*, 70 Ark. 434, 66 S. W. 915 (1902). This was a case out the Greenwood district of Sebastian County. The case arose in the county's coal mining industry. Mary Gabsky was a single mother of three children. The oldest was John, aged 11 in 1899. Mrs. Gabsky (she is referred to thus in court records, implying that she was a widow) supported herself and her children by various means, including taking in boarders. One of these, one Thomas Reskowski, was coal miner. Beginning on January 1, 1899, Reskowski brought young John to work with him in mine #51 near Huntington. Young Gabsky went there with the permission of his mother because the family needed the income. Reskowski assured the "pit boss" that John was 15. He looked older than his years. On January 28, 1899, John was killed in the mine when a large rock fell on him. Mrs. Gabsky brought suit under the terms of the Mining Act of April 4, 1893, which provided:

> *"... no person under the age of 14 years shall be permitted to enter any mine to work therein," and that, "for any injury to persons or property occasioned by willful violation of this act a right of action shall accrue to the party injured for any direct damages sustained thereby."*

The amount sued for was $2000 plus costs. Rowe found in favor of Mrs. Gabsky; the mining company, predictably, appealed his verdict.

Chief Justice Bunn wrote for the court that the Miners' Act did not apply to cases of death in that it included no provision for anyone but the injured person to recover. He ruled that the case should be remanded and the plaintiff be given opportunity to amend the pleadings to include the rule of survival in Lord Campbell's Act of 1846. Justice Riddick concurred on different grounds. He wrote that the general act on survival of actions and right of recovery by heirs at law would control. He concurred on the theory that the action was based on violation of the Mining Act

(Chapter 109, Section I of the Arkansas Code, Sandels and Hill *Digest*, 1894) and that the mother was as responsible for her son being in the mine as was the company and that she should not be able to recover against a fellow violator. This would not, however, have precluded an action for negligence.

Act 166 of 1903
10th Judicial Circuit
Consisting of Crawford, Franklin, Logan, Scott, and Sebastian Counties (Created Separate Courts of Chancery Statewide)

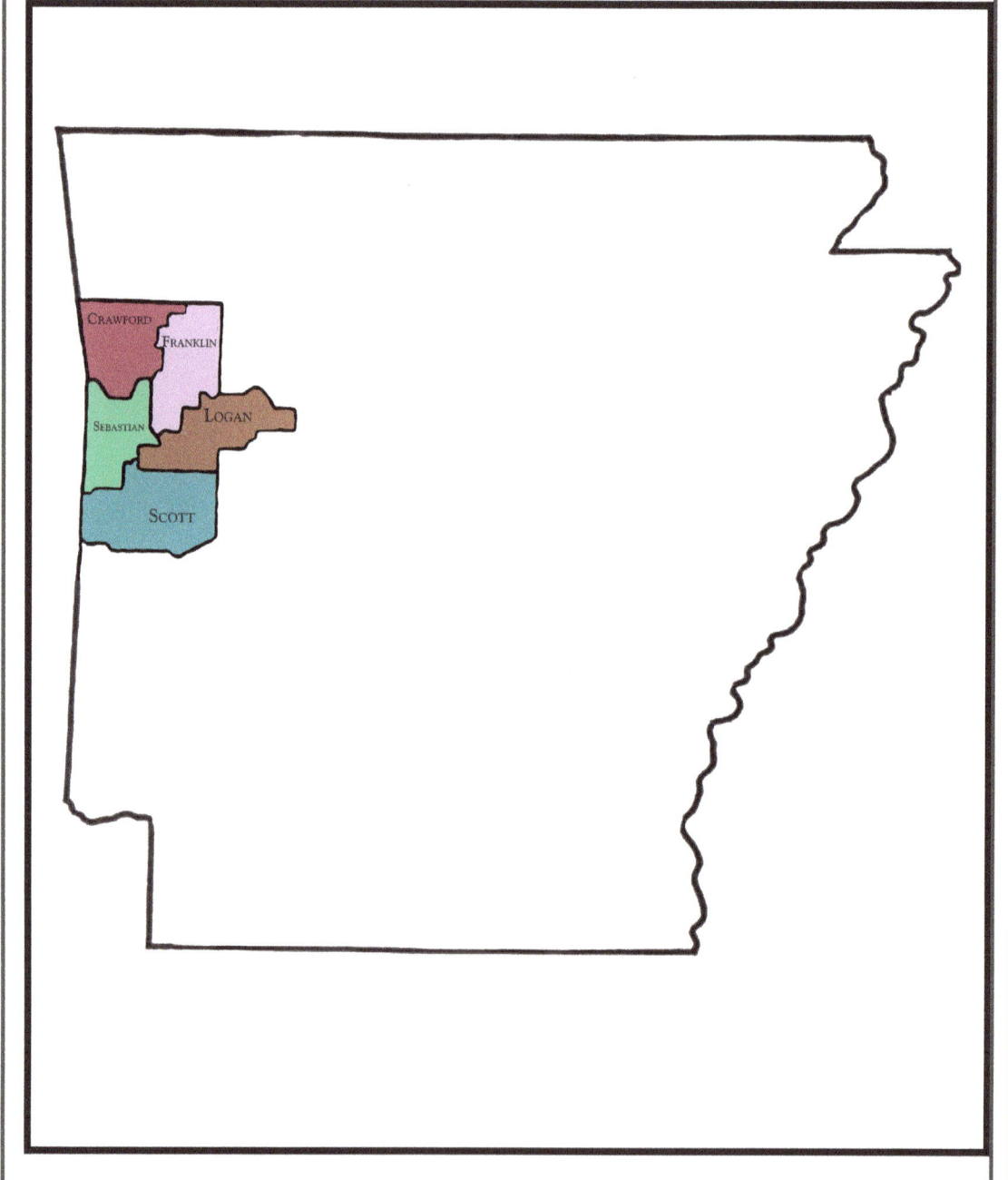

CHAPTER SIX

A New Century— and a New Court

Judge Franklin Wilder once stated that separate courts of chancery were created as a result of a campaign by Governor Jeff Davis. This may overstate things somewhat, but it has some merit. Every constitution since statehood had provided that such courts could be created by the General Assembly, should the need arise. A separate court of chancery in Pulaski County and others had been created earlier. Wilder reminds us, though, that Jeff Davis, while campaigning for governor, promise that if elected, he would see to it that the chancery courts would be created statewide and that he would appoint the first chancellors. This, naturally, had the effect of gaining political support for Davis among the ranks of the lawyers who might be appointed. He was elected and honored his promise: Separate courts of chancery were created by virtue of Act 166 of 1903. Under its terms, the state was divided into separate chancery circuits which had did not coincide with the circuit court circuits or districts.

Since chancery courts' duties have in recent years been rolled into those of general or common courts, a brief explanation of their origin and function is in order. Courts of chancery constituted a response to the limitations of the courts of common law, ones in which penalties or punishments were meted out but which did not restore equity—that is, fairness. These courts enjoyed jurisdiction over matters of equity, as opposed to matters of law. The distinction goes back to medieval England where the tradition developed of the Lord High Chancellor (one of the king's council of advisors) dealing with legal cases sent to the King. In 1280, King Edward I, feeling overwhelmed by requests for justice that might have been dealt with by others, ordained that:

> ...all petitions which touch the Seal shall come first to the Chancellor; and those which touch the Exchequer, to the Exchequer... [a]nd if the affairs are so great, or if they are of Grace, that the Chancellor and the others cannot

JUDGE JAMES V. BOURLAND
CIRCUIT JUDGE
1903-1912 AND 1919-1930
PHOTO COURTESY OF ARCHIVES

do it without the King, then they shall bring them with their own hands to the King to know his pleasure...

Over time, the Lord High Chancellor became seen as the leader of the Court of Chancery, rather than simply a representative of or substitute for the King. Early Chancery procedure mirrored the flexible and simple procedure of ecclesiastical courts. The Chancellor relied heavily on the common law but would do what his conscience perceived was morally right where the common law would cause hardship in a particular case. Although over time the English chancery courts became as formal and rule bound as courts of common law, the principle of fairness remained at their core.

In the United States, some states established separate common law and chancery courts but most, including Arkansas, opted to combine jurisdictions; until the adoption of Act 166 of 1903, the circuit courts would simply indicate, when hearing equity cases, that they were sitting in chancery. Injunctive relief and contract reformation along with certain land disputes have historically been matters for the court of equity; it was understood that common law and chancery were two distinct divisions of the law—but were presided over by judges in common.

Sebastian County was placed into the 10th Chancery Circuit. The 10th encompassed Crawford, Franklin, Logan, Scott and Sebastian Counties. The first chancery judge for this circuit was James V. Bourland. He was born at Lone Elm in Franklin County Arkansas on July 30, 1855. He was descended from an old Virginia family. His grandfather, Dubart Lee Bourland, had moved from Virginia to Tennessee before moving once again, this time to Franklin County Arkansas. He was the first Treasurer for that county and carried the public money in his saddle bags, evidence of how rural the Arkansas frontier was. Dubart married Malinda Robinson, a relative of General Robert E. Lee.

Their son, Ebenezer, was Judge Bourland's father. Ebenezer served in the Confederate Army and was later a merchant and blacksmith in Ozark. Ebenezer was a well-read man and a Mason. He married Rebecca Bruton of Pope County, the daughter of a prominent Baptist minister. Their son James attended Ozark schools and Cane Hill College. He got his legal education at Cumberland University in Lebanon, Tennessee. He graduated in 1876 and began the practice of law in Ozark, which he continued until 1903. In that year he was appointed Chancery Judge for the Tenth Chancery Circuit by Governor Davis. The appointment was for four years. He then was reelected to two consecutive six-year terms. He resigned in the fall of 1913 to accept an appointment as the United States Attorney for the Western District of Arkansas which he obtained through the influence of his political allies Governor James P. Clarke and Senator Jeff Davis. After four years of service in this position he practiced law in Fort Smith for a year and then was reelected Chancellor by a majority of 1,000 votes. He served in this position until 1930.

Judge Bourland was considered the best lawyer in western Arkansas. He was known for his strict enforcement of the divorce statutes. He was married on April 29, 1891, to Bonnie Jean Carter of Ozark, the daughter of a Franklin County physician. They had four children: Annie Marr, Mary Rebecca, Wallace Carter and James V. Jr.

A case decided by Judge Bourland that was later appealed to the Arkansas Supreme Court was *Southern Crawford Road Improvement District vs. Brown*, 156 Ark. 267, 245 S. W. 821 (1922). This was a case where jurisdiction of the chancery court was conferred by statute. It arose in Crawford County when the legislature created the ability to create road improvement districts. This case reflects the change in government and society brought on by that newfangled invention, the automobile. Road Improvement District #5 was created by the citizenry to (wait for it) improve roads in southern Crawford County. Some of the preliminary steps needed to begin this good work had been undertaken but no construction started when, in January 1920, a special session of the Legislature produced a special statute creating the "Southern Crawford Road District" of Crawford County. This statute called for the improvement of certain roads, including a portion of the roads authorized by District #5. The statute also abolished District #5 and provided that the new district would pay the debts of District #5, up to but not to exceed $5,000. It also said that if the newly created district did not in fact make the improvements, the preliminary expenses of the district would be a first lien upon all land in the district and would be paid by a levy of a tax thereon by the chancery court of Crawford County, to be collected by a receiver to be appointed by the court.

The new Southern Crawford Road District continued with the preliminary work and assumed responsibility for expenses incurred by the old district in the amount of $4609.90. It was ultimately determined, however, that the projected road construction would be too expensive; hence the commissioners of the district filed a petition in chancery court to complete the affairs of the district and pay their preliminary expenses, consisting primarily of engineering fees. The creditor engineers had been issued IOUs from the district and some of these had been subsequently negotiated to others. The commissioners had borrowed $8,000 from a bank and the bank thus also was a claimant. The property owners of the district (who would be taxed to pay the debts of both the original district and the one authorized in 1920) intervened and contested both the expenses and the constitutionality of the act.

Judge Bourland ruled that the act was unconstitutional because the Legislature had, in his view, improperly delegated legislative authority to the commission and because he deemed the method of payment of the preliminary expenses improper. The amount of the awards was not contested. Bourland approved payment to the claimants on a *quantum meruit* basis. He also honored the bank debt. The amounts allowed, it should be noted, were not the amounts claimed. The district appealed the constitutionality of Bourland's finding regarding the disallowal of the claims for expenses from the old district and the property owners appealed the portion that required them to pay the other preliminary expenses; it seems that no-one was happy with the results of this convoluted case.

The Supreme Court proved dissatisfied as well and reversed Judge Bourland's ruling. The court said that the Legislature had been within its rights and had not delegated legislative authority to the commission authorized by the 1920 measure; it had merely delegated the authority to the commission to determine the extent to which improvements to the roads should be made! The court also ruled that the bank loan taken out by the second commission had been a valid expense since the money borrowed was used to pay valid expenses. The court remanded the case with directions that the old expenses be paid, and the affairs of the defunct district be concluded, effectively telling the Commission and the district residents to work out their differences and pay the bills.

Another case decided by Judge Bourland that reached the Arkansas Supreme Court was *Lyric Theater vs. State*, 98 Ark. 437, 136 S. W. 174 (1911). There was at the time a law on the books prohibiting "Sabbath breaking," which included an assortment of practices, occupations and recreations which were considered by some to be inappropriate for Sundays. The Lyric Theater in Fort Smith advertised that they would offer vaudeville performances and moving pictures on a Sunday, both of which were prohibited. The prosecuting attorney advised the Lyric's management that he would prosecute if they did so. A parsing of the ordinance suggested, however, that the theater would violate the law only if it <u>sold</u> tickets to its Sunday shows. Therefore, they said, they would let people in free. The prosecutor then filed suit in chancery court seeking an injunction. It was alleged in the petition that the performances were legally and morally wrong and would tend to create a violation of the Sabbath breaking laws, that they would bring together a lawless and turbulent assembly of persons which would result in an injury to the morals and general welfare of the people of that community and that such performances constituted a public nuisance.

Nevertheless, the theater management persisted. On October 30, 1910, the Lyric advertised that on the following Sunday they would present these performances. True to the advertisement, on Sunday, December 4, the theater did so—running the risk that this might attract that "lawless and turbulent assembly of persons which would result in an injury to the morals and general welfare of the people"—and prosecution ensued.

The court's resume of the case described the illicit entertainment: "The performances were given in an enclosed building and consisted of moving pictures. The show was a portrayal of the life of Damon and Pythias, accompanied by a lecture thereon and sacred songs and music. Neither the moving pictures, songs or music were immoral or objectionable in any regard." The theater management, evidently, had opted to present a "vaudeville show" suitable for any Sunday School audience, the better to test the limits of the law. Judge Bourland, however, embraced the letter of the ordinance and permanently enjoined the giving of the performances on Sunday; the theater appealed. The Arkansas Supreme Court ultimately reversed and dismissed the case. They stated that the theater could not be enjoined from doing any act which was not in itself wrongful... and that these performances, with their high moral and improving tone, did not meet the definition of "wrongful." The fact that the theater had technically transgressed the criminal law was insufficient. Courts of equity, the Supreme Court's decision seemed to say, did not exercise their powers to enforce the criminal laws nor did they have the power to enforce the performance of moral duties solely as such. This case may seem to be nothing more than a quaint reflection on those past times. However, so-called "Blue Laws" that prohibited the sale of certain items or the conduct of some types of business on Sunday were enforced in Arkansas until the 1970s; they are still with us in the form of the prohibition of liquor sales by liquor stores on Sundays, and the customary practice of auto dealers remaining closed on Sundays.

In 1907, the district had a new circuit judge, the first not to exercise jurisdiction in equity cases. An interesting man by the name of Daniel Hon, he served from 1907 through 1914.

Daniel Hon was born near Waldron in Scott County on July 10, 1860. He was the son of farmer Jackson Hon who was born in Posey County Illinois, in 1815, and his third wife, Lucie Huie, a native of the Scott County area. Daniel was the grandson of Jonas Hahn (changed spelling) who immigrated from Darmstadt-Hessen, in present Germany in the 1770's. The date suggests the possibility that Jonas Hahn was a Hessian soldier, brought in by the British to fight in the Revolution, who chose to stay in a new and promising land. It is said that when Daniel Hon was a boy, during trips to town with his father, he would step into the courthouse to listen and wished that someday he could sit on the bench as a

JUDGE DANIEL HON
CIRCUIT JUDGE
1907-1914
PHOTO COURTESY OF POWELL WOODS

judge. Jackson Hon frequently gave young Daniel and his brother the choice of either studying or working the farm; Daniel Hon always chose study, while his brother tended to farm chores.

Daniel Hon proved to be an able and dedicated student. He was a member of the 1882 graduating class of the Arkansas Industrial University, now known as the University of Arkansas-Fayetteville. His transportation to the University was by "disciple's horses"; prior to the beginning of classes in the fall he would walk from Waldron to Fayetteville (a route of about 100 miles) and when school was over in the spring he would walk home. He next attended the Cumberland School of Law in Lebanon, Tennessee, enrolling for a one-year course of study that he completed in nine months!

Daniel Hon began his practice of law in Waldron in 1883, in partnership with a Mr. Lemming. Hon represented the Arkansas Western Railroad (a subsidiary of the Kansas City Southern line) railroad in some right of way matters and the railroad may have acknowledged this when it named the named the community of Hon, located just west of Waldron.

He was elected circuit judge in 1906 and reelected in 1910. Judge Hon was married to Margaret Pamela Gaines, a native of Montgomery County. Her father was Francis Cornelius "Buck" Gaines who served as sheriff of Montgomery County. Judge Hon was defeated for reelection in 1914, by Paul Little. He once again entered the practice of law, now with his son-in-law, John P. Woods. Mr. Woods left the practice to serve in the army during World War I. He later, along with Harry Daily, formed the Fort Smith practice that, to this day, retains the name Daily and Woods. Judge Hon served as bankruptcy referee in addition to his practice.

Judge Hon was an eccentric individual. He never permitted a desk telephone in his office or home; they had to be the wall mounted variety and of these he had two, because two different phone companies served Fort Smith: Bell and Pan. (One could not call a Bell system phone from one on the Pan lines, and vice versa). Neither Judge Hon nor his wife ever owned or operated an automobile. Judge Hon was a well-read and a particularly good speller. A century or more ago, communities commonly sponsored adult spelling bees and Judge Hon—if he chose to enter, and he frequently did—would usually win. The prize was normally a new hat. Each time there was such an event he was known to say, "This is where I get a new hat!" And each time he would indeed come home with a new hat. He was a convivial person who enjoyed a good story and was good at telling them. Hon did not hunt, fish or play golf or tennis; billiards was his game. His hobby was his vegetable garden and for this he was famous. His personal vices were modest: he liked root beer and tobacco. He became addicted to tobacco when he was a boy, growing up on a farm which grew...tobacco. His wife told their grandson Powell Woods that the Judge would smoke all day and if he had trouble sleeping, he would get up and smoke for several hours before going back to bed. Judge Hon passed away April 6, 1929, at the age of 68.

In 1910 the Fort Smith courthouse was 23 years old, and it had some structural defects as evidenced by falling plaster and instability caused by the massive bell tower. It was this instability that began one of the most bizarre episodes in the political and judicial history of Sebastian County. To better understand the story about to unfold the reader needs to understand the respective roles of the county judge and the quorum court under the 1874 Constitution. Professor Jay Barth, in *Arkansas Politics and Government*, notes that counties' quorum courts generally met but once a year and wielded little authority, even though they were charged to sit with and assist their respective county judges in levying county taxes and in making appropriations:

> *Annually the court members would assemble, answer the roll, give their unanimous consent to the judge's approximation of county expenditures for the coming year (which he frequently read aloud from a single sheet of paper), collect their ten-dollar fee, and retreat again to anonymity.... At no time...in any county did any quorum court exercise any real restraint over any county judge. In effect, then, the county judge exercised not only executive and judicial powers but legislative powers as well....in terms of county projects, property, employees, and funds the county judge became the closest thing to an uncrowned king that the American political system had to offer.*

It was this king-like authority that would spawn the conflict over the Fort Smith courthouse.

The Southwest American reported on May 6, 1910, that County Judge Jesse Harp had awarded E. R. Goodwin the contract to remove the tower from the courthouse:

> *"Investigation shows that the tower with its great weight swings to and fro during the wind and the movement is causing the plastering to fall in all the rooms on the first floor... It is with a view of preventing greater damage to the building that the tower will be removed."*

This work was done for the price of $465.00. So far, so good, but on May 18 the paper reported a rather humorous incident:

> **CLERKS GET NEW KIND OF SHOWER**. *It was not a shower that one would get to be given a bride. Neither was it one of those meteoric kind that may accompany*

Halley's Comet (which at the time was visible in the night sky) but it produced a hair raising foot race in the Sebastian County Clerk's office about 8 o'clock yesterday morning in which deputy clerk Luther Hopkins outdistanced clerk Ezra Hester by $\frac{1}{16}^{th}$ of a yard after a sprint of eight feet and $\frac{2}{7}^{th}$'s feet. The cause of this unusual piece of foot work was a deafening crash of laths and aged plastering. The third floor of the courthouse consists of a preparation of this kind. One of the workmen employed in tearing down the courthouse tower fell through the "ceiling" causing a shower of plaster and lath to fall in close proximity of the occupants of the clerk's office. At first it was thought the building was falling, but when the officials started an investigation, they saw a pair of feet slowly retreating out of the holes in the ceiling and they knew what the trouble was.

The work was completed by May 10, 1910 and the timbers removed from the tower were enough to fill two freight cars. They had to be cut up in order to get them down from the building and it was predicted that the wood would be used to fire the courthouse furnaces next winter.

The removal of the tower did not, however, solve the problem. On November 13, 1911, *The Southwest American* reported:

Temple of Justice Rocks Like Cradle During Wind, Possibility of Court House Tumbling Into Ruins Clearly In Evidence During Big Blow Yesterday-Officials Greatly Alarmed—Plastering Falls And Walls Crack. ...Saturday, suspicious new cracks opened in its walls...old ones widened, and the old structure trembled and shook like a thing of life as the wind beat against it in fitful, whirling gusts. County officials occupying the upper story grew alarmed when chunks of plastering began falling from the parting of partition walls and the breaking of ceilings. They watched closely the progress of the storm and threatened to vacate the building if the severity of the storm became much greater. Chiefly the trouble seemed to be confined to the southwestern section of the building—the one that has shown unmistakable signs of disintegrating for the past several years. Cracks and crevices mark this portion of the structure both inside and on the exterior. Some of these appeared during Saturday's storm, although the velocity of the wind, except for very brief gusts, did not exceed forty miles an hour, while some of the old defects were rendered more pronounced. Above the top landing of the stairway yesterday one long crevice between the ceiling and a partition wall increased to nearly two inches in width letting through pieces of plastering and quantities of pigeon feathers that had accumulated in the dovecote in the attic....A scrutiny of the exterior walls of the southwestern section of the building disclosed more pronounced sources of danger, perhaps, than appeared inside. The old cracks appeared perceptibly widened and at least one new crevice was added by the force of the storm. This appeared at the arch above a first story window and extended upward several feet. So pronounced was the opening that one brick at the nether side of the arch dropped out of place until it barely hung by one end between those immediately next to it. Higher up other defect appeared, one or more bricks being crushed by what seemed to be a concerted movement of one section of the building in a downward direction, the other portion remaining firm.

The report went on to discuss the removal of the tower and the architect's opinion at that time that the building was sound. The county judge told the reporter that he would appoint a commission consisting of architects and a builder to fully report on the real condition of the building. Harp told the reporter that, had the tower not been removed, the "big wind" would have caused collapse and many fatalities. The judge had a picture of the courthouse as it would look remodeled to his specifications with three stories and elevators with the walls of reinforced concrete. Harp estimated the remodeling to cost $70,000. Under the arrangement between the county and the city the former would bear two-thirds of the expense and the latter one-third.

On November 29, 1911, *The Southwest American* reported on the findings of the commission appointed by Judge Harp:

"Examiners Say Structure May Fall In Ruins, Commission Investigating Conditions At Court House Declare Building Is In Dangerous Condition—Faulty Foundation Is Believed To Be The Cause."

The commission consisted of architects J. T. W. Jennings and A. Klinginsmith and contractor Robert L. Paine. They opined that any unusual disturbance in the elements could bring it down. They suggested three solutions: first, underpin the foundation with concrete footing; rebuild the cracked portion of the brick walls and knit the whole mass together with an elaborate system of tie rods. The cost for this option would be $30,000; second, complete remodeling of the courthouse and conversion into a three-story building at a cost of $90,000. The third option was to raze the present structure and erect a $135,000 building "in keeping with the needs and greatness of the county and the city." They recommended that in the near term, a temporary system of braces and tie rods be applied. As for why the courthouse was in such dangerous condition, the commission suggested that a faulty foundation was the problem.

On December 24, 1911, *The Southwest American* reported that Judge Harp had opined that finances would not permit the building of a new courthouse. The county did not have the necessary funds and the state constitution forbade the issuance of interest-bearing bonds. The paper quoted Judge Daniel Hon as saying, "If the building should tumble into ruins tomorrow neither the county nor any other body could borrow a cent for rebuilding it. He (Judge Harp) could only issue non-interest-bearing scrip to hawk about generally at any old price."

For his part, Judge Harp dismissed any thought of a special quorum court session but did state that he would strengthen the walls to prevent disaster:

"The city appears to be in the notion of remodeling or rebuilding the structure, but just now the county cannot expend the money to meet the necessary two-thirds of the cost that would devolve upon it. The building of the new jail which cost nearly $25,000 cleaned us up. However, we will be on our feet again in the next few weeks with a few thousand dollars surplus, but there will not be enough to justify the expenditure of $50,000 or $75,000 more at this time. Our laws do not permit the securing of a loan for such purposes, hence the county judge gets "cussed" when there is no money in the treasury for "running scrip down, etc." regardless of how important the expenditures may be....The county cannot even buy groceries for its paupers, notwithstanding its millions of wealth. That may sound funny, but it is the law."

The co-tenant and owner of the land now came into the discussion. The city of Fort Smith, in a council meeting reported in the January 5, edition of *The Southwest American*, appointed a joint committee consisting of six members; three from the city council and three from the Fort Smith District Quorum Court to devise plans and means for building a new courthouse and city hall. The sentiment was practically solid for a new structure in line with the importance and wealth of the city and county. The cost estimate was now $250,000, up from the $135,000 estimated earlier by Judge Harp. Both anxieties o er the safety of the old courthouse and enthusiasm for a new one were so high that it was thought that construction could be started before the end of the year. No one attending the meeting favored repair of the existing building, which was referred to as dilapidated, dangerous, and out-of-date. A letter was presented to the group from County Judge Harp in which he advised that repairs could not be made without going into the foundation, which would cost several thousand dollars, and that the county could not afford the cost without issuing warrants that could not be paid from the treasury. He also expressed that he would not favor building a courthouse unless it would be a "good one." He said that it could be done by arranging with some "interests" to take care of warrants for this purpose. By interests he evidently meant some insurance or financial concerns.

The judge also reminded the council that the county was unable to increase its millage for this purpose as they were already taxing at the maximum five mils. He said that, at present, the county could pledge $20-25,000 per year to pay the warrants. Judge Harp also presented the council with the drawings of a proposed three-story building with a 240-foot frontage on 6th Street. Chancellor Bourland also addressed the group, indicating that he was for building this structure. He decried any attempt to foist a "hen coop" on the county. He related that Ozark had built a courthouse by issuing scrip and the people there had not felt the cost. Fort Smith Mayor Fagan Bourland also expressed a feeling that a new building was needed. He said if the county could afford $25,000 per year that the city could as well, keeping the city millage at 4 mils.

At this point the resolve for a new building seemed firm, reported the *Southwest American* on January 14. Alas, this firm support would later soften, and only the reluctant Judge Harp would want to press forward with the new courthouse enterprise. For now, though, the committee unanimously adopted a resolution in favor of the proposition and authorized Chairman John Howell to advertise for bids on construction and financing (authority to do this had been vested in the committee by the city council and the county judge).

It was noted that the city could pay cash but that the county would have to issue scrip (county IOU's or paper money that would be negotiable, non-interest-bearing instruments redeemable by the county at a designated time in the future at face value). A certain portion would be retired each year until the indebtedness was paid. The committee agreed that that numerous builders would be glad to enter into such an arrangement. The plan considered would be paid off in five years. It was mentioned that the county had a 99-year lease on the premises and the lease had 77 years left on it. The division of costs was that the county would be responsible for 3/5ths of the cost and the city for 2/5ths. All that remained, it seemed, was for the committee to wait on bids for the work.

It was at this point those problems started to develop.

The problem was funding and the already antiquated Arkansas Constitution, since amended, that forbade bonded indebtedness. It was reported on January 23 that the committee received a bid from James Black Masonry and Contracting Co. of St. Louis, the company that had constructed the First National Bank building in Fort Smith. They proposed a schedule of payments of $50,000 per year until paid at 10% annual interest. They would hold a mortgage on the property and title would revert to the city when the mortgage was paid. Mr. George Tilles, a local promoter and insurance executive, also attended the meeting and made a similar proposal but could not identify his backers. On January 30, a new proposal was reported from D.B. Ridpath of Oklahoma Quarries and Construction in Oklahoma City. On February 20 it was reported that the committee had held its final meeting and concluded that the only way for the project to proceed was for the county and the city to issue warrants and eliminate any bond issue. They recommended the hiring of an architect as well.

Another problem then surfaced. The legality of the joint commission appointed by the city and county was questioned. The Board of Public Affairs met with the commissioners, and it was not productive. They did agree on the hiring of an architect, but the discussion was that the Board of Public Affairs and the committee must both agree before the next step could be taken. The discussion was whether the county appointees could act for the county. The majority felt that the county judge had the authority to delegate such by his appointment of the members.

Judge Harp was in political trouble otherwise. He was being criticized and County Clerk Ezra Hester announced that he was a candidate to replace him. Hester was endorsed by *The Southwest American*. A story ran in that same edition concerning Harp assigning his salary to The Arkansas Valley Trust Co. to satisfy debt. He was also accused of reducing the taxes owed by Arkansas Valley Trust and it was noted that he had an office in the Arkansas Valley Trust Building. In the March primary election the citizenry was in a mood to throw the rascals out. State Senator John H. Holland, Governor George Donaghey and Judge Harp were all defeated. Harp came in third in a three-man race.

Now a lame duck, Harp's plans for a new courthouse were in jeopardy. On April 16, *The Southwest American* headlined: PLANS FOR NEW CITY HALL ARE GIVEN A SET-BACK. The Board of Public Affairs and the county commissioners gave approval of the plans of architect Jennings but Mayor Bourland said he personally and as a member of the board was not in favor until definite financial plans were made. Alderman Howell said the city council was not competent to approve the plans since they had not examined them. The proposal was tabled. On April 14 the *Titanic* had gone down and symbolically the plans for the courthouse had hit an iceberg as well. This iceberg was made of politics, personal animosity, and archaic law.

On May 21, the paper reported that the city council had adopted a resolution providing for the appointment of yet another committee to confer with the joint commission representing the city and the county and to report back to a special called meeting of the council. The purpose was to attempt to arrive at a solution to the problems that had kept the project dormant. A May 26, headline announced, COUNCIL PIDGEON HOLES PLAN FOR ERECTION OF COMBINED CITY HALL AND COURTHOUSE. The story related that the council did not dignify the project with so much as a comment. Judge Harp was quoted, "...[the] project now, insofar as the city acting in conjunction with the county is concerned seems to be as dead as the proverbial ten doornails." As background for this pronouncement the story related that Judge Harp had notified the city that if it did not see fit to cooperate with the county in the courthouse matter, the county would "seek a divorce" and undertake the building of a temple of justice alone. He had given the city until May 20, to decide.

One member of the council said that Judge Harp's ultimatum was received as a bluff and the aldermen called it. Harp addressed the council and advised that the county would go it alone. He stated that there would never be a time when the Fort Smith District would be able to pay cash. It was his opinion that some things should be done on faith in the future and let posterity help pay for improvements. Reasonable indebtedness was not a bad policy according to Harp. He also complained about the criticism received by his appointed commissioners and insisted that they were good people. He went on to say that the county could build a courthouse without an appropriation by the Quorum Court and that the county's lease on the premises had another 75 years to run and that he felt like the county should realize something from it. He was obviously upset.

Mayor Fagan Bourland opined,

> *"Someday we will have a new courthouse. If you don't want it now, say so and bury it. I am in favor of a joint building. This old building may stand a long time, but it seems to me the old cracks are getting larger all the time."*

By June 5 it was reported that PLAN FOR CITY HALL AND COURTHOUSE DEAD. All that remained was an unpaid architect bill of $500 to $1000, a set of plans, and a fine watercolor framed picture of a $250,000 courthouse which adorned the wall of the city clerk's office.

Jesse Harp, once reluctant concerning a new courthouse, was not going to let the idea die. The June 16, 1912, edition of *The Southwest American* headlined, COUNTY TO ASK CITY FOR COURT HOUSE LOCATION. Harp was requesting the northeast corner of the courthouse block, following the terms of the government grant for the purpose of constructing a courthouse. He quoted the grant of the block as being for this express purpose: "...grants to the city of Fort Smith...to be used for the erection of public buildings and county courthouse." If this was not granted, then the county would build elsewhere. The city council was now in favor of repairing the old building, according to the story, because it was cheaper. (The Gentle Reader should recall that the concept of a new courthouse had in fact originated with the Fort Smith city council.) Harp said that the law required a courthouse to be on land owned by the county and that the county would release any interest it had in the present building for a grant of the requested land for a courthouse. The confrontation had commenced.

By July 7, counsel was retained by Judge Harp to file a quiet title action in chancery court. The county had decided to claim the northeast corner of the courthouse block. The architect Jennings and Charles Jewett were appointed as commissioners to build the new courthouse on that site for a cost not to exceed $260,000. Judge Harp entered a detailed court order setting out the laws and justifications regarding the building of a courthouse. His main points were as follow: the Fort Smith District of Sebastian County does not have a good and adequate courthouse; the district enjoyed the right to build a courthouse; the real estate known as the "Courthouse Square" came by U.S. government patent to the City of Fort Smith in trust expressly for the building of a county courthouse and other public buildings; The City of Fort Smith had denied the Fort Smith District of Sebastian County the right to build a courthouse on this ground and, therefore the county court, Judge Harp presiding, would authorize the prosecution of an action at chancery to quiet title to the land in the county.

The particular property claimed was the northeast corner of the block on Rogers Avenue and 7th Street across from the Union train station (now the Holiday Inn) and measuring 160 by 110 feet. The cost of $260,000 was to be paid in 12 equal payments yearly until paid off. This was to be at no interest. The contractors would give a bond that they would not present the warrants for payment prematurely. The commissioners were to immediately present plans for the building. It should be noted that the main contention was that the city was not the fee owner of the property but merely a trustee for the benefit of the county. The object of the suit was to set aside any adverse claim the city might have enjoyed in the property. Judge Harp expected the contracts to be let and the construction to begin in a few weeks.

The city of Fort Smith did not sit idly by. The city council was in fact considering an ordinance to give the Courthouse Square land to the county in exchange for abandoning the claim to any interest in the existing court building. However, Mayor Bourland advised the council, that when Judge Harp had notified him of his intent to begin construction, he told Harp, "With the first shovel of dirt the city would apply for an injunction." The council unanimously approved the mayor's stand. By August 6, the council voted to take action. City Attorney Vincent Miles was instructed to file the injunctive proceedings to prevent the county judge from contracting for a new county building. This followed Councilman Garrett calling attention to the bid advertisement. The motion to seek the injunction passed without dissent.

By August 7, a suit was filed. It was not filed by the city but instead by a group of taxpayers represented by the law firm of Falconer, Youmans and Woods (Falconer was a former county judge and future chancery judge). Judge Bourland set the next day at 10:00 a. m. for a hearing. About the same time a suit was filed on behalf of the city. Judge Bourland consolidated them for trial. The grounds for the requested injunction were: the county had made no appropriation for the building; Harp's order of July 29 did not designate a location for the building; the county did not own the land, but the city did; the county did not have the money to pay for the building; the building would be too close to the train station and the noise would impede court proceedings; the city and county already owned a building and the city was willing to help repair said building; the county would lose any claim to the present building if the plan proceeded;

the predicted cost of the new court building would be $260,000 but the finished structure could not be worth more than $150,000; the county warrants would sell for .75 on the dollar and this fact, plus interest and fees, would make the expense on the new building come to a tidy $456,000.

The county had decided to let the city initiate the legal proceedings instead of seeking to quite title. The county's plan for the suit was to demur to the jurisdiction of the chancery court and plead that the exclusive jurisdiction of matters concerning the finance of a court building was with the county court.

Judge Bourland's ruling in the case was unique. He ruled that the injunction should be granted. The county was enjoined from building on the northeast corner as planned. However, on all other points he ruled in favor of the county! He ruled that the city did take the land in trust; however, the county had exercised its option and had built a courthouse on the land that the present building occupied. This land was owned now by the county and not the city and the county could do as it pleased with the building on that site. Tear it down and rebuild or remodel were the options and the city's only claim was a leasehold on the space it occupied in the building. The county judge was ruled to be the sole arbiter in the erection and maintenance of a courthouse building. The decision was a paradox.

Like a prairie cyclone, the issue quickly grew and threatened to run out of control. A town meeting was called by Judge Falconer, to demonstrate the attitude of Fort Smith's citizens toward the county's plans for a new home. About 100 people showed up in the circuit courtroom. A resolution passed by those in attendance was presented by Harry Daily, opposing a separate county building. Judge Harp, who was present, coolly stated that he intended to build a new building on the site of the old in accordance with the ruling of Judge Bourland.

On August 14th, it was reported that a special city council meeting resulted in a 4-2 vote in favor of a joint building. It was also noted that this was not the time to do it due to financing. There was one point on which all agreed: avoid litigation. Jesse Harp, however, forged ahead. An August 20 headline announced CONTRACT LET YESTERDAY FOR COUNTY COURT HOUSE. A contract had been let by Commissioner Jewett and approved by County Judge Harp for $257,225.00 with $4,125.00 paid in cash and the rest in county warrants. A deed of trust was filed after the court's 40-page order was entered. The contractor was the Falls City Construction Company of Louisville, Kentucky. The order of the county court contained all pertinent documents and history of the joint city/county building going back to 1888. As part of the order, the city of Fort Smith was given thirty days to remove all city-owned furnishings and files. Lon Norris, the sheriff of Sebastian County, was instructed to evict the city from the courthouse space after that time.

Justice Divided

"Down By The Court House" by John Bell, Jr. *Fort Smith, Arkansas*

1887 Fort Smith District Courthouse with Second Bell Tower

Harp, in his order, recited a lease agreement between the city and the county in 1888. He Harp opined that the lease was void as the county could not legally enter into a lease of the county courthouse. Citing Judge Bourland's opinion, Harp stated that the county was the sole owner of the land upon which the courthouse stood and that he was claiming a lot fronting on 6th Street in Block 515, in the northwest corner of that block 88 feet south of the corner of 6th Street and Rogers Avenue. It contained 17,720 square feet and included the site of the old courthouse. He asserted that the building was to be complete in fifteen months. He also provided that any delay caused by court action would not be chargeable and if enjoined by court action, the contract would be void. He also asserted the county's right to lease space during construction.

On the same day and in a story on the same page of the paper was the headline, COUNCIL ORDERS POLICE TO OPPOSE HARP'S ORDER. The story bruited about the possibility of open inter-governmental warfare, or at least a war of words. This ordinance provided that the police arrest any person who might seek to disturb the city's peaceful possession of the courthouse and charge them with trespass. This action was taken on the recommendation of the city attorney, who advised that seeking a court injunction would play into Harp's hands. He said, "It's not the city's job to protect the county from its county judge." The next day, August 21, the paper reported that J.B. McDonough, the lawyer for the county in the dispute, withdrew from the matter. He said that the contract signed by the commissioner and Jewett contained items of which he had not approved. Harp retorted that the contract followed the law. On August 24 there was a story that the county would rent space in the Grand Opera House for use during construction.

By the 28th the dispute was back in court. SUIT FILED TO ENJOIN HARP, read the headline. The suit pled that Judge Harp was acting illegally and as a private citizen in conspiracy with Charles Jewett. It was pled that the city owned all the courthouse block and that the contract with the construction company was illegal, thus null and void. On the 29th the lede was COURTHOUSE SQUABBLE NEARING LAST CHAPTER. The county had filed a cross-complaint to enjoin the city and a quiet title action to settle the title to the courthouse in the county; Chancellor Bourland arranged to hear the case that afternoon.

On August 30, the local paper trumpeted, CITY AND COUNTY BOTH ENJOINED FROM ACTING IN COURTHOUSE MATTER UNTIL COURT DECIDES QUESTION. Judge Bourland's order held that the county owned the ground on which the existing courthouse had been built; that the city of fort Smithy held an equitable interest in the building; that neither entity had the right to terminate the arrangement and that it was for a court of equity or chancery to determine when and how the arrangement might be terminated or changed absent an agreement of the parties.

On September 1, the paper revealed that Judge Harp had been enjoined from leasing the opera house for temporary space, considering Bourland's order and its implications.

If Bourland's order had been meant to slow the course of events, it soon became clear that the civic cyclone would not cooperate. On September 5, the *Southwest American* reported: HARP ORDERS HOPKINS AND HESTER JAILED... DEPUTY THOMPSON REFUSES; COURT HOUSE SQUABBLE REACHES ACUTE STAGE. It seemed that Harp had requested a county warrant to be filed in the county clerk's office to pay the architect, Jennings, $1200.00 on the contract entered by the county judge with the architect. Deputy Clerk Hopkins refused to do so. Harp then asked Clerk Ezra Hester (soon to become the county judge) to file the warrant and order of record; Hester likewise refused. Harp then ordered the deputy sheriff to arrest Hopkins and Hester; the deputy refused to do because the county court was not in session and therefore the judge had no authority to fine or imprison anyone. In addition, if he did so, he would be in contempt of Judge Bourland's injunction. Stymied by the county's clerical and law enforcement powers, Harp left the building; buy now, the good judge seemed out of control. In the same story, the paper helpfully reported that a group of citizens had now filed a lawsuit. They wanted the contract to build the building voided. It was time for cooler heads to prevail.

On September 7, *The Southwest American* published a story based on interviews with members of the quorum court. All of them were of a mind to stop and reconsider the reasons that the courthouse had become an issue. They felt requirements of the city and county should be addressed as well as the condition of the present building before any action was taken. They were of the opinion that the present building should be repaired, or a new joint city/county building be built. The very next day, the paper reported that MEMBERS OF CITY COUNCIL AGREE WITH QUORUM COURT ON COURTHOUSE. Dr. Eberle, a city councilman, referred to the quorum court as an advisory body which, in effect, it was before Amendment 55. Mayor Fagan Bourland opined that the repairs might be more extensive and expensive than believed but agreed that repairing the building was the best course. None of this reasonable talk had any effect, however, on the honorable Jesse Harp.

On September 18, the story lede was: AND THE COURTHOUSE WAR GOES MERRILY, MERRILY ON. The hot news was that Harp's orders for the payment to the architect and the county clerk's refusal were reaching the deadline imposed by Harp before fines and jail would result. The next day, following the deadline, he fined Hester an additional $50. On the 22nd it was noted that Judge Hon had postponed any consideration of the appeal of the county court order concerning the courthouse and the fines until after the October term of court. Thus, the matter would not be heard until two weeks prior to Harp leaving office and his nemesis Ezra Hester becoming county judge! (The reader is reminded that county terms of office began on October 31 in those days.)

On October 22, *The Southwest American* reported, ENJOINS HARP FROM OUSTING CITY OFFICERS. The city won a sweeping victory in chancery court and obtained a permanent injunction. It was ruled that the county could not tear down the present building. The contract to build the new building was void and the present courthouse was adequate for the needs of the district. The previous holding that the county owned the land the present courthouse occupied was overruled.

The new ruling stated that the city owned the block in fee simple. The court also ruled that the condition of the building was uncertain but there was no immediate danger, and it could be repaired. This quietus put an end to the Jesse Harp courthouse project. On October 31 the headline read, NEW COUNTY OFFICERS TAKE OVER; HESTER COUNTY JUDGE. Hester immediately undertook to undo all Harp had done concerning the construction of a new courthouse and, of course, set aside the orders fining and jailing himself for failing to do the bidding of Judge Harp.

All this set-in motion a case decided in Judge Hon's court that made its way on appeal to the Arkansas Supreme Court: *Jennings vs. Fort Smith District of Sebastian County*, 115 Ark. 130, 171 S. W. 920 (1914). This case dealt with the courthouse in Fort Smith. The reader will recall that it was built in 1887, on land donated to the city by the Federal government. The courthouse was constructed thereon as a joint enterprise with the Fort Smith city government and the Fort Smith District of Sebastian County. The reader will also recall that Mr. Jennings, the plaintiff in the present suit, was hired as an architect to design the new county courthouse on the site of the old city/county building. The chancery court had ruled preliminarily that the county owned that site but later held that The City of Fort Smith was the owner in fee simple of all the block of land. In this ruling the court held that the county might not construct a building on the city's land. The court enjoined the county from "...*entering upon said ground for the purposes named, and from contracting with any persons, partnership or corporation, or otherwise, for the construction or erection of a public building upon the northeast corner of said block, or upon any other unoccupied portion of said block.*"

After this preliminary order, Mr. Jewett, the sole commissioner appointed for the purpose, awarded a contract for constructing the courthouse, not on the site enjoined by the order of the court, but on the site occupied by the present courthouse building. This had been specifically ruled the property of the county. As noted, the court reversed its preliminary order and held that the property all belonged to the city. When Judge Ezra Hester took office, he directed that all appeals of the chancellor's orders be dismissed. This ended the claim of ownership of the courthouse property by the county.

In August of 1912, the county court (Judge Harp overseeing) had directed that Jennings be paid $1200 for his services as architect on the ill-fated project. Later the balance of his bill of $4620 was ordered paid along with the previously approved amount. The previous order for a partial payment was set aside and the full amount of $5820 was authorized. Judge Hester, on the motion of a taxpayer, set aside the order to pay Jennings and Jennings then sued to collect his fee in circuit court. To confuse matters further, the Supreme Court's account of the case and decision indicated that the case, so rooted in the politics and civic importance of Fort Smith, originated in...the Greenwood District! This must have been an error unless the plaintiff Jennings was a resident of that district.

Judge Hon ruled that the contract for the services of an architect was illegal. Since the county could not build the building, they could not enter into a valid contract for plans. Jennings pled that he was not a party to the previous lawsuit but that was of no importance. He knew of the dispute and the court said he had constructive notice that the county could not build on land it did not own. Jennings had also been one of the two commissioners appointed for the construction of the building and had shortly thereafter resigned. This was most probably for the purpose of obtaining the contract to design the building. The court said he could not even get the $1200 earlier approved, as he had acquiesced in this order being set aside and incorporated in the order for full payment, that Hester, the new county judge set aside. The Supreme Court affirmed Judge Hon in all respects.

On June 7, 1913, *The Southwest American* reported that a joint city/county courthouse committee was meeting and discussing whether to add onto the existing courthouse and make improvements or to build a new structure. This was a continuation of the conversation that had been ongoing since 1911. A new county judge, Ezra Hester, was in office absent the baggage of the old controversy. The committee made a tentative agreement based on the two-year-old report recommending modifications. They proposed to construct a new foundation, partially rebuild and reinforce the walls and construct some fireproof vaults. The projected cost was about $28,000. It was undecided whether the addition would be on the south or east of the building. It was noted that a considerable number of the city commissioners and the quorum court still wanted a new structure. One quorum court member was quoted as saying that he had remodeled and built onto his home and when it was completed, over budget, he still had... an old house.

Evidently the project proceeded without problem because a news story in the *Southwest American* on August 20,1913, reported that the workmen found the foundations to the building to be sound and not the cause of the deterioration of the building's walls on the south and west sides. The foundation was found to be of massive stones quarried from the Bailey Hill area which contained the best and hardest building rock in the area. These blocks were one foot thick and three to five feet square.

By October 3, 1913, the contractors had completed the south wall to the second story and the west wall was nearly as far along. The masons were relaying the interior walls and the arched wall in the chancery courtroom had been removed and nearly re-laid. The two-story vault in the county clerk's office was completed except for the upper vault door. Both vaults were reported to be of brick and reinforced concrete throughout and were, thankfully, fireproof. The third story rooms were practically ready for lath and plaster. It was noted that there was plenty of unused space on the third floor for future expansion.

On October 18, the new walls on the courthouse had reached the top of the second story and the outside walls were completed up to the cornice lines, making the building practically enclosed. The inside work was gradually covering the entire building. The partitions over the doors had been replaced and steel girders put in upon which the new walls were to be built. The probable cost was estimated to be $25,000 to $30,000. This was in line with the original estimates.

It was also reported that the city had issued over $1000 in warrants to date and would have to issue an additional $7000 in warrants to cover its portion of the expense. The reluctance of using scrip to finance construction by the city had evidently been overcome. The rebuilt structure, along with a new bell tower, was hoped to be ready for occupancy around the first of 1914.

A story in the paper on January 13, 1914, headlined COURTHOUSE PLEASES QUORUM COURT. The story went on to report that the cost for the renovations was $26,000 which was more than the appropriation but easily handled. Following the quorum court meeting they inspected the building and all expressed satisfaction with the results. The paper quoted quorum court members' reactions: *"The building is a stronger, more attractive and serviceable one than when it was first built." "We are well served and a great deal better off than if we had saddled the district with a $300,000 building."* This newly remodeled building

This Is The First Picture Shown of Our Newly Remodeled Court House at a Savings of Over $250,000 to the Tax-Payers

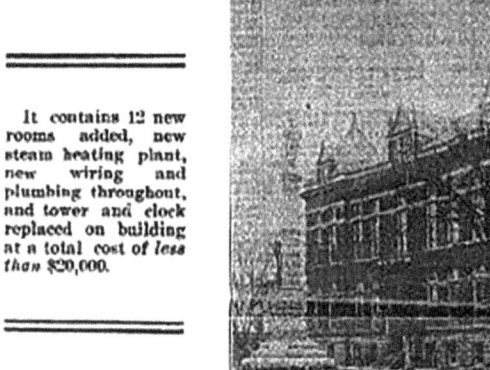

It contains 12 new rooms added, new steam heating plant, new wiring and plumbing throughout, and tower and clock replaced on building at a total cost of *less than* $20,000.

When Ezra Hester became your county judge he found plans and contract in existence for a new court house, at a cost of $257,225, plus $9,700 architect fees, $15,000 commissioner fees and $2,000 attorney fees, or a total of $283,925.

SOME COURT HOUSE HISTORY

On September 4, 1912, Ezra Hester, acting as your county clerk, was fined $50 and sentenced to 24 hours in jail for refusing to issue warrants on the treasury allowing architects' fees for a new court house.

On September 18, 1912, Judge Hester was again fined $50 and sentenced to 24 hours in jail in the same case.

Ex-County Judge Harp mortgaged the county's claim on the block on which the court house stands to the Falls City Construction Co., to secure payment of the quarter million dollar contract price of the proposed new court house.

On October 31, 1912, Judge Hester's first day in the county judge's office, he made an order setting aside all contracts for a new court house.

On November 12, 1912, the Quorum Court of Sebastian county took their stand with Judge Hester in preventing this enormous, useless expenditure, by passing the following resolution:

"In the matter of a new court house, Justice Clifton introduced the following resolution: Resolved, That the Quorum Court condemns as unwise and inexpedient the contract entered into by the late County Judge, Jesse A. Harp, and the Court House Commissioner, C. J. Jewett, with the Falls City Construction Company, and we indorse the action of Judge Hester in attempting to defeat this contract, which resolution being seconded by Justice Kuper was by a unanimous vote in court adopted.

Vote For Judge Hester, For His Second Term as County Judge

Greenwood District Courthouse, Dedicated 1916

The 1916 Greenwood Courthouse Under Construction

was the main claim for Judge Hester in his re-election bid in March 1914; Hester and his boosters were so proud of the remodeling feat that they took out a full-page campaign ad in the *Southwest American* on March 15, 1914, booming his role in the project.

While the plans for a new courthouse in Fort Smith were thwarted, the same was not true for Greenwood. In 1916 construction on the fifth courthouse to serve Greenwood was commenced under the leadership of Judge Hester. The new courthouse was to be located on the south side of the square and was to measure 65 by 98½ feet. The builder was T. T. Reddick and the cost was $62,500. It was financed by a bond issue passed by the voters of the Greenwood district and without a consequent tax increase. It was to be a beautiful red brick and stone building, two stories high with a clock tower. A story in *The Southwest American* in July said that the bids were to be opened on July 19. It described the proposed building as a "handsome, commodious and substantial structure." The two-story building would have a basement where the steam heating plant, water and supply equipment would be located as well as the jail. The first floor would contain the County Courtroom which was to be 19 by 25 feet, the offices of the County Judge, Treasurer, County Clerk, Sheriff and Grand Jury room. It was to have two vaults on this floor as well. One was in the clerk's office and one in the Circuit Clerk's rooms. The second floor would contain the Circuit Courtroom which measured 40 by 60 feet, judge's chambers, prosecuting attorney's office, the County School Superintendent, two witness rooms and two jury rooms. A corridor would run on two sides of the courtroom to serve all offices and there would be "imposing entrances" in front and back of the building.

A story published on July 14 revealed that not all, however, were in favor of a new courthouse in Greenwood although the old one was regarded as extremely unsafe. Some parties wanted the new courthouse to be built elsewhere. This time, the contestant was not Fort Smith seeking to be the sole county seat, but the thriving coal towns of Hartford and Midland. Citizens of these towns had requested that their little burgs be considered for the new courthouse and thereby win the appellation of "county seat". The Quorum Court had initially disregarded them, but an appeal was lodged with the Circuit Court. They also filed for an injunction with the Chancery Court. Judge Falconer had set a hearing and over one hundred citizens showed up for it. Falconer dismissed the petition as the matter was pending in Circuit Court. Meanwhile, developments on the new Greenwood courthouse proceeded. On July 20 it was reported that the contract had gone to T.T. Reddick of Fort Smith, who had built the Peabody and Duval Schools in Fort Smith and well as the new high school auditorium (the present Darby Jr. High auditorium). There was never a report of a ruling by Judge Little on the Circuit appeal before the groundbreaking.

The cornerstone was laid on Friday November 24, 1916. Marshall Strozier, the Grand Master of the local Masonic lodge, presided. The principal address was made by Circuit Judge Paul Little, before what was estimated to be to be the largest gathering in the history of the county. Fort Smith brought several hundred persons and Darby's Band of that city provided music for the occasion (it should be noted that that the Darby mentioned is Percy Darby, father of Brig. Gen. William O. Darby, who may have played in the band that day).

Over 1,000 people showed up and the Masonic delegation from over the state marched from the Masonic Hall, which was across the street to the south of the present courthouse, to the site of the laying of the cornerstone. Grand Master Strozier paid eloquent tribute to County Judge Ezra Hester, who had just been elected to the state senate, and members of the Quorum Court for providing the district with a modern temple for justice. He referred to Hester as a "doer of things" who was keeping pace with the times of progress by providing the people with the things which they need. He gave a history of the county and of the creation of the first courthouse in Fort Smith in 1817 down to the present time. He told of the heated political feuds that the county seat fight between Greenwood and Fort Smith had caused and referred to them, perhaps optimistically, as having passed away, never to return.

Strozier's eloquence was matched by that of Judge Little, who declared that "Law and government is nothing else than crystallized sentiment that rise up yonder in the equator of God's infinite love and flows around the world, human life would be robbed of its happiness and its bloom and human endeavors would be cold and frozen on the bleak and barren bosom of despair" [but for the law]. Little went on to say that liquor traffic created more lawlessness than any other element and endorsed women's suffrage, asserting that with the enfranchisement of women the liquor traffic would be more speedily driven from the county. Rev. John Tatum (Little's uncle and later a circuit judge)' one of the most beloved ministers in the county, offered a prayer. A copy box was placed in the cornerstone and the contents were listed; they included former Governor "Bass" Little's inaugural address, a biography of the late Judge Styles Rowe who had been a Grand Master of the Masons, assorted rosters and business cards of officials, copies of *The Greenwood Democrat* and documents pertaining to the building itself. The building would be complete in the spring of 1917 and served until April 19, 1968, when it was destroyed by a tornado.

The old courthouse, built in 1882, was demolished after the new one was completed. The square in which it stood was turned into a public park which remains in this use today.

JUDGE PAUL LITTLE
CIRCUIT JUDGE
1915-1919
PHOTO COURTESY OF FREED LITTLE

❦ ❦ ❦

A new circuit judge, and the orator at the dedication of the courthouse, had taken office the year before: Paul Little, a name that echoes through the judicial history of Sebastian County: Little. He was the son of former judge, then Governor, J. S. "Bass" Little, and the great-grandson of the father of Sebastian County, Eaton Tatum. He served as circuit judge for the 12th judicial circuit from 1915 until his tragic death in 1919. Paul Little was born in Greenwood on November 2, 1878. As Greenwood had no high school, he attended the University of Arkansas High School in Fayetteville. He spent several years as an undergraduate at the University of Arkansas and graduated from Georgetown University School of Law in Washington, D. C. He served as private secretary to his father while his father served in Congress, 1893-1903. He returned to Fort Smith and was in the private practice of law until his father was elected governor in 1906. He again served his father as private secretary until Governor Little resigned, a few days after his inaugural, due to poor health. He returned to Fort Smith, served two terms as prosecuting attorney, and was elected circuit judge in 1914. He had been elected to his second term as judge and there was talk of him running for Congress at the time of his death. Judge Little was married to Ada Jones of Greenwood, and they had one child, Katherine.

The story of Judge Little's demise is one of the most intriguing stories in the history of Fort Smith. It was ruled an accident, a case of mistaken identity but, at the time, there were rumors that this was not the case (these rumors were repeated to this writer by Judge Franklin Wilder, many years later). Judge Little's court reporter, Guy Williams (who served from 1943 to 1949 as Arkansas's Attorney General), was also his brother-in-law. On the night of October 29, 1919, around 9:30 p. m., Judge Little went to the home of Mr. Williams on Alabama Street in Fort Smith. Mr. and Mrs. Williams had gone to bed. The house was dark when Little arrived, and he went to the bedroom window and knocked or rattled it. Williams fired a shotgun through the window, critically wounding Judge Little. The good judge later died while being transported, via train, to St. Louis for medical treatment. The rumors, according to Freed Little, his great-nephew, were spread by his political enemies.

This killing was the subject of a case that was presided over by his successor, Judge John Brizzolara, concerning insurance proceeds that will later be discussed.

A case that was heard in Judge Little's court was *Bourland vs. Baker*, 141 Ark. 280, 216 S. W. 707 (1919). This is a case of a woman driver and a kid in the back seat. As it occurred on September 17,1918, it must have been one of the first such cases. The facts were that Queen Bourland, wife of James Bourland (not to be confused with Chancellor James V. Bourland), was driving her car on North 13th Street, between the suburban railway tracks and North "O" Street at approximately 2:30 in the afternoon. She was in the front seat and her infant child and little boy were in the back. The car was described as a "chummy roadster." She was driving on the wrong side of the street and in violation of a city ordinance. The distance between the tracks and "O" Street was about 200 yards of straight road. A Mr. Baker was walking in the roadway going the same direction and near the left curb. The evidence was conflicting as to the speed she was driving. In 1918, 20 miles per hour could have been considered too fast. As she crossed the tracks, she looked into the back seat to check on the baby and told her young son to sit down (modern parents must remember that there were no car seats or infant carriers or, for that matter, seat belts, in 1918). When she looked up Baker was in front of the car and she instantly shut off the engine, put on the brakes with both feet and stopped the car. The front wheel ran over Baker but the back wheel stopped just as it reached him. He was severely injured, and a lawsuit resulted, naming both Bourlands. The jury returned a verdict against Queen Bourland and her husband for $2000. The judgment was affirmed as to Mrs. Bourland but the winds of women's rights had apparently been blowing through the halls of the Legislature and the verdict against Mr. Bourland was reversed.

The verdict against Mr. Bourland had been based solely on the common law theory that a husband is responsible for the torts committed by his wife, even in his absence. The reason for the common law rule was the legal unity incident to the marriage relationship. It was reasoned that, because of this unity, the husband could control his wife absolutely in and out of her presence. Therefore, because of the control, he could prevent his wife from committing a tort on another, even if the tort in question consisted of running a man down with the family's roadster, unaccompanied by her husband. Talk about a legal fiction! Judge Little instructed the jury inaccurately on this and the court reversed him.

The Court's tone seemed to regret the change brought about by Act 159 of 1915, known as *The Married Woman's Act*. They had ruled earlier that it had the effect of *"absolutely and completely destroying the legal unity founded upon the nuptial contract"*. This was so complete that now the wife might sue the husband for a tort committed by him against her person. The opinion by Justice Humphreys seemed to be a lament. The Court's decision explained that the act did not make women the equal to men in the eyes of the law. This act merely restored to married women the rights they would possess as single women including, evidently, the right to be held responsible for the consequences of their own inattentive driving.

※ ※ ※

When Chancellor Bourland left to become the United States District Attorney, Judge William Armistead Falconer (pronounced FAWK-NER) became chancellor. He only served one elected term. He was in office from 1913 when he was appointed by Governor Futrell and then from his election in a special election in August of that year through 1918. He was born at Charleston, Franklin County, Arkansas, on June 16, 1869. He attended the University of Arkansas and the University of Virginia where he earned his law degree. He served as principal of the Charleston High School in 1892-93. He practiced with Judge Joseph M. Hill in Fort Smith beginning in 1894. That same year he married Miss Nattie Gilmore. He also served as a justice of the peace. During his term as justice of the peace he was instrumental in breaking up a gang of toughs known as *"The Texas Road Gang"* which had terrorized Fort Smith for several years. He also put some junk dealers out of business who had gotten some young boys to steal scrap metal for them.

In 1902 he was elected County and Probate Judge. During his administration the first mile of macadamized road was constructed in the county and by the end of his term there were over 30 miles of macadamized road as well as many new bridges. He forced the saloons and lunchrooms to be separate and closed the saloons on Sunday. He also had slot machines removed from the saloons. He was appointed to the Railroad Commission in 1909 and served as chairman. He required Sunday passenger service between Fort Smith and Paris and daily service between Waldron and Fort Smith. He had the Iron Mountain Line build a rock depot in Ozark and helped to obtain lower fares. He was president of the Woodrow Wilson Democratic Club in Fort Smith during the 1912 election. In 1913 he was the attorney for the citizens and taxpayers in their fight against County Judge Jesse Harp and the Falls City Construction Co. in the "unwise and ill-considered" scheme to build a $250,000 courthouse. In addition, Falconer was quite the classical scholar: He translated Cicero's *De Senectute, De Amicitia,* and *De Divinatore. (On Old Age, On Friendship, On Divination)* These were published in 1923 in the Loeb Classical Library series. In the preface, Falconer wrote:

"When my uncle, then in his eighty-first year, was confined to his room by a serious illness, he received a letter of consolation from a friend, who quoted from Shuckburgh's translation of the De Senectute. This quotation, though short, brought solace and cheer to the invalid and made him eager to hear more of Cicero's views on old age, and as a result, he asked me to bring him the essay in the Latin and read it to him. Twenty years had passed since I had read the tractate at the University of Virginia under my revered old professor, Dr. Wm E. Peters, and hence my rendering at first sight must have done

JUDGE WILLIAM A. FALCONER
CHANCERY JUDGE
1913-1918
PHOTO COURTESY OF SEBASTIAN COUNTY

violence to the original in many places; but just as 'honour peereth in the meanest habit' so the light of Cicero's genius was not wholly obscured by the medium through which it had passed. At any rate, when I had finished, my uncle begged me-more, I think, for my good than for his own pleasure-to write out a translation of the entire treatise. I pleaded that my Latin was too rusty and that my judicial duties did not leave me leisure for such a task. He replied that my Latin would brighten with use and that an hour or half-hour spent upon it now and then would not be missed and would afford me needed recreation. In his earnestness he exacted a promise which his death a few months later made only the more sacred. And so, on the trains as I went about the circuit, in hotels at night after trying cases all day, I strove to redeem that promise."

This is evidence of a genteel and civilized way of life, now lost forever.

A case decided by Chancellor Falconer that made its way to the Supreme Court was *Fenolio vs. Sebastian Bridge District*, 133 Ark. 380, 200 S. W. 501 (1917). This case involved the construction of the bridge at the foot of Garrison Avenue into Oklahoma. The legislature passed a measure in 1913, providing that the property owners or voters of the Fort Smith District of Sebastian County could form a commission and pass a levy to construct a bridge into Oklahoma. The plan for the bridge called for it to begin its approach to the river 300 feet from the banks of the river. This was because there was—and is—a steep decline from about 2nd Street to the river bank. This would require the bridge to be constructed in the middle of Garrison Avenue, beginning at 2nd Street; consequently, the businesses in the block of Garrison from 1st to 2d Streets would then have a bridge rather than a wide street in their front doors.

Much of the property in that block was owned by the Fenolio family. According to pictures in Stan Kujawa's *Garrison Avenue, Fort Smith Arkansas*, the Fenolio Hotel was at 109 1/2 Garrison and the Fenolio Wholesale Liquor and Saloon was at 111 Garrison. The Fenolios were not happy with the prospect of the bridge being built and filed a petition in chancery court seeking to enjoin the construction. The injunction was denied by Judge Falconer and Fenolio appealed. He attacked the validity of the legislative act on several grounds, beginning with the assertion that the Legislative Assembly, by authorizing a commission to construct the bridge, had unconstitutionally delegated its duties.

The Supreme Court rejected this and all Fenolio's arguments. It held that the act only prescribed the conditions under which the powers <u>might</u> be exercised. The second contention rejected was that the act expired within two years and was now void and that a subsequent act in 1915 could not revive it. This was rejected. The legislature had reenacted the entire bill in 1915 and changed the dates. This was perfectly proper. Also, any actions taken after the expiration of the first act were proper as the act was not void, only in need of an extension of time. The court also held that the legislature was not prohibited from authorizing construction of a bridge into another state and that the Arkansas act was not void because the Oklahoma act had been held unconstitutional. They also said that the plan to begin the construction from 2nd Street did not violate the act which called for the bridge to be constructed from the foot of Garrison Avenue as the approach from 2nd Street was merely an extension of Garrison Avenue. The court directed that Fenolio, if he felt he had lost value in his property due to the construction of the bridge, could bring suit for damages. An image in Mr. Kujawa's book shows the bridge, which opened in 1922, with the Fenolio properties to the north side; apparently it had not been fatal to the family's interests! There has always been someone trying to stop progress in Fort Smith for self-serving reasons.

The next circuit judge to serve Sebastian County and the 12th Judicial Circuit was John Brizzolara. He was appointed by Governor Charles Brough in 1919, upon the death of Paul Little. He only served out the term of Judge Little. He was never elected to office. He was the son of James Brizzolara and his second wife, Mary Lane. He was born March 12, 1886. He had a half brother, James, who was the product of his father's first marriage, and a sister, Anna, who married a Mr. Vaccara, and resided in Memphis at the time of her father's death in 1913.

His father, James Brizzolara, had been born in Virginia in 1848. He studied in Milan, Italy and in Pennsylvania. He fought with Garibaldi in Italy and practiced law in Memphis before coming to Fort Smith. He left Memphis after fighting a duel with a Mr. Phelan in which Brizzolara was injured. He was prominent in local politics, serving as U. S. Commissioner and mayor of Fort Smith. For several years he practiced law with William H. H. Clayton under the name of Clayton and Brizzolara. It later became Clayton, Brizzolara and Forrester, and, in 1897, became Hill and Brizzolara with Judge Joseph M. Hill as partner. This later became Hill, Brizzolara and Fitzhugh. The youngest member was H. L. Fitzhugh.

Young John Brizzolara joined his father's firm after being admitted to the bar. Judge Brizzolara never married and lived in the family home at 2116 South P Street with his stepmother, Stella Brizzolara, until her death in 1949; he died in 1955. Judge Brizzolara was a highly respected lawyer and jurist, the very quiet son of a very flamboyant father.

The case selected that arose in Judge Brizzolara's court was previously mentioned: *Aetna Life Insurance Co. vs. Little*, 146 Ark. 70, 225 S. W. 298 (1920). This was the appeal of the claim on the life insurance policy on the life of Judge Paul Little who had been killed by his court reporter. The death occurred when Judge Little showed up at the home of the court reporter Guy Williams (who was also the judge's brother-in-law), at 9:30 p.m. on the evening of Wednesday,

JUDGE JOHN BRIZZOLARA
CIRCUIT JUDGE
1919-1922
PHOTO COURTESY OF BRIZZOLARA FAMILY

October 29, 1919. Williams and his wife had gone to bed and the lights in the house were out. Judge Little went around to the bedroom window of the house and knocked on the window or rattled it. Williams fired a shotgun blast through the window and fatally injured Judge Little.

The Aetna policy insured against loss from bodily injuries affected solely through external, violent and accidental means. The insurance company predictably insisted that the death had been no accident. They claimed that had Little wanted to talk to Williams, he could have called him on the phone as both homes had telephones. They claimed also that he could have approached the home in the usual way, ringing the doobell. Little had apparently caused Williams to believe that someone was attempting to enter the home with an unlawful or wrongful purpose, and that Williams knew that person to be Judge Little. Little did not try to enter the home. He merely tried to get the attention of the occupants. In this he indubitably and fatefully succeeded.

The Supreme Court, through Justice Smith, opined that if Judge Little had an improper motive, there were only two possibilities: burglary or assignation; that is, that he was there to see Mrs. Williams and unaware that Mr. Williams was home. There was no testimony or evidence to support either theory with burglary being the most remote. The arguments trotted out to support the "assignation theory" were that Williams had only recently bought the shotgun, and also the testimony of Frank Hines, a neighbor, who was sitting on his porch (located a block and a half away). Hines claimed that he had heard a shot fired, then called Williams to ask what the trouble was. Williams replied that he had shot Judge Little. The phone call took place about five minutes after the shot was fired and Hines subsequently went to the Williams household. Hines said he got there just as the ambulance was leaving and that Mr. and Mrs. Williams left for the hospital about five minutes later. Other witnesses testified that when they arrived on the scene before Hines, they informed Williams whom he had shot and that it had been about fifteen minutes before the ambulance got there. In short, there was doubt as to the chronology of the event.

Judge Brizzolara directed a verdict in favor of the plaintiff. There was no doubt, he opined, that Judge Little died by a violent means and therefore the insurance company had the burden to prove that it was not an accident. This, he ruled, they had not done; there was not sufficient evidence to go to the jury. The Supreme Court evidently recognized common sense when they encountered it, and affirmed Judge Brizzolara.

Rumors were rampant after the incident concerning a possible relationship between Little and Mrs. Williams. According to Judge Franklin Wilder (speaking to the author many decades after the events had taken place), Judge Little had had every reason to believe that Mr. Williams was not home: Judge Little, according to Wilder, had dispatched Williams to the court house in Greenwood to file some papers. Little watched Williams get on the train to Greenwood knowing that he could not return until the following day on the return train. This was all rumor and conjecture, as pointed out in the Supreme Court opinion. It also noted by some that Williams did not testify at the trial, he was in Texas at the time. The clouds of rumor did not prevent Guy Williams, the court reporter who shot and killed Judge Little, from serving as Attorney General of Arkansas in the 1940s.

The next person to serve as circuit judge for Sebastian County and the 12th Judicial Circuit was John Eaton Tatum another member of the famous Tatum-Little family. John E. Tatum was the son of Eaton Tatum, that aforementioned "Father of Sebastian County," who helped establish his claim to the title by having three different families with three wives. Judge John E. Tatum was "Bass" Little's uncle and Paul Little's cousin. He was born April 25, 1862, his mother was Eaton Tatum's second wife, Josia Ann Brown Tatum. He joined the Baptist church and became a schoolteacher at age 17. He did this for ten years and farmed and studied law under his nephew, Judge John S. Little, who was eleven years his senior. John E. Tatum married Mary Caldwell Yadon on June 13, 1889. Of this marriage ten children were born, six boys and four girls. They were: Eaton, Wilkins T., George Y., Mark T., John E. Jr., Preston E., Bonnie T., Josia Ann, Mary Lee, and Evangel Lucile.

A few years after his marriage, he began the practice of law in Greenwood. A forceful and magnetic speaker, he was elected state representative in 1896 and again in 1898. In 1899 he formed a partnership with Melvin Cornish for the practice of law. Mr. Cornish had been private secretary to J. S. Little when he served in Congress. Cornish was later named as the clerk to the Dawes Indian Affairs Committee and this ended the partnership. John Tatum served as city attorney for Greenwood for two years and was then elected circuit clerk for Sebastian County and served into his third term. He resigned to enter the law practice once again, this time with Thomas B. Pryor; Pryor later became assistant general counsel for the Iron Mountain Railroad.

John Tatum again left the law practice when he was elected president of the Concord Missionary Baptist Association. He reorganized this association and got it on its feet. He then took up pastoral work. He served as pastor of the First Baptist Church in Greenwood and concluded his ministry as pastor of the First Baptist Church in Stiller, Oklahoma. His son in law, Eugene M. Bartlett, was a

JUDGE JOHN EATON TATUM
CIRCUIT JUDGE
1923-1926
PHOTO COURTESY OF FREED LITTLE

famous composer of gospel music and is a member of the Gospel Music Hall of Fame. He is best remembered for writing the song, *Victory in Jesus*.

Following his ministry, Judge Tatum reentered politics. He served as a deputy prosecuting attorney under his cousin Paul Little. Elected circuit judge in 1922, he served from 1923 through 1926. On January 1, 1927, he formed the law firm of Rowe and Tatum. It is assumed that his partner was the son of Judge Styles T. Rowe. Judge Tatum died on April 9, 1932, at age 70. He is buried in The Greenwood Memorial Cemetery.

A case decided by Judge Tatum that was appealed to the Arkansas Supreme Court is *Bevers vs. Bradstreet*, 170 Ark. 650, 280 S. W. 667 (1926). This was a case brought by a wife against another woman for alienation of affections. It is not exactly the type of case one would wish to defend in front of a Baptist preacher! Mrs. T. W. Bradstreet brought the suit against Mrs. Carrie Bevers. Mr. and Mrs. Bradstreet had been married forty-four years. He left his home at Ramona, Oklahoma and moved to a Bartlesville, Oklahoma hotel operated by Mrs. Bevers. When Mr. Bradstreet moved out, Mrs. Bradstreet did some investigation and found where a certain "Mr. and Mrs. Bradley" had registered at The Dixon Hotel in Kansas City, Missouri, on August 25, 1922. She also found where a "Mr. and Mrs. W. O. Wilson" registered in a hotel in Abilene, Kansas on August 9, 1922. Both of these registrations were in the handwriting of her husband. She produced a letter on the letterhead of The Dixon Hotel, addressed to no one, which read. *"Between the 10th of August and the 1st of September, 1922, I registered at the Hotel Sexton at Kansas City, Missouri, under the name of Mr. and Mrs. Bradley. Mrs. Carrie Bevers of the Alameda Hotel in Bartlesville, Oklahoma, was the woman that stayed with me there."* It was signed T. W. Bradstreet. The jury returned a verdict against Mrs. Bevers in the amount of $4000.

Appeal was taken and the Arkansas Supreme Court reversed the lower court and remanded for a new trial. They stated that the secondhand testimony about the hotel registers was inadmissible; it was not the best evidence. The registers themselves must be produced and it was beyond the jurisdiction of the court to order production. They also ruled that the unsigned letter was inadmissible as hearsay. Evidently Mr. Bradstreet was not present to testify but, even had he been, the court stated that his testimony was incompetent. This disallowal was made based on the presumption of collusion between spouses. In such a situation one spouse could not be made testify against another in a subsequent perjury case. Therefore, such testimony was to be considered incompetent. The court also reversed on an instruction given by Judge Tatum. The offending instruction read:

> *Should you believe from the evidence that plaintiff and her husband were living together in such relation, and were happy and affectionate towards each other, and that the defendant, by her conduct, won the attention and affection of plaintiffs husband, and that thereafter plaintiff's husband showed to plaintiff no love or affection, became unhappy and discontented with plaintiff, brought on by reason of defendant Bevers' attention toward plaintiff's husband, then your verdict should be for the plaintiff, Bradstreet.*

The court ruled that instruction erroneous in that it did not direct that the plaintiff must have acted purposely to cause such alienation. They acknowledged that where the alienation was by means of adultery, malice could be inferred. This fact was not mentioned in the instruction and therefore it was incorrect. What was not explained in the opinion was why the case was in Arkansas. All parties at the time lived in the state of Oklahoma, and all the acts mentioned in the case occurred elsewhere as well!

The judiciary in Arkansas underwent a change in 1924. Amendment 9 to the Constitution of 1874 was approved. This expanded the Arkansas Supreme Court to five members, provided that they could sit in divisions of three, and allowed the legislature to increase the number to seven justices. This the legislature did by Act 205 of 1925. Since that time the Arkansas Supreme Court has consisted of seven justices. In 1927, the legislature, by Act 18, realigned the 10th Chancery Circuit. Scott and Logan Counties were reassigned, and the circuit consisted of Crawford, Franklin, and Sebastian Counties. It would remain this way until 1977.

The next circuit judge to serve Sebastian County and the 12th Judicial Circuit was J. Sam Wood. Judge Wood served an unprecedented 26 years as circuit judge, from 1927 through 1954. Judge Wood was born John Sam Wood on November 9, 1889, at Paris, Arkansas. He was the youngest son of Charles Fox Wood Sr. and Mary Melinda Spangler Wood. He had eight brothers and one sister. The family moved to Fort Smith in 1900, from Roseville, Arkansas, where his father had run a mercantile store. He attended Fort Smith Public Schools and graduated from Fort Smith High School in 1907. He graduated from The University of Arkansas in 1912 and received his law degree from Columbia University in New York City in 1915. During his time at Columbia, he never came home, as money was tight. Instead, he worked part-time in Yankee Stadium as an usher to help make ends meet. The rest of the money he borrowed from his brothers and paid back after he began law practice in the firm of Hill and Brizzolara. From that time until his death on November 25, 1974, he was directly

Act 18 of 1928
10th Chancery Circuit
Consisting of Crawford, Franklin, and Sebastian Counties

JUDGE JOHN SAM WOOD
CIRCUIT JUDGE
1927-1954
PHOTO COURTESY OF J. SAM WOOD JR

involved as a lawyer or judge in the administration of justice in western Arkansas except for a period in 1917-18, when he served in World War I.

After war was declared on April 6, 1917, he was the fourth man from Fort Smith to enlist. This was on April 9; his brother, Roy Wood, was the third man to join the colors. He went to the first officer's training camp held at Fort Logan H. Roots near Little Rock, Arkansas. He was commissioned a 2nd Lieutenant after a 90-day training period and assigned to the 2nd Battery, 335th Field Artillery, 87th Division. He was assigned to Camp Pike, Arkansas, where the unit remained until about the 1st of August 1918. The division was then transferred to Fort Dix, New Jersey, where they remained until embarkation for England aboard S.S. *Lancaster*. It was a small ship; the seas were rough, and they had to transverse an area of the Atlantic heavily infested with German U-boats. Judge Wood reported that he was seasick the entire trip. They landed at Liverpool on September 13, 1918, and spent three days at rest camp at Ramsey, England. They then marched to South Hampton and boarded a large ferry boat which took them across the English Channel to Le Havre, where they boarded a French freight train on which they rode for three days and nights having French bread and canned tomatoes as their only rations. They arrived at Camp Montierchaum near Chateurue, France. There the unit remained until the signing of the Armistice on November 11, 1918.

The unit had nothing to do but await orders to return home. During that period, he had several leaves. He and his brother Roy visited London and Scotland. He also traveled to Italy and spent several days in Rome. He visited Paris many times, sometimes as long as a week at a time. He toured Belgium spending the most time in Brussels. In late July 1919, he joined Roy at Bordeaux, France, and sat there waiting about three days for transportation home. They landed at Philadelphia on August 3, 1919, almost one year to the day from their embarkation. He received two weeks leave and transportation to Fort Smith. On August 19, 1919, he was discharged at Camp Pike. All in all, the future Judge Wood had enjoyed a great tour of Europe, courtesy of the United States Army.

Upon returning from the service, he joined the firm of Read and McDonough. In 1920, he ran for and was elected prosecuting attorney for the 12th Judicial Circuit. After six years in this position, he was elected circuit judge in 1926. On March 31, 1929, he married Lillian A. Richmond of Conway, Arkansas. She was a graduate of Arkansas State Teacher's College, now called The University of Central Arkansas. She had been a teacher at Belle Grove School in Fort Smith. Their only child was J. Sam Wood Jr., who was born February 22, 1931, in Sparks Hospital.

Judge Wood was defeated for reelection in 1954 by Judge Paul Wolfe, after serving for 27 years. He was a very religious man and belonged to the First

Christian and First Methodist Churches. Early in his life he was a golfer and was one of the twenty-five founding members of the Hardscrabble Country Club. He also, from his childhood days, kept a love of farming. In 1920, he bought a farm located at Greenwood Junction, Oklahoma. He actively ran that farm as an absentee landowner until his death. Whenever he had a tough case to decide he would go to the farm, saddle his horse, ride out into the fields, and burn a stump as he deliberated. If one wanted to find him, all a person had to do was to look for a spiral of smoke. He once ran for Congress to fill the unexpired term of William B. Cravens who had died. He carried Sebastian and Scott Counties but lost the others in the district to the congressman's son, Fadjo.

As a judge he maintained decorum in the courts and the dignity of the office, and yet did not lose "the common touch". He presided during the transition from court room battles of free- swinging ingenious oratory and surprise to the modern practice of full disclosure of facts and law. As a person, he enjoyed all people. He could and did laugh with them at their foibles and absurdities whether they were defendants he was prosecuting or persons standing before him as litigants. To friends and associates he always appeared to have a twinkle in his eye. More importantly, he could and did laugh at himself when the occasion arose.

He loved his profession and the courts. While on the bench he was admitted to practice before the United States Supreme Court, not because he anticipated appearing before that court but because it was the highest court in the land, and he loved the profession. He also did not feel it demeaned his dignity to practice in the Municipal Court. He served as city prosecutor for Fort Smith after leaving the bench with the zest and vigor of an ambitious young lawyer, but with the sagacity and compassion of his long experience. At the time of his death someone wrote on the visitor's book at Putman Funeral Home, "The black people of Fort Smith loved you." That says it all about equality and fairness.

Ballentine vs. State, 198 Ark. 1037, 132 S. W. 2d 384 (1939), was a case heard in Judge Wood's court and later appealed to the Arkansas Supreme Court. *Ballentine* was a murder case. The facts were that the deceased, Albert Honea, was an old man who operated some type of "joint" at the foot of the Frisco Bridge into Fort Smith, in an area known as Coke Hill. The appellant and others had gathered at his place and were playing poker and shooting dice. They were all more or less intoxicated from drinking bay rum. The appellant got mad over the craps game and attacked Honea, who was not a part of the game. He struck him with his fists, knocked him down, picked him up, knocked him down again, kicked and stomped him. Honea died at the hospital.

Dr. T. P. Foltz, the father of Circuit Judge Harry Foltz, testified that Honea had lacerations and bruises over his entire body, cranial skull fractures, fractures of both right and left lower and upper jaws, a broken vertebra, a broken neck, and ribs on the right side which were fractured to such an extent that fragments pierced his lung which produced a hemorrhage. The officers who arrested Ballantine examined his shoes and found gray hairs around the protruding tacks in the soles.

The jury convicted Ballantine of second-degree murder and sentenced him to 21 years in the penitentiary. He had been charged with first degree murder and the judge offered the lesser included offense in the instructions as well. This was the alleged error in the trial. Ballantine said there was no proof of any malice or intent to kill on his part and that he was guilty at most of involuntary manslaughter. The court, citing precedent, ruled that no specific intent to kill was necessary to constitute the crime of second-degree murder and the intention to drink might fully supply the place of malice aforethought, so that if one voluntarily became too drunk to know his own intentions, then without provocation assaulted and beat another to death, he would commit murder, the same as if he were sober. They then stated the evidence was sufficient to sustain a verdict for first degree murder and therefore the court did not err in submitting the lesser charge to the jury.

The reader should remember that Chancellor J. V. Bourland served in Chancery District 10 at two separate times, before and after Chancellor Falconer. Bourland's second term ran through 1934; in that year, Columbus Maynard Wofford was elected to this job, and he served through 1954. Chancellor Wofford was born in Gainesville, Georgia, on February 3, 1881. He graduated from Uniontown High School and Ouachita College. He was admitted to the bar in 1913 and served as Crawford County Clerk from 1910 through 1914. He was the prosecuting attorney for the 15th Judicial Circuit, which included Crawford County, from 1918 through 1929, and city attorney for Van Buren from 1921 through 1930. He was elected Chancellor for the 10th Chancery Circuit in 1930, and served for 24 years, retiring in 1955. Judge Wofford was a Mason and a member of the Sebastian County Red Cross chapter for many years and a member of The Noon Civics Club and First Baptist Church. He passed away on September 17, 1958. He left surviving him his wife, two daughters, three brothers, four sisters and two grandchildren. He is buried in the Forest Park Cemetery.

A case decided by Judge Wofford that was appealed to the Arkansas Supreme Court is *Pruitt vs. Sebastian County Coal and Mining*, 215 Ark. 673, 222 S. W. 2d 50 (1949). This is a fascinating case going back to the founding of Sebastian

JUDGE C. M. WOFFORD
CHANCERY JUDGE
1931-1954
PHOTO COURTESY OF SEBASTIAN COUNTY

County itself. It involved the boundary line between Sebastian and Scott Counties. The lawsuit was over title to some land between one Pruitt and the named mining company. Sebastian County Coal and Mining Company filed suit claiming ownership of the disputed tract of land. The suit claimed that Pruitt had trespassed and cut timber on their property. The company asked for an injunction against Pruitt and damages for cutting their timber. Pruitt admitted that he cut the timber but that he owned the land under a Scott County tax title and that the land in question was in Scott County. The suit was required to be filed in the county in which the land was located. It was first incumbent on the court to make that determination. Judge Wofford ruled that the land was in Sebastian County and issued the injunction and awarded damages. Pruitt appealed.

The court first ruled that, based on a long line of precedent, the court could determine the boundary line of a county without the county being a party to the suit. The court then recited the history of the founding of Sebastian County. They in fact referenced the act of the Arkansas Territorial Legislature of November 5, 1833, that established the boundary of Scott and Crawford Counties as being, "the line between townships 3 and 4 North of the Baseline." This line, insofar as the involved land was concerned, remained the same through a Territorial Act on October 24, 1835, and an Act of the Arkansas General Assembly on December 16, 1838. Sebastian County was created by the General Assembly on January 6, 1851, assembled from parts of Crawford, Polk and Scott Counties. It took a thirteen-mile-wide and eighteen-mile-long strip of Scott County land adjoining the border of the Indian Territory. All the territory was south of the north line of Township Three in Ranges 31, 32 and 33. This, Pruitt claimed, was unconstitutional for the General Assembly to have done as it reduced Scott County to less than the minimum area allowed for a county, which was 900 square miles. An ordinance of June 1, 1861, by the Arkansas Secession Convention returned to Scott County all of Sebastian County that was south of the Poteau Mountain. The mining company claimed that the top of the mountain was the boundary, but Pruitt claimed that description was too vague to be valid.

The court affirmed Judge Wofford in all respects. The court ruled that Pruitt's claim that the creation of Sebastian County had been invalid, insofar as it reduced Scott below the area minimum, failed since Pruitt's brief did not acknowledge that Scott County had been enlarged by an act of October 24, 1835, before Sebastian County was created. This added area had remained a part of Scott County until Sarber County (now Logan) was created in 1871. The court also noted that no one had complained from 1851, until this lawsuit. The court also noted that the Constitution of 1874 had reduced the necessary area of a county to 600 square miles. This obviated any previous deficiency.

The court, on its own, addressed the validity of the 1861 act (adopted by the Confederate legislature and convention). Concern existed because the secessionist government had later been declared illegal, and many of its enactments had been questioned, including the 1861 measure act that returned all the land in Sebastian to Scott County that lay south of Poteau Mountain. The Arkansas High Court referred to an opinion of the U.S. Supreme Court of The United States, authored by John Marshall Harlan Sr. Justice Harlan had ruled that acts of the Confederate legislatures were valid if not hostile in their purpose or mode of enforcement to the authority of the national government, and did not impair the rights of citizens under the Constitution. This act had obviously not impaired rights, interfered with Federal authorities or embodied hostile purpose, thus was valid.

Pruitt's next argument was that the description in the 1861 Act was too indefinite, i.e. "the top of the Poteau Mountain". The court noted that there was only one main range of the Poteau Mountain in the affected area and that established law was where a boundary follows mountains or hills, the water divide constitutes the frontier. Therefore, the mining company was right: the line was the top of the mountain.

Pruitt also argued that subsequent legislation (he cited six legislative enactments) had recognized the boundary as being the north line of Township Three. The court noted that each of the acts dealt with some special matter and did not attempt to change the boundary line. Since it was not the purpose of any of the six measures to change the boundary line, none had had that effect.

Pruitt's claim ultimately came down to an argument that the boundary between the counties had been established by recognition and acquiescence. That is to say, that everyone involved, save Pruitt, had always thought that the land was in Scott County and therefore it was. This was based on a theory of limitations and that does not apply against the Sovereign, that is, the state. That theory could only apply when there existed uncertainty in the legal description. In this case, the High Court held, such uncertainty was lacking, except (perhaps) in Pruitt's understanding. This case holds particular interest due to its examination of how Sebastian County had been constituted, combined with a good dose of common sense! This is a virtue seldom used in the dispute of courthouses in Sebastian County.

CHAPTER SEVEN

A NEW COURTHOUSE AND A NEW ERA

FRANKLIN D. ROOSEVELT WAS ELECTED president in 1932 and soon told the people that all they had to fear was fear itself. He was talking about the Great Depression that had paralyzed the country since "Black Thursday" in 1929. In the first 100 days of his presidency, Congress approved a series of measures, which became known as the "New Deal," to help the country out of the depression. One of the programs in this package was the Public Works Administration or PWA. It was the job of the PWA to finance work on needed public buildings around the country and thereby funnel money into the moribund economy. Many courthouses around the country are a product of this program, including the present building in Fort Smith.

There had been interest for some time in Fort Smith for a new courthouse to replace the 1887 building. There was still dissatisfaction with the old building notwithstanding the 1914 renovations. A citizens' committee had been appointed to plan and promote the building of a new city offices/courthouse in the Fort Smith District of Sebastian County utilizing the PWA program. The reader will recall that the Fort Smith and Greenwood Districts were, in essence, two separate counties within a single county. There was a separate Quorum Court for each of the districts and each district was responsible for the finances of that district.

The reader will recall the difficulty the county had in financing the proposed new courthouse in 1912. The county could not issue bonds to cover the expense but had to rely on issuing IOU's called script. Amendment 11 to the Arkansas Constitution remedied this. In *Jewett vs. Norris*, 170 Ark. 71, 278 S.W.652 (1926), the Arkansas Supreme Court established that the Fort Smith District of Sebastian County might issue bonds under the provision in the Constitution establishing two separate county courts within the county. This holding reinforced the unique status of Sebastian County. This case, originally decided by

Chancellor J.V. Bourland, held that the provisions of Amendment 11 applied to the Fort Smith District as if it were a separate county.

The committee appointed to investigate possibilities for a new courthouse consisted of the members of the Fort Smith District Quorum Court: C.N. Geren, H.L. Benning, S. Birnie Harper, Luther Hodges, Lamar Moore, Walter Hennig, Geo. E. Ellefson, A.N. Sicard and R.T. Hunt, along with citizens Frank W. Youmans, Walter N. Hinton, Margaret A. Sortet, Henry C. Armstrong, Stella Brizzolara, J.R. Woods, Dess Garrett, R.J. Ross and Allen Henderson.

The Southwest American reported, on September 9, 1935, that the committee had upon unanimous approval of the preliminary architectural plans, authorized Fred Armstrong with the assistance of the architects E. Chester Nelson and Carnall Wheeler of the firm of Basham and Wheeler, to file the application with the PWA for the funds with which to construct the new courthouse. The plans were similarly approved by County Judge R.P. Strozier. The committee also tentatively set September 17 as the date for an election to authorize the required county bonds. The news story related that the plans called for an Art Deco-styled edifice, five stories tall, served by three elevators (one reserved for prisoner transfers), with the top two stories being a city/county jail with accommodations for up to 160 prisoners. The building was to be faced up to the first story with crystalline limestone and the remainder of the facing to be oolitic limestone. The ground floor was to house the sheriff and the chief of police as well as provide a large assembly room for public meetings. The majority of the city and county offices would be on the first floor including the county judge, assessor, tax collector, county clerk and city offices including the mayor and city commissioners (at this time Fort Smith enjoyed a city commission form of governance), the city water department and a city council room. The second floor housed the large chancery, circuit and municipal courtrooms along with ample chambers for the judges and the circuit clerk's office. The third floor housed the prosecutor's office, jury room and grand jury room.

On September 15, *The Southwest American* reported no organized opposition had developed to the bond proposal. The ballot issue did not contain a dollar amount for the bonds, so as to allow flexibility in the issue. The women of the community, by way of various women's organizations, actively campaigned for the passage of the issue. On election day the newspaper reported that the women had established a campaign headquarters at 1217 Garrison and were providing rides to the polls. The day following the election, the headline read: VOTERS FAVOR COURTHOUSE PROPOSAL, ALL PRECINCTS IN CITY WANT PROJECT. The vote was 1415 for and 315 against. The officials noted in that story that the real fight would be to gain approval by The Public Works Administration.

The financing mechanism for such a project was the issuance of bonds by the county under the auspices of the PWA. This was the subject of the election. Following final approval of the project by the PWA the bonds were to be offered for public sale and usually the PWA purchased the bonds at par plus accrued interest. Following approval of the project, the PWA was to give the Fort Smith District a grant of 45% of the total construction cost or $222,000. The total cost of the project was anticipated to be $491,000. The grant money was to be paid to the county as the work progressed. When the bonds for the Fort Smith City/County Building were offered in January 1936, PWA officials were surprised when more than half of the $269,000 offering was purchased by a joint enterprise between The First National Bank of Fort Smith (through its vice-president McCloud Sicard) and the president of Merchants' National Bank, W.J. Echols. The bonds were 30-year bonds, to be paid annually at $10,750-$15,000 amounts. The paper pointed out that this was only the second PWA project in the state in which any private investors had bid on the bonds. The other was a $55,000 school offering in Little Rock. A few weeks later, First National, acting on behalf of the Little Rock brokerage firm of Vinson, Hill and Co., purchased the remaining bonds totaling $134,000 making this the first Arkansas PWA project totally financed by private money...excluding, of course, the $222,000 grant given to the county!

The reasoning given for willingness of private investors to buy the bonds was the fiscal stability of the Fort Smith District of Sebastian County. Except for these bonds, the district was debt free and had operated on a cash basis the previous year, ending the year with a substantial cash balance. This status was remarkable in that this was in the midst of the depression. The fact that the bonds were all purchased by private investors also speeded the project toward completion. Had the PWA been the default purchaser the process would have delayed the project. "The whole thing should be underway in about 60 days" Judge Strozier stated.

On Tuesday, March 10, 1936 Judge Strozier presented the final plans and specifications for the new courthouse to PWA officials in Little Rock. The citizens committee and the architects had given final approval a few days before. On March 29, the *Southwest American* reported that the plans had been approved by the PWA and that the date to receive construction bids had been set by Judge Strozier to be May 1, 1936 at 1:00 p.m. in the Judge's office. Legal notice would be published on April 1 and April 8. Strozier advised that as soon as the bids were opened a work order could be issued. The article went on to say that the building would be up to date in all respects and would be centered on the courthouse block on 6th Street where the old courthouse was located. There would be an entrance on all four sides. "One of the features of the new courthouse will be detention quarters for girls and children separate from the jail", Strozier stated.

It was also noted that the labor cost to be paid would be $150,000. This was most likely noted because of the Depression and the need for workers to have jobs that paid a good wage.

The bids were opened at 1:30 p.m. on Friday May 1, 1936. They were divided into five areas of the work; general construction, jail equipment, plumbing, heating and electrical wiring. Manhattan Construction Co. of Muskogee was the low bidder on general construction with a bid of $324,627. The jail bid went to Southern Prison Co. of San Antonio, Texas in the amount of $30,858. John Patton and Son of Morrilton was the low bidder for plumbing and heating in the amount of $52,470 and Hunt Electric Co. of Fort Smith was the low bidder for the electrical work at $12,807.

Judge Strozier and the citizens' jail committee met the next day and tentatively awarded the contracts to the low bidders as the bids did not exceed the amounts set aside by the PWA for the projects. *The Southwest American* noted that Manhattan Construction Co. was also doing work on the new high school football stadium (Mayo-Thompson) and a new nurse's home at St. Edward Hospital.

It was estimated that the construction on the new courthouse would take 290 days. Following the tentative awarding of the contracts, the committee and the judge signed and sealed the bonds previously purchased by First National and Merchants National Banks making them ready for delivery Monday morning. The monies in the bonded amount would be immediately available. Once final approval of the contracts was obtained from PWA, work could commence. On May 5, the paper reported that Judge Strozier was to present the plans and contracts for the project to Alexander Allaire, the state WPA administrator in Little Rock, and to also ask for 25% of the government grant for the project. Allaire was then to leave with the documents for Washington to get final approval along with a request for an extension of the time in which to complete the project. This was necessary because the President had placed a December 1, 1936, deadline on completion of projects such as this. No difficulty was expected. *The Southwest American* reported on May 26 that the extension had been granted until June 1, 1937. "As far as I know there is nothing else that can delay work getting under way," Judge Strozier was quoted as saying. *The Southwest American* reported on May 27 that the work orders had been issued by Judge Strozier. The city and county offices then began relocating to the Geren Building where temporary facilities had been secured. The government offices were located on all three floors of that structure with Circuit and Chancery Court being on the third floor. Municipal Court was located across the street in a building at 512 ½ Rogers Avenue. The contractor was advised to begin the razing of the old building on June 1, 1936.

The Southwest American on June 17, 1936 ran a three-picture story on the front page of the 140' clock tower of the old courthouse being pulled down. This signaled the end of an era. The story related:

> *The old clock tower is no more! Tuesday, at noon, with several hundred people congregated about the safety lines, the old sentinel that long has stood guard over the county's capital building, was toppled from its high perch to smash against the walk at the east entrance to the building, which is being demolished. The veteran tower had withstood an earlier attempt to pull it to earth. The contractors wrecking the courthouse had twice attempted early Sunday morning, in the absence of crowds, to pull the tower down, but the spliced cable parted. Tuesday, when the effort was successful, the old structure, although it appeared weak after the protective brick wall had been removed, did not give way as many spectators expected, but tower and supporting structure came down in one piece, the tower standing on its head with its wooden supports high in the air as if making a last defiance to its wreckers. With the superstructure down work demolishing the old building will be rushed and within a few days there will be nothing left of the building that for 49 years housed the official families of Sebastian County and the city of Fort Smith.*

The cornerstone was laid for the new building on March 20, 1937. A story on the front page of *The Southwest American* on March 19 reviewed the history of this new building. The story reminded the reader that the first courthouse had been constructed 50 years ago on the same site, on land given to the city by the Federal government from the old military reservation and that it was two stories tall and was a joint city-county effort. According to County Judge Strozier, thanks to the PWA program's contribution, the new building would cost the taxpayers of the Fort Smith District less than the building it replaced (The original building required a 3-mill tax to finance and the new one a 1-mill tax.).

The story quoted Mr. Harry Kelley concerning progress in Fort Smith. Kelley recalled that the people in 1887 were just as proud of that new building as were the people today. He discussed the fact that civic progress had always required a fight in Fort Smith. When he came to Fort Smith in the 1880s the needs had been sewers, pavement and factories. He stated that people had opposed taxes even more then. The water supply of that past day came from Mill Creek, which was not suitable to drink. Kelly related that he was the most unpopular man in Fort Smith because he fought for civic improvements. He mentioned the paving of Garrison Avenue. Mr. J. H. Clendening, as head of the Chamber of Commerce, and the banker Samuel McCloud were noted by him as progressive leaders. The story mentioned that the population of Fort Smith when the courthouse was opened in 1887, had been 4,500; the population in 1937 was 39,000.

SDAY MORNING, JUNE 17, 1936

Time's March Overtakes Old Sebastian Landmark

Courthouse Clock Tower Is Dragged From Lofty Perch

WORK OF CERTIFYING BONUS BONDS SPEEDED

TEMPERATURE SOARS TO 101-DEGREE MARK

The Southwest American, for Sunday, March 21, 1937, carried the story of the ceremony surrounding the laying of the cornerstone. At 1:00 P.M. a parade started from the Masonic Temple on 11th Street led by the Fort Smith High School Band which proceeded up 11th Street to Garrison and down Garrison to 6th Street and to the site of the new building. There were over 200 people in the parade including local dignitaries and a contingent of Spanish-American War Veterans, The Veterans of Foreign Wars, Battery C of the 142nd Field Artillery and the Headquarters Battery of the 2nd Battalion Combat Train, consisting of 4 trucks, two mounted guns and 40 men. At 2 p. m. the ceremony began; the account made it clear that it was a Masonic affair. The band played several selections and a choir from Fort Smith's First Methodist Church sang hymns. The ceremony was conducted by Gene Bly of Fort Smith, who served as Grand Master for the state of Arkansas. Also in attendance were leading Masons from around the state. Within the cornerstone were placed some 100 documents including lists of officials and newspapers. One of these was a copy of *The Elevator* dated December 14,1887, that had been removed from the old box that was placed in the corner stone of the old courthouse (a list of the items was preserved by the county, perhaps as insurance against the "time capsule" being overlooked). The main speaker was Judge Joseph M. Hill. He reminded the audience that the building, as fine as it was, was "but stone and brass" unless there was true justice dispensed within its walls by upright judges and honest juries. He reminded the audience that it was "within their province" to supply the same.

Also on the program that day was the Reverend B.F. Neal, a Methodist Episcopal minister, speaking on behalf of Fort Smith's Black community. The previously mentioned file listing the items placed in the courthouse also contained the text of Neal's remarks, including this hopeful passage:

> *To the honorable County Judge, Quorum Court, and eminent citizens who conceived the idea and executed the same, of erecting this lasting monument, we extend our congratulations, and wish to assure you that we pledge our loyalty and ourselves to this shrine, and to this cornerstone that represents the foundation of justice, equity and liberty. We pray that upon you shall be built a lasting structure of brotherhood and that no soul shall ever have cause to point to you with enmity, because of having received injustice. We pray that you may ever stand as a building for the people, of the people and by the people.*

This author has seen the blue prints calling for colored restrooms and vividly remembers the water fountain with two faucets: one for Whites and one for Blacks. In hindsight, Mr. Neal's words seem a bit ironic.

The building opened for business later that summer. The aluminum plate inside the west entrance of the courthouse tells out the names of the elected officials serving at that time: In addition to Judges Wofford and Wood the honorables included: Harrell Harper, prosecutor; Jess McConnell, assessor; Jerry Bell, county clerk; Paul Lynch, circuit clerk; Loyd Been, treasurer; Jack Pace, sheriff and R.P. Strozier, county judge. As it was a joint city and county building, the city officials are also listed. They were: J.K. Jordan, mayor; Frances Buck, commissioner number one, H.S. Peck, commissioner number two, and James A. Gallagher, municipal judge.

The year 1938 brought a change in the court structure in Arkansas. Prior to that time the county judge served as the probate judge. Amendment 24 to the state constitution changed this and assigned the probate court to the court having equity jurisdiction in the county. That, of course, was the chancery court. This remained the case until Amendment 80 which unified the state's court system in 2001.

World War II began in 1939, and America entered after Pearl Harbor was attacked in late 1941. This conflict brought a lot of changes to Sebastian County. The major one was the creation of Camp Chaffee to the east of Fort Smith. This new reservation swallowed up a good portion of the county and brought with it an influx of personnel and government monies. Its creation involved the next person to serve as circuit judge, Paul Wolfe. He would not become circuit judge until 1955, but he served as prosecuting attorney prior to the war.

Paul Wolfe was born January 5, 1908, in Weir, Kansas. He was the son of John and Myra Wolfe. The Wolfes moved to Fort Smith when Paul was a lad. He attended Fort Smith schools and graduated from Fort Smith High School in 1926. He attended the University of Arkansas and obtained a law degree. He took and passed the bar while still in school. His score was so high that one of the examiners offered him a job in his firm. He turned this down and stayed in school and obtained his degree in 1933. He married Jean Johnson on January 12, 1932. From this marriage three children were born: Jean, Cynthia, and Myra Lynn.

He practiced law for six years and was then elected prosecuting attorney for the 12th Judicial Circuit in 1938. He was elected to a second term in 1940, but resigned in 1942, to take a position in the Judge Advocate Corps in the army. He had previously been serving as Post Judge Advocate for Camp Robinson, Arkansas, during its period of expansion in preparation for the military buildup. He later was transferred to Camp Chaffee and was involved in the acquisition and construction of the base. It was the Wolfe family flag that first flew over Camp Chaffee. He was still serving in the position of prosecuting attorney while

Fort Smith Courthouse, Dedicated 1937

in the Army and this drew at least one complaint from the citizenry, prompting his resignation in 1942. In 1976, he donated the family flag to Fort Chaffee.

In May 1942, he went into the service full time and was assigned to Washington, D. C. where he handled all the legal matters for the newly formed Women's Auxiliary Corps (WACS) and the Army Specialist Corps. In August 1942, he was assigned as Division Judge Advocate to the 3rd Army Division of the 1st Army. He served with that division through the D-Day invasion of Normandy, the Battle of the Bulge, and was the first Judge Advocate to step onto German soil. Although he was invited to participate in the Nuremburg war crimes trials, he chose to return home to Fort Smith. He was awarded the Bronze Star for his exemplary service, two Purple Hearts, and an Army Commendation Medal. His stay in civilian life was cut short as he was recalled to the service during the Korean Conflict. From his recall in 1950, until 1952, he served as staff judge advocate at Fort Bragg, North Carolina, and then at Munich, Germany.

Following his second military discharge he rejoined his family in Fort Smith that now consisted of his second wife, the former Mrs. Jim Henderson, whom he had married in 1947, and their child, Jim Paul Wolfe. He was appointed Assistant United States Attorney for the Western District of Arkansas and later resigned that position to make a run for circuit judge. He took on the longtime incumbent, J. Sam Wood. He defeated Judge Wood in the 1954 election with the slogan, "Twenty-eight Years is Long Enough."

He married for the third time in 1959. His third wife was Ruth Flanagin Gramlich, the sister of Betty Bumpers whose husband Dale was elected the governor of Arkansas in 1970 and United States Senator in 1974.

Upon Judge Wolfe's recommendation, the Joint Committee for the Effective Administration of Justice undertook the project to write a book for the benefit of new state trial judges. He chaired the authoring committee. The book was used as a textbook by the National Conference of State Trial Judges. Also during his tenure on the bench, he chaired the Arkansas Supreme Court's Model Jury Instruction Committee that produced the first model civil jury instructions in Arkansas. As president of the Public Historical Association beginning in 1955, he spearheaded the project to restore Judge Isaac Parker's courtroom and gallows. The clearing of Coke Hill and the establishment of the area of Belle Pointe and the old fort as a national historic site were part of this project. He chaired the committee for the Butterfield Overland Mail Centennial Celebration overseeing the preparations and implementation of many special activities that took place on September 19, 1958. For several years he also served as president and umpire in Fort Smith Church League Baseball. After twenty years on the bench he retired in December 1974. After his retirement he was instrumental in writing the Federal Speedy Trial Act and joined the Sparks Medical Center TeleMed program as a volunteer. He died on October 26, 1976, leaving his widow Ruth Wolfe and his children; Jean Sizemore, Cynthia Wolfe, Myra Lynn Vest and Jim Paul Wolfe, along with two stepchildren, Ginger Gramlich and Lou Gramlich.

A case heard by Judge Wolfe and later appealed to the Arkansas Supreme Court was *Rush vs. State*, 238 Ark. 149, 379 S. W. 2d 29 (1964). This was one of the most notorious murder cases ever to plague the city. Mr. Freddy Rush was convicted of first-degree murder and was sentenced to life in prison. From this conviction, Rush naturally appealed.

The victim of the crime was his stepfather, Paul Rush, who had adopted Freddy. The state contended that there was a conspiracy that included Freddy's cousin Raymond Wood and one Carolyn Brown. The killing took place about 11 p.m. the night of May 13, 1962. Earlier that night, the state contended, Freddy Rush went by V&R Sales Company, a furniture factory operated by the Rush family in Fort Smith, and intentionally left a light burning on the third floor. Later he drove by the factory with his wife and children of a former marriage, and pretended to discover the light burning. This gave Freddy Rush, the state contended, a pretext to drive over to his father's apartment and ask the elder Rush to go to the factory with him to investigate the burning light. In furtherance of the conspiracy, Raymond Wood waited, hiding, in the building, armed with a

JUDGE PAUL WOLFE
CIRCUIT JUDGE
1955-1974

PHOTO COURTESY OF SEBASTIAN COUNTY

.22 caliber rifle. Carolyn Brown was waiting for Wood in an automobile outside the factory, to help Wood escape after having killed Paul. Wood did kill Paul Rush and escaped as planned. In addition to fatally shooting Paul in the neck, Wood also shot Freddy in the shoulder to allay any suspicion that the younger Ruch had been involved. Rush was questioned at the hospital by the police where he was being treated for the gunshot wound.

Freddy Rush was married at the time but also had a girlfriend named Pat Taylor, a cousin to Carolyn Brown. Taylor and Brown both lived in a Fort Smith motel. The day after the killing, Taylor, Brown and Raymond Wood were all questioned by the police in the first installment of interrogations that continued, sporadically, for the next few months. All denied any knowledge of the killing, but they nevertheless remained persons of interest to the investigation.

This unsettled condition might have continued indefinitely, had it not been for Freddy Rush's roving eye. About nine months after the killing, he left Pat Taylor and took up with a new girlfriend, Louise Bromley. In February, 1963, he left Fort Smith with Louise and Carolyn Brown. This trio relocated to Houston, Texas, where they all lived together in an apartment, leaving Pat Taylor, "a woman scorned," behind them, which was a major miscalculation. Taylor contacted one Burnside, a bondsman and private detective who had been hired by Paul Rush's heirs, and told her tale. She then (presumably at Burnside's suggestion) went to the police and sang her song: she explained Freddy's plan and explained that it had been worked out in her motel room and in her presence: she had, in short, the goods. Based on her testimony, Freddy Rush was brought back from Texas, arraigned, tried and convicted, after which an appeal was filed.

The basis for the appeal was that the court had denied Rush's motion for a change of venue. The appeals court agreed as the state offered no counter-affidavits or rebuttal testimony on this question as required. The court also said Judge Wolfe erred in not striking a juror who had talked to a witness (with whom he was acquainted) prior to being summoned as a juror, stating that he had formed an opinion that would take evidence to remove. This lapse was not cured by Judge Wolfe having been assured by the juror that he could set aside any prejudice. Judge Wolfe also apparently had erred in admitting into evidence a pistol which was not alleged to have been the murder weapon. The state's theory on this was that Carolyn Brown and Wood had borrowed the pistol from Freddy Rush and that, in some way, corroborated Taylor's testimony. The court also ruled that Pat Taylor was an accessory to the crime and that her testimony must be corroborated. She had testified that the preparations for the killing were made in her apartment; that Raymond Wood's hair was dyed by Carolyn Brown, that Rush had cut strips of adhesive tape to put on car tires to disguise the tracks and that a license tag was altered. She also said that she helped in removing the dye from Wood's hair. These actions, taken together, made her an accessory, whose testimony could not be relied upon without corroboration. The instruction on this point was not properly objected to at trial and not preserved for appeal. The case was reversed and remanded for a new trial.

On retrial the case was sent to Scott County on a change of venue. That case, also presided over by Judge Wolfe, ended in a conviction of Mr. Rush for 2nd degree murder. That conviction was also appealed and reversed! The citation in question is *Rush vs. State*, 239 Ark. 878, 395 S. W.2d 3 (1965). The facts set out in this appeal revealed that Carolyn Brown and Raymond Wood were tried separately and each acquitted. The case was submitted to the jury only on an instruction for first degree murder. After the jury had deliberated from 2:00PM until 8:00PM the jury reported that it was deadlocked. The court asked how the jury stood and was told 10-2. The jury was sent back for further deliberation and then to a motel for a night's rest. They returned for more deliberations at 9:00 the next morning, which was a Saturday. At 11:30AM the jury was asked as to their progress and they replied they were deadlocked. The court then gave the "get together" instruction. They began deliberating again until 12:45PM. They broke for lunch and returned to work some more. At 3:50PM they returned to the court room and announced they were hung.

Judge Wolfe then engaged in a discussion with the foreman. Judge Wolfe explained that he could not expand on the instructions given but could explain some legal terms. The jury took a break and then, once again, began deliberating. At 6:00PM the court called the jury in and, over the objection of the defendant, instructed them on the offenses of 2nd degree murder and manslaughter. One hour later the jury came back with a verdict of guilty of 2nd degree murder. The jury had deliberated for over twenty-six hours.

The court found this to be reversible error. The court said that the instruction of 2nd degree murder should have been given but not after the jury had been deliberating on the charge of 1st degree murder only and the court had ascertained that the jury was hopelessly deadlocked on the charge of 1st degree murder. The court said that it was the same as the court bargaining with the jury. This was a case of first impression. This they ruled was improper and had violated the rights of the defendant. The case was remanded once again. This time, Rush was acquitted.

In 1955, the 12th Judicial Circuit and the 10th Chancery Circuit both had new judges. This was something of a novelty as Judge Wood had served as circuit judge since 1927 and Chancellor Wofford had served since 1931. The new chancellor was Franklin Wilder. Judge Wilder served one term, while Judge Wolfe served five terms. A scandal-filled reelection campaign shortened Wilder's tenure.

Franklin Wilder was born August 18, 1913, the son of Solon and Mary Elizabeth Miles Wilder. He was the grandson of Oscar Miles, a prominent early day lawyer who was awarded a silver cup by the Arkansas Supreme Court for outstanding service. This cup was a memento that Judge Wilder cherished. He also had an uncle, Seaborn Holt, who served on the Arkansas Supreme Court. Judge Wilder graduated from Fort Smith High School in 1929 and attended Fort Smith Junior College which at the time was located beneath the stadium at what is now Northside High School. While in high school and junior college Judge Wilder became the agent for Curtis Publishing Co. This company put out such magazines as *Look* and *The Saturday Evening Post*. He began this when he was 16 years old. He took the circulation in his area from 500 to 3000 and had other boys working under him selling subscriptions. He had a very good offer from Curtis but turned them down to pursue a career in law. He graduated at the top of his law school class in the late Thirties and returned to Fort Smith to practice law. He opened an office with Vincent Narisi but they were not partners; they simply shared office space and expenses. He married his wife Bernice in 1941. They had three children, Frankie, Sheila, and Robert. Robert was killed in an automobile accident in 1965, and Sheila died after suffering from severe arthritis for many years. Judge and Mrs. Wilder adopted Sheila's son Robert Phillips when her condition deteriorated. During World War II Judge Wilder served in the FBI. The Wilders resided in Philadelphia during most of this time. After the war he reentered the practice of law in Fort Smith. He was always a solo practitioner. He was elected chancery judge for the 10th Chancery Circuit in 1954. The lawyers appreciated the fact that he brought the docket current when there had been a great backlog.

The election of 1960 was memorable and bitter. Judge Wilder's opponent was the Fort Smith Municipal Judge, James Langston. A newspaper story accused Judge Langston of some sexual impropriety with a female defendant in his court. Judge Langston vehemently denied this and blamed the story on Judge Wilder and his political supporters, one of whom was the editor of the paper in question, *The Fort Smithian*. The anger of the electorate was such that both Judge Wilder and Judge Langston were defeated. The winner of the Democratic primary was defeated by an independent write-in named Hugh Bland in the general election.

Judge Wilder had a distinguished career following his judgeship practicing law. He was very active in civic affairs helping, among others, The Sebastian County Humane Society, The Fort Smith National Cemetery, and Fort Smith Junior College (now The University of Arkansas - Fort Smith). Judge Wilder

JUDGE FRANKLIN WILDER
CHANCERY JUDGE
1955-1960
PHOTO COURTESY OF SEBASTIAN COUNTY

was very active in his church, First United Methodist of Fort Smith, and the Methodist Church in general. He was also an accomplished author and historian. He wrote mainly about Methodism, the Wesleys and religious matters. He wrote a biography of Susanna Wesley, the mother of John and Charles. Other of his works include *The Layman's Guide to the Life of Christ* and *The Devil Died Last Night?* His last book, released following his death, was entitled *John Wesley Rides Again.*

Judge Wilder made one more try at politics in 1974. He was an unsuccessful candidate against John Holland in a race for circuit judge to replace the retiring Judge Paul Wolfe. Judge Wilder died on September 4, 1995 and is buried at Oak Cemetery. He left surviving him his wife Bernice, his son Frank, two sisters, Mary Frances Borengasser and Lucille Wilder and a brother, the Rev. William Wilder.

A case heard and decided by Judge Wilder that was appealed to the Arkansas Supreme Court was *Jones vs. Oz-Ark-Val Poultry Co.* 228 Ark. 76, 306 S. W. 2d 111 (1957). This was a water rights case involving subsurface water, which also touched on issues of family farms facing corporate operations and the growth and power of a major agricultural industry.

The facts were that Mr. and Mrs. Jones and a Mrs. Ward owned land near Bloomer, Arkansas, in the Greenwood district. The A.T. Crouch Creamery owned adjacent land. In 1954 and 1955, wells were drilled on the Crouch property and water from these wells was conveyed by pipeline to chicken processing plants owned by Oz-Ark-Val Poultry Co. The poultry company held a lease on the water rights of the Crouch Creamery property.

The poultry company first drilled two wells in 1954. During a test of the new wells' capacity, existing wells on the Jones and Ward properties went dry within two hours. After the new wells were capped, water returned to the Jones and Ward wells.

In July 1955, the Crouch Creamery wells were put to use in the poultry processing business and the Jones and Ward wells promptly went dry again. In September 1955, Jones extended his forty-eight foot well to one hundred fifty feet. It had water until January 1956, when the poultry company dug five more wells; Quickly, the deepened well on the Jones farm went dry. Every time the chicken processing plant used the well water, the Jones and Ward wells went dry, and every time they stopped using the water the Jones and Ward wells had water, suggesting a causal relationship. Jones and Ward sued in chancery court seeking an injunction and damages.

Judge Wilder ruled against Jones and Ward. The poultry company had an expert witness who testified that the poultry company's use of the water was not the cause of the Jones and Ward wells going dry. Mr. Rutledge, the witness, was a registered engineer. He contended it was the severe drought, which had lasted from 1952 to 1955, that had lowered the water table and that the amount of water taken by the poultry company was inconsequential. He further testified that water in the wells on the Crouch property came from a different source than the water in the Jones and Ward wells.

The appellants, Jones and Ward, had relied on common sense, and it was justified: the Arkansas Supreme Court ruled for Jones and Ward. The Court's decision recited the history of the area's plentiful water existing prior to the poultry company's wells. They reviewed the law concerning the rights of adjoining landowners to underground percolating waters. They stated that Arkansas had adopted the reasonable use rule in regard to riparian owners, that is, users of surface water from rivers and creeks, and saw no sense in not applying it to underground percolating waters. These are waters that move underground without a definite channel and are not shown to be supplied by a definite flowing stream. The "English Rule" had traditionally been that one could take all he could extract from under his own ground. In contrast, the "American Rule" was based on the principle of reasonable usage: everyone has a right to the water needed for his or her purposes. The court stated that without a supply of water for their domestic purposes, the Ward and Jones property had become unsuitable as a place to live. The poultry company was taking 36,000 gallons of water daily to process 12,000 chickens. They reversed Judge Wilder and enjoined the poultry company from taking the amount of water that they had been taking.

In 1960, Judge Wilder was up for re-election. Municipal judge James L. Langston filed for the office as well. This set the stage for the most infamous judicial race in the history of this circuit. It began with no particular indication of what "fun" was to come. One notable change from past races was that live television speeches were a big part of it; newspaper advertisements touted the events, inviting readers to "see and hear" the respective candidates or their representatives on television that night. The candidates could depend on viewers, because they enjoyed a captive audience: there was no cable television in 1960, and Fort Smith was served by a single channel, which carried shows from all three networks.

"The scandal" became public on June 24. Edgar Ramey was the publisher of a weekly "advertiser" newspaper called *The Fort Smithian*. In it appeared a column entitled *Fort Smith in a Nutshell*. Ramey wrote the column under the pen name "The Kernel." In the June 24 issue, Ramey accused, without naming names, Judge Langston of having had an improper relationship with a female minor. As might be expected, this started a firestorm of talk in the community. Interestingly the local newspaper, *The Southwest American*, made no mention of it until a grand jury returned indictments. There was never an editorial or a news story other than a report of the testimony. This would hardly be the case today!

The tawdry saga began when the young lady in question, one Sue Ann Wentz, age 17, visited Judge Langston in his office in the courthouse in Fort Smith. She had married at age 15 and she was seeking advice on an annulment of her marriage. According to Miss Wentz, they began meeting for coffee and breakfast at cafes. Langston telephoned her several mornings and came to the Temple Theater where she worked. He took her on two separate trips to Oklahoma and made what she termed improper advances. Each time he drove on when another car approached where he had stopped on the side of the road.

The Temple Theater was located in the Masonic Temple on North "B" Street. This was about a block from the Grand Supermarket on Grand Avenue. An employee of that store, Jimmy Pratt, became aware of what Miss Wentz was claiming. After a talk with Sue Wentz, Pratt resolved that he would "do anything I could to get Langston out of office." That "anything" involved making Judge Wilder, Edgar Ramey and Pratt's employer (and uncle) J.O. Sellars aware of her Wentz's allegations. Ramey and Pratt then proceeded to arrange for Wentz to make notarized statements to Rev. Braxton B. Sawyer (an independent evangelist with an office at The Grand Avenue Baptist Church), the Sebastian County Bar Association and to a group including two ministers and Edgar Ramey. Armed with these statements, Wilder made a comment to Otis Harris, the Sebastian County Circuit Clerk, "It's going to hit the fan (referring to future edition of the weekly) We're going to run Langston out of town."

The campaign of television speeches began on July 3. A newspaper ad asked readers to *"Hear James L. "Jim" Langston speak in his behalf."* On July 6, Wilder ran an ad asking the readers to *"See Judge Franklin Wilder"* on Channel 5 that evening. He ran with the slogan of "One good term deserves another." Wilder also ran television ads in which Mark Woolsey, a noted lawyer and speaker, would speak for him, as well as comparison ads; it was obvious that a heated campaign was underway. On July 21, 1960, the two-horse race expanded: a front-page story in *The Southwest American* announced: "Hugh Bland Chancellor Candidate." A former U. S. Commissioner and assistant district attorney, Hugh Bland announced that he would be an independent candidate for chancery judge in the November general election. He would face the winner of the Democratic primary, either Langston or Wilder. In making his announcement Bland explained what had prompted his candidacy:

> *Because of certain developments in the race for chancery judge of the 10th Chancery Circuit which have occurred after the closing date for filing in the*

Democratic primary, and in response to the urging of many friends and colleagues, I have decided to enter the race for the office of chancery judge as an independent candidate in the November 1960, general election.

A story in the July 24th edition of the paper noted that for Bland to qualify as an independent candidate, he must secure signatures on a petition equal to 15% of the votes cast for governor in the last election from the three-county district. This district consisted of Sebastian, Crawford and Franklin. In the meantime, the ads continued touting the qualifications (and lack thereof) of the candidates. Wilder compared the jurisdiction of the municipal court to a combination police and justice of the peace court. He said in his July 24th ad that the only reason that Langston was running for the post was so he could get a better job. On the same day Langston ran an ad stating that Wilder was not licensed to practice before the U. S. Supreme Court. On that same date Bland ran an ad that said that his announcement had been received in an enthusiastic manner. He was quoted as saying: "My entry into this race is my answer to the necessity of preserving the dignity of this important office."

The primary election was held on July 26th and the headline in the next morning's paper reported that Wilder was out front. The final tally was Wilder winning by 3,149 votes. On August 9, *The Southwest American* reported Bland saying he had 1000 signatures:

I will need about 3500 signatures but I have 38 more days before the deadline and hope to get as many as 5000. I announced (before the primary) so I could not be accused of running against either candidate for the Democratic nomination. I meant to run against the winner of the primary and not just one candidate. I got into the race because of developments after the deadline for filing in the primary.

It was noted that several groups were carrying petitions in the three-county district.

The next event was the convening of a grand jury to investigate the circumstances of the accusations made in the chancellor's race. A news story on August 10, related that the grand jury had been requested by Prosecutor Lyman Mikel and called by Circuit Judge Paul Wolfe. It was to convene at 10 a.m. on that day. There was no reference by name to either candidate. The calling of the grand jury as a result of an election campaign is and was extraordinary and the speculation was active and spirited as to why. Testimony in a later trial provided a little enlightenment: On October 11, Sue Wentz testified that she went to Prosecutor Mikel's office and took a copy of her complaint. Pratt and Mrs. Louise Williams accompanied her to the meeting. Mikel refused to take the complaint unless her father or grandfather was present. There was some mention of her father not believing her at some point. It seems that Mikel and possibly Judge Wolfe were very put off by the whole sordid affair and took it on themselves to throw all the rascals out. At this remove, it is difficult to determine exactly where loyalties lay between the chancery judge, prosecutor and circuit judge, but it may be reasonably suspected that there was no love lost.

Don Flanders was selected as the foreman of the grand jury. He urged anyone having any information concerning the situation to contact the prosecuting attorney. They took testimony from 32 persons and returned a sealed report. On August 18th the sealed report was opened: The grand jury had indicted Langston for contributing to the delinquency of a minor and determined that there had been, in addition, a conspiracy to cause the character and reputation of a female minor to be held up to public scandal and degradation. They were, however, unable to determine who may have been the conspirators.

On August 20, the paper reported that Bland had established a headquarters in the First National Bank. Bland told the reporter that "Developments this week resulted in the speedup of the petition drive."

The grand jury had not been dismissed and continued to work through a four-person investigatory committee. This, again, was—and remains—very extraordinary for a grand jury to continue its investigation by committee. The import was serious enough to cause Langston to step down as municipal judge until the situation could be cleared up.

On September 1, a news story reported that Bland had secured more than 5000 signatures and paid a filing fee of $3. Loyd Been, the county treasurer, said it was the first filing as an independent since he first got into county government in 1934.

On September 3, *The Southwest American* headlines trumpeted: GRAND JURY CHARGES FOUR WITH CONSPIRACY. Named in the indictment were none other than Franklin Wilder, Edgar Ramey, J. O. Sellars and Jimmy Pratt. The indictment for the misdemeanor charge read: "The defendants did on the 28th of June 1960, unlawfully and maliciously conspire to deceitfully induce a female minor to make a statement degrading her name and character with the intent that such statement would be publicized to further the conspirator's ends and that such was done to her injury." It is noted that this charge was not found in the Arkansas Statutes, but was instead resurrected from English common law. Also note that "truth is not a defense," even if it could be proved that the allegations be proven true. This again raises the suspicion that the prosecutor and circuit judge were more than just disinterested cogs in the wheel of justice.

Wilder wanted an immediate trial so that all the facts could be known to the public. Ramey stated that "If I am guilty of anything it is reporting the news as I see it irrespective of time or individuals." A special prosecutor was requested as two of the accused—both Langston and Wilder— were office holders. This was apparently denied. The stage was now set for the climatic trials of each of the contestants in the Democratic primary.

Langston's trial was set for October 3rd. His attorneys were former Circuit Judge J. Sam Wood and future Chancery Judge Charles R. Garner. Sue Ann Wentz was the first to testify and she repeated her story, as earlier related. Judge Langston told the court that he first met Sue Wentz before April 25. She had called for an appointment. She wanted to know if her father could send her to a correctional school because she wasn't living with her husband. Her father wanted her to move home and she was living with friends. Judge Langston told her that he could not help her. He later ran into her near the courthouse and she was complaining of a toothache. He made arrangements for her to see Ted Skokos, a local dentist. He also testified that he later helped her to get a driver's license. Langston said that he first heard of the stories about him on June 16. This was before the article appeared in *The Fort Smithian*. He then went to see the prosecutor, Lyman Mikel. Fran Langston, Judge Langston's wife, told of running into Sue Wentz at Brady's Shoe Repair. She confronted her and Sue replied; "I didn't do it Mrs. Langston, Jimmy Pratt did it." There was also testimony about Langston being seen with Wentz and some testimony from a Fort Smith policeman about Langston trying to arrange a double date for the two of them with Sue and one of her friends. The headlines the next day read: "Judge Langston Acquitted; Jury Out Only 55 Minutes; Cheer Fills Courtroom When Verdict Returned."

The trial for the alleged conspirators began on October 10. Prosecutor Mikel's opening statement related that the previous June, Sue Wentz had made statements concerning Judge Jim Langston and the state would show who was present and how the arrangements to secure the statement had been made. G. C. Hardin, one of the six defense attorneys, reminded the jury that the charges relate only to the alleged conspiracy in obtaining the statements and that Judge Langston did not enter into the case in any way. This seemed to acknowledge public sympathy with Langston. It was also noted by Hardin that Sue Ann Wentz was not named in the indictment and that she had made the statements of her own free will.

As in Langston's trial, the first witness was Sue Ann Wentz. She testified that after her statement was transcribed, it was notarized in a local café by one Cecil Knight. Present were Wentz, Pratt, Ramey, "Red" Williams and Peggy Williams. Cecil Knight testified that he saw Wilder and Sellars in another portion of the café. E. V. Sellars, a brother of J. O. Sellars and the operator of the café, testified that the café was separated by a hallway and he did not see Wilder and Sellars with the others. Wentz, during her testimony stated that Ramey had promised not to use her name and in fact had honored his promise. She further said that no inducements were made to get her to make the statement and the first time she heard her name mentioned it was on television by Judge Langston. She said she was not deceived by any of the defendants but stated she was afraid of Langston. The defense offered no witnesses.

On October 12, Judge Wolfe granted a directed verdict of acquittal in favor of Sellars. The next day the jury returned a verdict of not guilty in favor of Wilder and were unable to reach a verdict on Pratt and Ramey. A mistrial was granted as to them and the criminal cases resulting from the judicial election of 1960 finally came to an end.

The election, however, was not over. The general election was set for November 8 (this was the same Election Day on which John F. Kennedy won the presidency). The competing ads on television and in the newspaper resumed. On October 26, Bland ran an ad stating that he would be on television that night and had the slogan, "The Basic Qualification of a Judge is Good Character." On November 4, Bland invited the people to hear him that night and stated, "Hugh Bland will return dignity to the Chancery Court." A Wilder ad of the same day said, "An office of dignity demands a man of dignity." It also reminded readers that Wilder had been endorsed by more than 11,800 voters in the primary election. On November 5, Wilder parroted back Bland's slogan, "The Basic Qualification of a Judge is Character." On the 6th, Bland responded with an ad saying that "A Judge reflects the Character of Those He Serves. I have lived by the rules of fair play and as Chancery Judge I will not turn my back on these principals." On the 7th, Election Eve, Wilder's ad told the voters that "We need to keep a good chancery judge who is old enough to have the necessary experience, yet young enough to have the necessary energy"—a pompously snarky reference to Bland's age.

On the day, Hugh Bland proved to be the winner. The decision by Wilder or his backers to make much of the allegations associated with Sue Ann Wentz ended up having the unintended result of both Langston and Wilder being defeated; a person who most likely would have never run for the office otherwise became chancery judge for the 10th Chancery Circuit!

Chancery Judge Hugh Bland served from 1961 through 1966. In that year he was appointed to the Arkansas Supreme Court. Hugh Bland was born on a farm near Springdale, Arkansas, on November 1, 1898. He was the son of

JUDGE HUGH M. BLAND
CHANCERY JUDGE
1961-1966
PHOTO COURTESY OF SEBASTIAN COUNTY

Mr. and Mrs. Frank Bland. The family farm is now covered by Beaver Lake. When he was just one the family moved by covered wagon to near Oolahgah, Indian Territory. They returned to Arkansas in the same wagon a few years later and settled on a farm near Cane Hill. He graduated from Cane Hill High School and then the family moved again to Tahlequah, Oklahoma. He attended Northeastern State Teacher's College and graduated in 1917. He taught school for a while and then enlisted in the army for World War I on March 27, 1918. He was in the 28th Division Field Artillery. He never made it to France and was discharged at Camp Zachary Taylor, Kentucky, on November 28, 1918, just eighteen days following the armistice. He then attended The University of Oklahoma and studied law. He obtained his law degree in 1922 and began practice. He was elected Cherokee County Judge the same year. He practiced at Muskogee and Oklahoma City before moving to Fort Smith in 1939. He chose Fort Smith because some Cane Hill friends had prospered there. He said Fort Smith offered him an opportunity to practice near the scenes of his boyhood. He married in June 1941, to Ann Johnson, a native of Alabama. They had no children.

In 1949, he was elected president of The Sebastian County Bar Association. He also served on many committees including the Coke Hill Project, now the Fort Smith National Historic Site. He was elected as an independent to be chancellor in 1960, following the raucous primary between Chancery Judge Franklin Wilder and Municipal Judge Jim Langston. During the campaign he set out his own criteria for a judgeship: "*He must be fair and impartial, and seek always the truth so that justice might be done. He must do justice, love mercy, and walk humbly with his God.*" In the final year of his term he was appointed to the Arkansas Supreme Court by Governor Orval Faubus to fill out the term of Jim Johnson who had resigned in order to run for governor, a race eventually won by Winthrop Rockefeller. Judge Bland's health began to fail later that year due to cancer. He left the bench in January of 1967. He died on April 1 of that year and is buried in Oak Cemetery.

A case decided by Judge Bland that was appealed to the Arkansas Supreme Court is *Arkansas State Highway Commission vs. Scott*, 238 Ark. 883, 385 S. W. 2d 636 (1965). This was a right of way case over property in Fort Smith. The legal issue was whether Judge Bland should have granted the demurrer to the evidence presented at the conclusion of the highway department's case. A demurrer to the evidence is the same as a motion for a directed verdict in circuit court; that is, that the evidence presented by the plaintiff in his case in chief is considered in the most advantageous light for the plaintiff. If this evidence fails to make a *prima facie* case the matter must be dismissed. Judge Bland granted the demurrer and ruled in favor of Scott and denied the declaratory judgment sought by the highway department.

The facts of the case involved the route of Highway 71 in south Fort Smith. This route is better known as Towson Avenue and Zero Street. Testimony established that prior to 1927, Highway 71 turned where Phoenix Village is today and traveled east. This apparently is Phoenix Avenue. On September 3, 1927, the county court entered an order without notice, taking the land in question in a 70 foot right of way. The law allowed this procedure and gave the landowner one year from the date of the actual entering onto the land to file his claim for compensation. The landowner, one Scott, failed to do so. The width of the right of way of Highway 71 is what was contested. The entirety of Highway 71 in this location is all new road since 1927. It is the land where Towson Avenue turns to the east and becomes Zero that was the subject of the controversy. It is most likely the old "curve" that goes behind The Stonewall Jackson Inn and not the new "curve" that goes north of that location. The old road is still there as well. The county court ordinance set the right of way at 70 feet. Evidently the road actually built did not take up the entire right of way and Scott had built a gas station and grocery store that encroached on the right of way. At the time the road was built the land was unimproved pasture. The issue was whether the landowner, Scott, had notice of the taking and entry onto the property. The law is that when the government builds the road that constitutes notice. The taking extends to the entire described right of way even if actual entry is made on only a portion. Judge Bland's ruling was reversed and the cause remanded for trial. Dicta indicates that since Scott did not file his claim within one year, there was no remaining claim for compensation.

The next person to serve the 10th Chancery Circuit and Sebastian County as chancery judge was Ralph "Cotton" Robinson. He was appointed by Governor Orval Faubus to fill out the term of Judge Bland when he was appointed to the Supreme Court. Judge Robinson only served from the date of his appointment in 1966, until the end of the year when Judge Bland's term expired. Ralph Walter "Cotton" Robinson was born December 29, 1909, in Crawford County Arkansas. he was the son of Marshall and Mattie Robinson and was one of a well-known Crawford County family. The family consisted of six sons and one daughter. He graduated from Van Buren High School in 1928, where he was a fine student and athlete. He was president of his senior class and played center on one of the few Pointer football teams to defeat Fort Smith. He attended The University of Arkansas on a football scholarship and completed law school. He passed the bar and was licensed in 1932. He served as the court reporter for Circuit Judge J.O. Kincannon of the 15th Judicial Circuit, which included Crawford County. He was

Judge Ralph "Cotton" Robinson
Chancery Judge
1966
photo courtesy of Sebastian County

elected prosecuting attorney for the 15th Judicial Circuit and served from 1937 through 1943. He then entered private practice and developed into an excellent orator and trial attorney representing individuals. He truly embodied the ideal of a "people's lawyer." He enjoyed helping people and being their friend. He represented clients who could pay and those who could not. His uncollected fees would represent a substantial amount if he had kept records of such. When poor health required that he give up his active practice his most difficult task was to say to his longtime clients and friends that he could go no further with them.

During World War II he performed investigative work for the Civil Service Commission and was stationed in Washington D.C., Houston, and New Orleans at various times. He returned to private practice in Van Buren after the war. He was selected as Chairman of the Democratic Party in Crawford County and served in that capacity for several years. He became successful financially and owned a great deal of property. He was also a political power in the county, district, state and even nationally, through patronage. His political influence was able to obtain many benefits for his county and its people. This included the expansion of Highway 64 into a true two-lane surfaced road, the designation of Cave City Road as a state highway, the opening up of a beautiful area to Devil's Den State Park and the improvement of Kibler Road, which became a state highway leading to Alma. In early 1966, he was appointed by Governor Faubus to be chancery judge for the 10th Chancery Circuit to replace Judge Hugh Bland. He served until January 1, 1967. He was married to Virginia Meeks who predeceased him. He left surviving his son Ralph Walter Jr., his daughter Martha, and his two grandchildren; Ross and Lisa whom he had adopted and reared as his own children. He was a member of the First Baptist Church of Van Buren. He died on August 6, 1979, at age 69.

A case decided by Chancellor Robinson from the Fort Smith District of Sebastian County that was appealed to the Arkansas Supreme Court is *Plastics Research and Development Corp. vs. Bill Norman et al*, 243 Ark. 780, 422 S. W. 2d 121 (1967).

The facts of this case were as follow: Bill Norman was an employee of Plastics Research and Development Corp. He was a department head in the division that designed, manufactured and marketed fishing lures. Norman had a contract that paid him $800 per month base salary and a bonus of 4% of the net profits of the lure department. Evidently things were not going well in the arrangement concerning Norman's bonus compensation; Norman responded by starting a competing business, "Rebel Manufacturing Company, Inc." while still working for Plastics Research. When this became known, Plastics Research fired Norman. Prior to this termination, Norman solicited Plastics Research sales representatives to withhold orders until his startup company got into production with virtually identical products. It should be mentioned that the signature lure manufactured by Plastics Research, dubbed "the Rebel," was itself nearly identical to the Finnish-made "Rapala" lure. It was packaged in a blue and white box marked with the letter "R," with a Confederate flag in the top of the letter and marketed under the names "Rebel Minnow" and the "Amazing Rebel Minnow". Norman marketed his copycat lure as "Reb-1" and "Amazing Minnow". He also used a blue and white box bearing crossed Confederate flags.

Norman sued Plastics Research, seeking payment under his contract and an accounting of the bonus which he felt was owed him. Plastics sued Norman, claiming breach of contract and alleging unfair competition; they sought an injunction against Norman manufacturing a fishing lure similar to the "Rebel" lure and using any information he might have acquired while employed by Plastics Research in the manufacture, promotion or sale of fishing lures. They also asked that Norman be enjoined from using the name "Rebel" or "Rebel Minnow" directly or indirectly in his business. Judge Robinson found in favor of Norman; he entered a judgment for the bonus income that he determined was due Norman and denied the injunctive relief requested by Norman's former employer. Not surprisingly, Plastics Research appealed.

The court spent most of its discussion analyzing the accounting in the record and concluded that they were unable to say that the findings of the trial court, as well as the award of $14,689.26, were not supported by substantial evidence. They further ruled that the court was correct in not enjoining the manufacture of a copy of an unpatented fishing lure that was in fact itself a copy of another lure and, further, enjoining Norman from making disparaging remarks as to the financial condition of Plastics Research. The court did, however, reverse Judge Robinson and found that he should have enjoined Norman from using the name "Rebel", "Reb-1" or "Amazing" in its literature, packaging and advertising. They also enjoined Norman from naming his company "Rebel Manufacturing." They said that confusion was the natural and probable result of Norman's conduct in the packaging of his product. The Supreme Court ruled that it was impermissible for Norman to use the same model or stock numbers to designate color and size of his lures. Norman eventually sold out to Plastics Research, his old employer; the company is today one of the world's largest manufacturers of fishing lures and other outdoor equipment, now known as "Pradco Outdoor Brands," a division of the EBSCO Corporation.

In the year 1967, the Arkansas General Assembly adopted Act 304. This changed the 12th Judicial Circuit's boundaries to include only Sebastian County.

Act 304 of 1967
12th Judicial Circuit
Consisting of Sebastian County

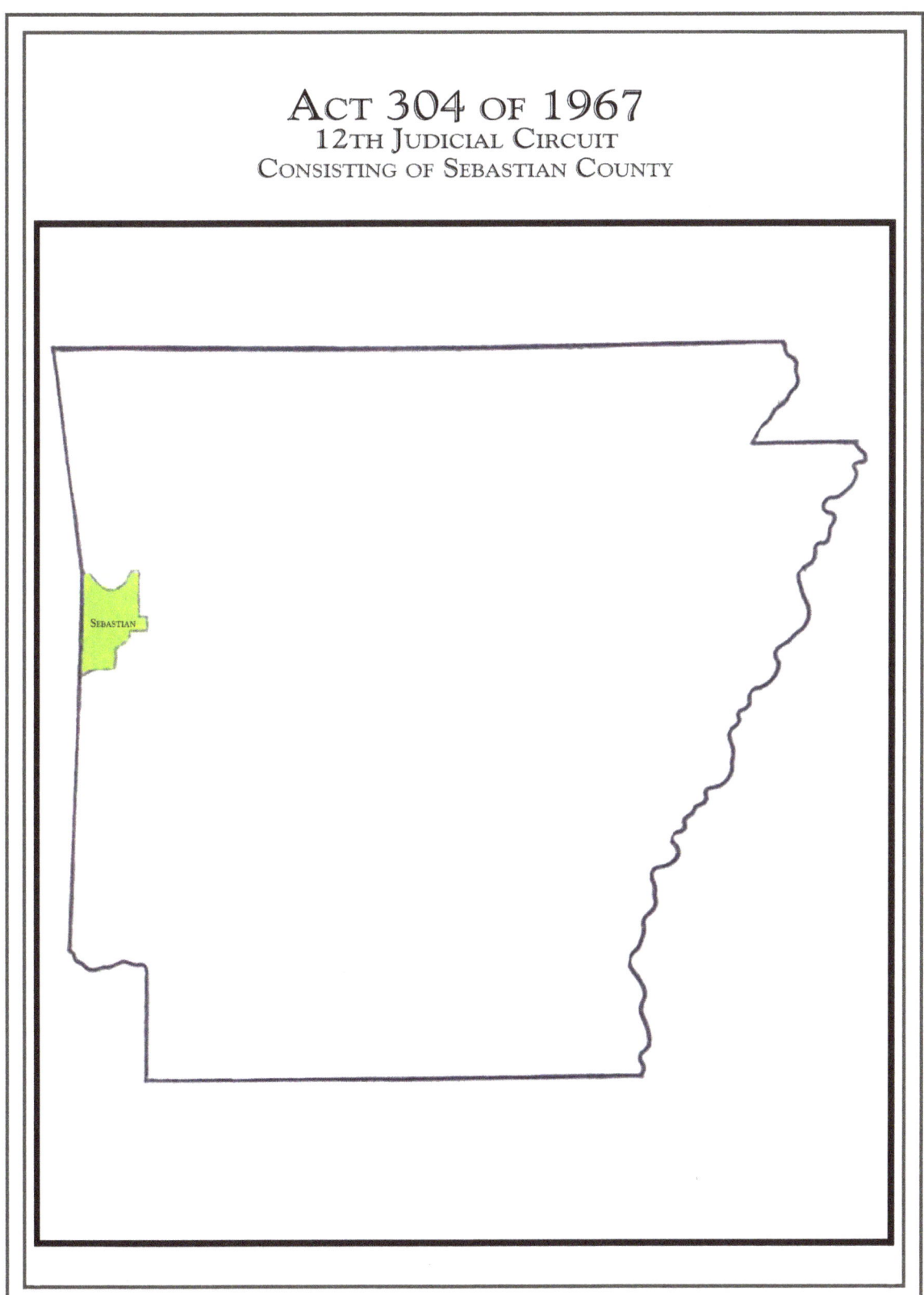

Scott County was added to the 15th Judicial Circuit. This did not change the 10th Chancery Circuit.

The year, 1967, also brought a new chancellor to the 10th Circuit: Warren O. Kimbrough who would serve in that position until the end of 1996. Judge Kimbrough was born in Lafayette, Louisiana, on November 29, 1923. He was the son of William Clair Kimbrough, a native of South Carolina, and Juliette Oakley Kimbrough, a native of Tennessee. He had two brothers, W. Bradley and Richard A. Kimbrough. Judge Kimbrough attended public schools in Lafayette and later attended Southwest Louisiana State College at Lafayette from 1940 until 1943. He entered the United States Navy in World War II and served from 1943 until 1946. He continued to serve in the United States Naval Reserve and retired with the rank of captain. Following the war he attended Hendrix College in Conway following his family's move to Ozark, Arkansas in 1947. He graduated from that institution in 1949 with a degree in history and political science. He obtained his law degree from Vanderbilt University School of Law in Nashville, Tennessee, in 1953. He returned to Ozark where he entered the family business. In 1954, he moved to Fort Smith to practice law. He also operated the area office of the Central Adjustment Company. He practiced general law and served as assistant city attorney for Fort Smith. He later became deputy prosecuting attorney for the 12th Judicial Circuit. Thereafter he returned to the practice of law in the firm of Garner, Shaw and Kimbrough. Judge Kimbrough was admitted to practice before the Arkansas and United States Supreme Courts, the United States Court of Appeals for the 8th Circuit; the United States District Courts for the Eastern and Western Districts of Arkansas and the United States Court of Military Appeals. He was a member of the American and Arkansas Bar Associations and the American Trial Judges Association. In 1966, he was elected chancery judge for the 10th Chancery Circuit and served in that position through the change to the 12th Judicial District until his retirement at the end of 1996.

During his service he served as president of the Arkansas Judicial Council and on various committees. He was also a member of the National Conference of State Trial Judges of the American Bar Association and became the first chairman of the State Trial Judge's Alternative Dispute Resolution Committee. He was active in The Arkansas Bar Association in developing the Arkansas Alternative Dispute Resolution Committee. He was involved in getting legislation passed in Arkansas concerning alternative dispute resolution. He was active in establishing and running the Third District Trial Practice Seminar. He belonged to the W. B. Putman American Inns of Court in Fayetteville. He was on the board of his church and was a member of the Fort Smith Chamber of Commerce. He was the recipient of the Arkansas Judicial Council's Community Service Award and was a member of the Sebastian County Senior Citizens Association. He was a past

JUDGE WARREN O. KIMBROUGH
CHANCERY JUDGE
1967-1996
photo courtesy of Sebastian County

member of the board of The Western Arkansas Alzheimer's Association and The Methodist Nursing Home and Village, Incorporated. He was also a member of Sebastian County Volunteer Attorneys Program, a board member of Project Compassion Incorporated and of the Naval Fleet Reserve Association. He was also a member of The National Cemetery Acquisition Committee and served as chairman of the Arkansas Child Support Committee and several Masonic bodies as well as the Harbor House board. He served also on the Fort Smith Art Center board, the Trolley Museum and the Fort Smith Museum of History boards, as well as Board of Trustees of Hendrix College. Following his retirement he engaged in the practice of law and mediation in Fort Smith.

On August 21, 1949, he married Rebecca Conaster, a native of Ozark, Arkansas, who for many years served as his court reporter. They had six children: Warren Carter, James Bryan, Kevin Alexander, Karen Elizabeth, Beverly Claire and Sarah Jane. Judge Kimbrough died at his home in Fort Smith on September 2, 2002 and is buried in the Fort Smith National Cemetery.

A case that was decided by Judge Kimbrough, then later appealed to the Arkansas Court of Appeals was *Vicki Korolko (Kanady) vs. Joseph Korolko*, 33 Ark. App. 194, 803 S. W. 2d 948 (1991). This was, for Judge Kimbrough, "The Case from Hell". Before it was over Ms. Korolko was appearing on CNN's "Larry King Live" as a celebrity due to the notoriety this case received. It started as a divorce case with the custody of the minor female child in controversy. The father was eventually awarded custody. At some point Ms. Korolko accused Mr. Korolko of inappropriate behavior with the child. The basis for this accusation was never established. On July 4, 1988, Ms. Korolko took the child, Sarah, on a ten-day visit. She then fled the state with Sarah and concealed her whereabouts until February 9, 1990. She was cited for contempt and, following a hearing held before Judge Kimbrough, Ms. Korolko, now going by the name of Kanady, was sentenced to six months in the Sebastian County jail. This sentence was appealed to the Court of Appeals.

The basis for the appeal was that the chancellor did not recite the burden of proof necessary to find one guilty of criminal contempt. That burden of proof is "beyond a reasonable doubt". The Court of Appeals rejected this and said it was not necessary to recite this and a failure to do so does not indicate that the chancellor was unaware of the burden. The decision was also contested on the grounds that Judge Kimbrough was not impartial, since Ms. Korolko's lawyer had sent him a letter informing the judge that a complaint had been filed against him with the judicial discipline committee, and that he should have disqualified himself from the case. The court also rejected this argument as judges are presumed impartial and disqualification is discretionary. To show a judge to be biased requires a substantial burden of proof in this regard. The court also noted that while the appellate court has the authority to reduce a sentence for contempt that this was not a proper case to do so as Ms. Korolko, now Kanady, hid the child from the father and the court for a year and a half. They did not feel a sentence of six months in jail was excessive. Judge Kimbrough was affirmed in all respects.

This proved to be an ongoing, complex saga. This appeal was but one chapter in it. Judge Kimbrough did eventually recuse from the case and Judge John Lineberger from Fayetteville was assigned in his stead. There were several hearings in the matter before the child finally reached the age of majority. This may seem to have been an "inconclusive conclusion" but it is sometimes so, even in the most emotional domestic relations cases. Eventually the children reach age eighteen and the court is no longer a part of their lives.

CHAPTER EIGHT

The Winds of Change

Aprl has been a devastating month as far as court buildings go in Sebastian County. At about 3:00 p.m. on April 19, 1968, from a library window at Arkansas Tech some 80 miles from Greenwood, this writer noticed the western sky turn midnight black. A devastating tornado tore through that city. Children were just getting out of school as a giant tornado funnel dropped from the sky, killed 14 people, obliterated the town square and tossed the deer that were kept there like plastic toys. The Sebastian County Courthouse, built there in 1916, was destroyed. *The Southwest Times Record* of April 20 reported that the tornado cut a 200-foot-wide swath through the center of the town. It generally followed Highway 10 east. The clocks in the town were stopped from between 3:10 and 3:14PM. An eyewitness reported: "Then it hit the courthouse. The steeple with its old clock crashed three floors to the ground—the upper story was virtually ripped apart. The building just popped out—like exploding dynamite."

Fortunately, the building was insured and the County Judge, Ben Geren, put in an application for Federal Disaster Relief funds to help with the reconstruction. On July 22, 1968, the County Court authorized the reconstruction of the Greenwood District courthouse. The order specified that, with the insurance and disaster relief funds, no special tax would be required. The order also set a special election that was required by Amendment 17 to the Arkansas Constitution to proceed with the reconstruction. The date for the election was set as September 3, 1968. The result of the election was 3555 for reconstruction and 21 against. The citizens of the Greenwood District certainly wanted to rebuild. Until the new building was ready to occupy, the county offices would occupy various spaces in the community and the Quorum court would meet in the Scott-Sebastian Library in Greenwood pending the completion of the courthouse.

By the court order that recognized the election result, the architecture firm of Nelson, Laser and Cheyne was employed to design the new building. James G. Cheyne was appointed by Judge Geren to be the commissioner in charge of the construction. There was some delay noted by the county judge in commencing the construction as there was a delay in securing the Federal funds. On December 23, 1968, an agreement was reached between the county and D&W Construction Company to remove the brick from the rubble of the old courthouse. The contractor was to pay $8.00 per thousand brick and he was to clean, stack and palletize the brick for confirmation prior payment. This was to be accomplished in 30 days.

The plans for the new building called for an orange brick and pre-cast concrete structure measuring 138 feet 8 inches in width and 64 feet deep. It was of a modern design, in contrast to the classically styled building it was to replace. The circuit/chancery courtroom was on the second floor and was 53 feet 6 inches deep with a 31-foot width. The plans called for restrooms, the prosecuting attorney's office, witness room and two jury rooms along with the judge's chambers, court reporter's office and attorney room, all on the second floor (the floor currently holds the law library, district court clerk and district court chambers, juvenile court offices and one jury room). The first floor had a county court room to the left of the front entrance, which is now a small circuit court room. The county judge's office, also on the first floor, today serves as chambers for the circuit court. Across the hall were secretarial offices along with offices for the assessor, collector, and sheriff. The circuit clerk, county clerk and treasurer's office were to the front of these and facing from the hallway perpendicular to the entryway. A vault was provided for each of these offices. There were also offices provided for the state revenue office, the county health nurse, along with an examination room, the county school superintendent, the county agent, the demonstration agent, and secretarial space. These, along with restrooms, completed the layout.

The county agent, demonstration agent, and county health nurse have all either moved or are now non-existent. The county judge now has his office where the county health nurse held sway and the old county court chambers are the chambers for the circuit court when more than one judge is holding court in Greenwood. The assessor today is where the revenue office once conducted business and the sheriff occupies all the space formerly reserved for the assessor, collector and clerical staff.

The commissioner reported that the estimated price for the new building would be $387,712.50. This was approved and bids were opened on February 14, 1969. The low bid was by Pharoah Construction Company, for $408,408.00. This bid exceeded the estimate and the parties negotiated an elimination of some elements to bring the price down to $357,000.00. I believe that one of the items eliminated was the elevator; one was later installed to comply with the Americans with Disabilities Act.

Greenwood Courthouse After Devastating 1968 Tornado

Greenwood Courthouse, Dedicated 1970

Court orders reflect a series of partial payments to the contractor as the building progressed. Judge Geren commented in a Quorum Court meeting in November that the construction was nearing completion. The contracts for furnishings and equipment were awarded to Fort Smith Office Supply in the amount of $14,203.88 and to Yoes' Office Supplies and Furnishings in the amount of $10,407.04. These amounts were paid in April 1970. The final payment was made to the contractor on April 24, 1970. Most of this was approved by the Quorum Court in special meeting in the new courthouse on April 23, 1970.

A month earlier, on March 14, 1970, *The Southwest Times Record* reported in a caption underneath a photo of the new courthouse on page one above the masthead that the building would be dedicated that day, debt free. It was the only courthouse to be so dedicated in modern times. This was due to the old building being insured and the Federal Disaster Relief money. The caption also stated that Tom Harper of Fort Smith would give the dedicatory address. Former county judges Ezra Hester of Poteau, Oklahoma and Marshall Strozier of Tulsa, Oklahoma, would preside over the cornerstone ceremonies. They had presided over the cornerstone ceremonies of the former structure that had been destroyed by the tornado 54 years previously on November 26, 1916. The reader will recall that Hester was the county judge and Stozier was an officer of the Masons. Also present were Sebastian County Judge Ben Geren, Means Wilkinson (father of Circuit Judge Norman Wilkinson), Dr. James Burgess, Mayor Ed Hall and Irvin Quillman. It was a good day for Greenwood following a tragedy.

In the early 1970s the 10th Chancery Circuit, which consisted of Crawford, Franklin and Sebastian Counties, experienced an increased caseload and it was determined that an additional chancery judge was needed to handle it. The General Assembly passed Act 34 of 1973, early in that session, to provide a second chancery judge. The act took effect on July 1, 1973. Governor Dale Bumpers appointed a retired Veterans Administration lawyer from Van Buren to that position to serve until January 1, 1975, when the new chancellor, who would be elected in 1974, would assume office. This "appointed man" was Horace Zed Gant.

Judge Gant was born April 1, 1914, at the home of his parents, George and Ida Gant, in the Oliver Springs community in Crawford County, where they had moved in 1911. His father engaged in several occupations as Zed grew up: produce buyer, grocery operator, deputy sheriff, jailer, chief of police, and real estate trader. During the depression years, he operated a restaurant in the Anheuser-Busch Building on Main Street in Van Buren.

JUDGE H. ZED GANT
CHANCERY JUDGE
1973-1974
PHOTO COURTESY OF SEBASTIAN COUNTY

Judge Gant attended the Van Buren schools and graduated from Van Buren High School in 1931. After one year in Fort Smith Junior College, he transferred to The University of Arkansas where he completed his law degree in 1936. While there he met Imogene Farabough of Rogers, Arkansas; they married in 1937. Four children were born to them in the years to follow: Alice Margaret, Linda Beth, Zed George and Paul David.

His first law related job following his graduation was deputy prosecuting attorney and municipal court clerk in Van Buren. During World War II he was appointed as an attorney for the War Relocation Authority and accompanied his former law professor, Robert Leflar, to Washington D.C. It was in Washington that he volunteered for the Navy. He was assigned as a gunnery officer to oil tankers that moved supplies to the Navy fleet around the world. He was on sea duty for 26 months. His final military assignment was as legal officer at the naval base in New Orleans before being released from active duty. He then transferred to inactive reserve and held the rank of Lieutenant Commander. In 1947, he returned briefly to Washington as an opinion writer for solicitor's office in the Department of the Interior. He later transferred to work out of the Veterans Administration Regional Office as a field attorney. For nearly 30 years he serviced the legal needs of veterans living in the northwest corner of the state. It was from this position that he retired in 1973, shortly before his appointment as chancery judge.

Following his service as chancellor he was appointed to serve as Master in Chancery to hear uncontested divorce cases. In this position he served from 1976 until 1991. He also joined his son Paul in the practice of law in Van Buren under the firm name of Gant and Gant. He was active in his church, First Baptist of Van Buren, serving as Sunday school superintendent, trustee, and ordained deacon. He chaired the building committee in 1950 and oversaw the completion of a new auditorium and a three-story education building. He was the oldest living Past Master of Van Buren's Masonic Lodge #6. He was also active in many community groups: board member for Gateway House, the Mental Health Association and Western Arkansas Legal Services. He served as chairman and president of many of these boards. He was also chair of the board of trustees for Boggan Educational Scholarship Trust Fund which provides educational grants to students from Crawford County.

Zed and Imogene lost three children to death. Alice Margaret Schoolcraft was killed in an automobile accident while attending the University of Arkansas. She left four children who all completed college degrees with the help of their grandfather. They also lost their son Zed, who was handicapped. He was blind and suffered many seizures which weakened him until his death. The love, concern and care given this son by Zed and Imogene is a testament to the character and faith of these fine Christian people. Their son Paul was an attorney in Van Buren and practiced with his dad. Sadly, Paul passed away from cancer following the death of his parents. The surviving child is Linda Beth Harwood a retired teacher from Southside High School in Fort Smith. Paul has a daughter who is a graduate of Baylor and Linda has two children; a daughter who lives in Texas and a son who is a fireman in Springdale. At the time of this writing Judge Gant had nine great-grandchildren. Judge Gant passed away on January 13, 2002. Not long after, he was joined in death by his wife, Imogene.

A case first was heard by Judge Gant that was appealed to the Arkansas Supreme Court was from the Probate Court of the Fort Smith District of Sebastian County: *James R. McWilliams and Dottie Ann Kimes vs. Marjorie Tinder, Executrix of the Estate of Velpoe Petty McWilliams, Deceased*, 256 Ark. 994, 511 S. W. 2d 480 (1974).

This was a will contest. The issue was competency and undue influence. Velpoe McWilliams had left a will leaving his estate to his only surviving daughter, Marjorie Tinder. He had two other children that predeceased him: Audrey McWilliams, the father of appellant James McWilliams, and Bernard McWilliams, the father of appellant Dottie Ann Kimes. Following the death of Velpoe's second wife he lived alone for the last eight or nine years of his life. He had an electric bell arrangement so that he could summon his son-in-law, Carl Tinder. Marjorie took care of his cooking and washing. In 1970, allegations were made that Carl was forging some checks on Mr. McWilliams. Audrey McWilliams and Marjorie Tinder filed simultaneous petitions for the appointment of themselves as his guardian. Audrey was appointed.

Submitted in evidence was a letter from Dr. Kemal Kutait, dated August 31, 1970 which basically said that, at times, Mr. McWilliams was not competent and other times he was. Dr. Kutait opined that McWilliams was incompetent to care for his financial affairs and personal affairs. Mr. McWilliams was still driving at the time of the guardianship hearing. On November 17, 1972, Dr. Kutait wrote that Velpoe was oriented to time, place, and person and of sound mind. He also noted that he did not want to have social or financial contact with his son Audrey. After Audrey died, Velpoe was sent to Dr. Max Baker, a psychiatrist. Dr. Baker's opinion was not much different. He noted in his report that Audrey had become upset that his dad was giving too much money to Marjorie. Dr. Baker noted that Velpoe did this because it was Marjorie that was helping him. All the others wanted something if they did anything for him. Dr. Baker said that Velpoe had a clear understanding of the extent of his property and an awareness of the objects of his bounty. Dr. Baker said that the guardianship should be canceled.

The contention was that the state of his mind, although acknowledged to be adequate for testamentary capacity, coupled with the undue influence of Marjorie would be sufficient to defeat the will. The Supreme Court disagreed. The court ruled that the only kind of influence that is considered is that which would result in fear, coercion or any cause that deprives the testator of his free agency. The influence which results from natural affection, or which is acquired by kind offices does not count. The court also criticized the appellant's lawyer, former chancellor Franklin Wilder, for testifying in the case while he was still an advocate. Judge Gant was affirmed.

�� �� ��

The person elected to this new chancery judgeship was Bernice Lichty Kizer. She served from 1975 until her retirement in 1986. Judge Kizer was born in Fort Smith, Arkansas on August 14, 1915, to Earnest and Opal Lichty. Bernice was influenced at an early age when, in 1932, she saw Hattie Carraway and Huey P. Long of Louisiana at Andrews Field in Fort Smith during Senator Carraway's campaign for the United States Senate in Arkansas. Mrs. Carraway had been appointed to fill out the term of her late husband Senator Thaddeus Carraway, who had died in office. Surprising everyone and with the help of the Louisiana populist, Hattie Carraway became the first woman ever elected to serve in the United States Senate. An inspired Bernice Lichty began running and serving in various offices when she was in high school and did not cease doing so until she was 77 years of age.

Hard work was the norm for her growing up. As a young girl she sacked groceries at a local Fort Smith grocery for twelve dollars a week. She graduated from Fort Smith High School in 1932. She attended Stephens College in Columbia, Missouri, and while there she waited tables to pay her way. She also ran and held student office. She then attended the University of Arkansas in Fayetteville and earned her baccalaureate.

While her first husband, James M. Parker, the grandson of the famous United States District Judge Isaac C. Parker, was serving in the Navy during World War II, she returned to the University with two young children. She was one of the first five women to enroll in the University of Arkansas School of Law. She graduated in 1947 but did not immediately enter practice.

Following her husband's death, she began the practice of law in 1957 with Jack Rose, a former Navy pilot. She was married to Harlan Kizer in October 1959; they remained happily married until Harlan Kizer's death in February of 1996.

JUDGE BERNICE LICHTY KIZER
CHANCERY JUDGE
1975-1986
PHOTO COURTESY OF SEBASTIAN COUNTY

Judge Kizer was a member of the Arkansas General Assembly from 1959 until 1974. She served as the first woman chairman of any legislative committee (Labor) and was the first woman to serve on the Arkansas Legislative Council. She was also vice chairman of the Joint Budget Committee, and was a member of the Rules Committee, Savings and Loan Committee and Banking Committee. She was quoted in the *Southwest Times Record* in 1999 as saying, "I never cared whether I got credit for any bill that was passed or defeated, I only wanted to know it was good legislation." She claimed that she read every bill she voted on.

Upon completing 14 years in the House, she ran and was elected Chancery Judge, Division II for the 10th Chancery Circuit. She was the first female elected to a trial judgeship in Arkansas. This writer has been told by Donna Gay, formerly an official with the Arkansas Administrative Office of the Courts, that Judge Kizer was her inspiration, just as Hattie Caraway had been Kizer's.

After retiring from the bench, Judge Kizer again sought public office and was elected to the Fort Smith Board of Directors. While her opponent campaigned, she took a trip to Australia. She was elected handily! She served in this capacity from 1988 until 1992. As reflected by her life, Judge Kizer did not stop there. At age 84, she began taking cases on assignment as a retired judge. Judge Kizer passed away Monday January 16, 2005 at the age of 90. Her funeral was in St. John's Episcopal Church and she was interred in the columbarium at St. John's.

The case selected from Judge Kizer's court is one in which she was the defendant or respondent in a petition for a writ of prohibition. *Deborah Fay Rapp vs. Bernice L. Kizer*, 260 Ark. 656, 543 S. W. 2d 458 (1976). This was a case based on obsolete law, although the law remained on the books at the time. The petitioner was Deborah Rapp who had been married to one Fred Rapp. They divorced on October 30, 1973. Subsequent to the divorce they cohabited, and a child was born out of wedlock on September 12, 1974. Fred Rapp filed suit in chancery court seeking custody and, in the alternative, visitation with the child. Deborah filed a writ of prohibition with the Supreme Court. Not reflected in the court's opinion was the fact that the law concerning bastardy did not allow the father the relief requested in county court. The fact of extramarital paternity was acknowledged by all concerned; the only issue was whether chancery court had any jurisdiction in the matter as there was no adequate remedy at law.

The court held that the Arkansas Constitution placed jurisdiction for all matters relating to bastardy in the County Court. The fact that paternity was not an issue was irrelevant according to Justice Byrd. The writ was granted and Mr. Rapp found no remedy. Subsequent law has changed all this, but it is an interesting look back in time, not so long ago, to see how our laws and society have changed. This writer, now retired former chancery and later circuit judge, regularly heard paternity, not bastardy, cases filed by putative fathers; sometimes they were even granted custody.

In 1974, Sebastian County had elected two new judges: Bernice Kizer in the 10th Chancery Circuit, and John Gray Holland in the 12th Judicial Circuit. John Holland served as circuit judge from 1975, until his retirement at the end of his term in 1998. Judge Holland was born October 20, 1925, the son of Cleveland and Bertha Gray Holland. He attended Fort Smith public schools and graduated from Fort Smith Senior High School in 1943. Judge Holland enjoyed a strong legal heritage. His grandfather, John H. Holland, was admitted to the Arkansas bar in 1882 and served as Sebastian County Judge from 1892 until the end of his term in 1896. He then served as state representative from 1901 through 1904, and state senator from 1905 through 1912. His uncle, Chester Holland, was admitted to the bar in 1905, following his graduation from the University of Arkansas. He served as Greenwood city attorney and assistant prosecuting attorney for the 12th Judicial Circuit from 1927 through 1932. As if this heritage were not enough, Judge Holland's father, Cleveland Holland, was admitted to the bar in 1911. He served as Sebastian County Judge from 1917 until 1921. He also served as president of the Arkansas County Judge's Association from 1920 through 1923.

In high school, Judge Holland lettered in three sports: football, track, and basketball. He had the nickname as a running back of "Hipper Dipper Holland." He was also president of the student body. Following his graduation from high school in 1943, he enlisted in the United States Army that December. This was during World War II. He was a combat infantryman in France and Germany serving in Company H, 399th Infantry Regiment, 100th Division of the Seventh Army. They were south of Patton's Third Army and had to cover its flank and rear when Patton turned north to counterattack the Germans during the Battle of the Bulge. They repulsed a German offensive of their own during this same time. This action gets very little attention from historians due to The Bulge overshadowing it. He was awarded the Bronze Star and the Combat Infantryman's Badge before his discharge in 1946.

John G. Holland entered the University of Arkansas in the fall of 1946 and enrolled in the law school when he had sufficient undergraduate hours. He graduated from the law school in 1951 and began his law practice with Jack Rose. A short time later he went into practice with his father under the firm name of Holland and Holland. He continued this practice until his father's death in 1958. Judge Holland also served as assistant city attorney for Fort Smith, prosecuting in Municipal Court. He also was The United States Magistrate and referee for the Arkansas Workmen's Compensation Commission. Both positions were part time and he carried on his law practice as well. In 1974, he was elected circuit judge for the 12th Judicial Circuit, defeating former chancery judge Franklin Wilder handily. He served until his retirement at the end of 1998. Judge Holland married Ann Brady of Enola, Arkansas, on July 6, 1968. They have two children: Leslie Ann, born October 5, 1970, and John Eric, born November 2, 1974. Judge Holland is now enjoying his well-earned retirement.

A case heard by Judge Holland that was appealed to the Arkansas Supreme Court is *H. Clay Robinson vs. Greenwood District, Sebastian County Quorum Court*, 258 Ark. 798, 528 S. W. 2d 930 (1975). This case concerns the enactment of Amendment 55 to the Arkansas Constitution. The reader will recall the strange arrangement of Sebastian County that was memorialized in the Arkansas Constitution of 1874. Amendment 55, ratified in the 1974 general election, radically reorganized county government in Arkansas. In 1975, the Legislative Assembly adopted enabling legislation (Act 128) to put the amendment in effect. Section 13 of the act provided for separate quorum courts for the Greenwood and Fort Smith Districts of Sebastian County. This was consistent with practice and with the provisions peculiar to Sebastian County that were set out in the 1874 constitution. This section states:

> *"Notwithstanding any other provision of this Act, any county in the State which on the effective date of this Act is divided into two districts and has a separate levying or quorum court for each district, shall continue to have separate levying or quorum court for each district and the provisions of this Act relating to the quorum court shall be applied in each district of such counties the same as if such districts were separate counties."*

This case came about when the Greenwood District Quorum Court petitioned Judge Holland for a Writ of Mandamus directing the Sebastian County Election Commission, H. Clay Robinson, chairman, to create two separate quorum court districts in the county pursuant to Act 128, section 13. The election commission refused, stating that the provision of the Act upon which the Greenwood District relied was unconstitutional. Judge Holland was cognizant of the feelings of the people in the Greenwood District and followed the statutory provision. He granted the Writ of Mandamus; the election commission appealed.

The Supreme Court recognized that, historically and legally, the two districts had been treated as two separate counties. They noted that this was patently inconsistent with Amendment 55. They pointed out that the amendment talks in many places about *"the quorum court"*. It should be noted that the amendment in question is a self-rule amendment for counties, which provided for the quorum court to make decisions affecting the entire county and not just adopting budgets, levying taxes and passing appropriations as in the past (as in the time of Judge Jesse Harp, discussed in an earlier chapter, when the county judge was basically a king). The fact that the minimum and maximum numbers of the

JUDGE JOHN G. HOLLAND
CIRCUIT JUDGE
1975-1998

PHOTO COURTESY OF JOHN HOLLAND

quorum court are set by the amendment is inconsistent with there being two separate quorum courts. To the suggestion that the failure to provide for Sebastian County's unique position was an oversight that could be corrected by this legislation, the court responded that it could not. The Supreme Court reversed Judge Holland.

Since that time, Sebastian County has been unified, at least to the extent that there is one law-making body. The two districts, however, remain.

∽ ∽ ∽

The year 1977 brought about great changes in the judiciary of Arkansas. Until that year the state had been divided into separate judicial subdivisions; one for circuit courts and one for chancery courts. Sebastian County was the 12th Judicial Circuit and was part of the 10th Chancery Circuit along with Crawford, and Franklin Counties. Act 432 of 1977 combined the judicial circuits and chancery circuits into judicial districts. Sebastian along with Crawford became the new 12th Judicial District. This was much to the chagrin of Crawford County which, until this time, had been the dominant county within the judicial district to which it was assigned.

The act became effective on January 1, 1979, following the election for district offices in 1978. Judge David O. Partain, who had been circuit judge in the 15th Judicial Circuit since 1971, was elected with no opposition. In the district there were now two circuit judges and two chancery judges. The district had Judge Kimbrough and Judge Kizer as the chancellors and Judge Holland and Judge Partain as circuit judges.

In 1978, a proposed constitutional amendment, which became Amendment 58, was also successfully referred to the voters. It established the Arkansas Court of Appeals. The appellate work for the Supreme Court had become overwhelming. This amendment created an intermediate appellate level and originally had six judges. Its jurisdiction was set by the Supreme Court and the legislature could establish the number and divisions thereof.

Judge David O. Partain served the 12th Judicial District and Sebastian County as circuit judge from 1979 until his retirement in 1986. He was born in Ozark, Franklin County, Arkansas, on August 10, 1919. He was the son of Mr. and Mrs. David Sidney Partain. His father was a lawyer practicing in Ozark but in 1924, the family moved to Van Buren. There Mr. Partain practiced law with Theron Agee under the firm name of Partain and Agee. Young David attended Van Buren schools and graduated from high school in 1936. He then attended the University of Arkansas and graduated with a law degree in 1942.

Act 432 of 1977
Twelfth Judicial Circuit
Crawford and Sebastian Counties
Circuit and Chancery Circuits Unified: Effective 1/1/79

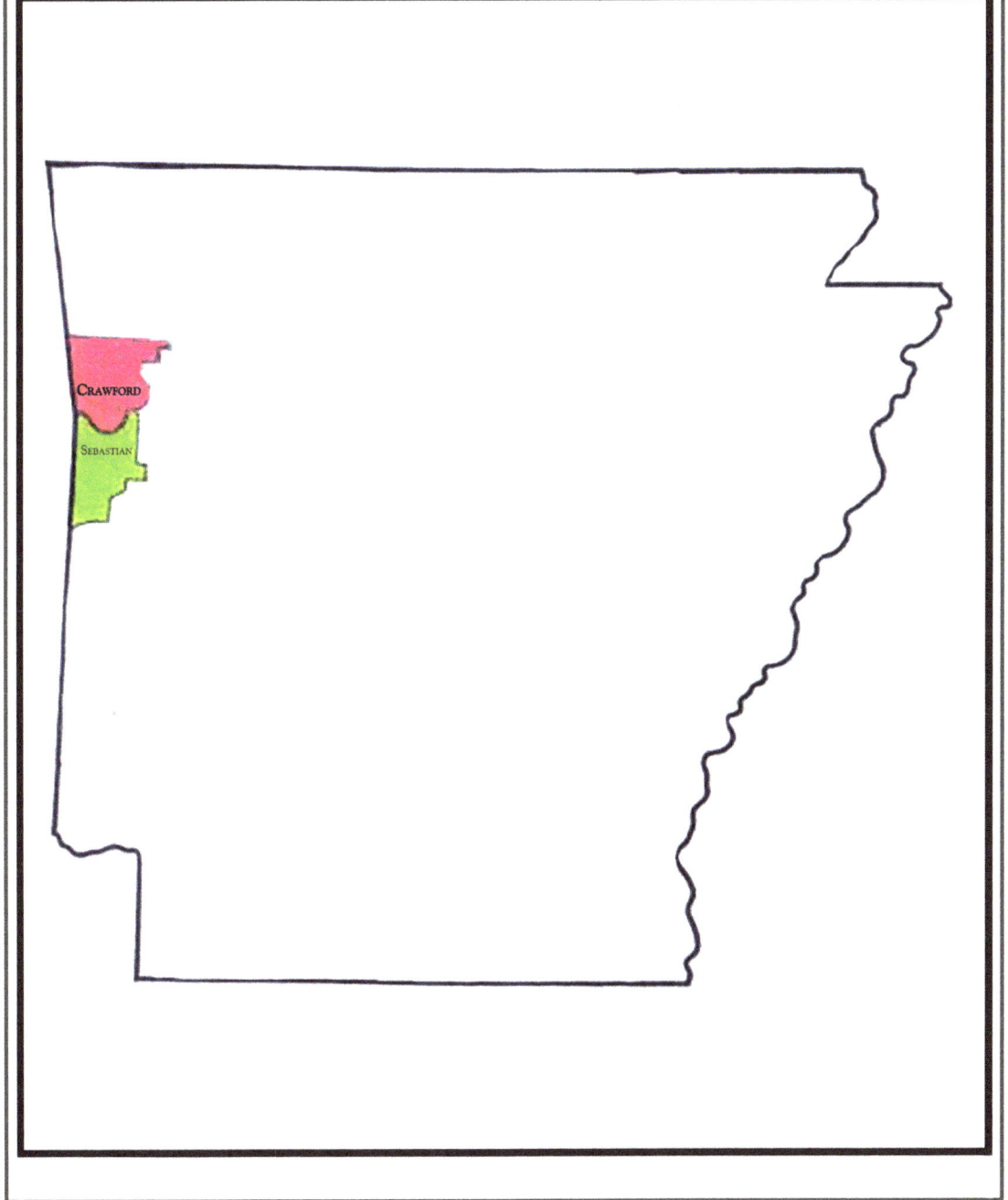

Partain, along with Judge Holland, Judge Gant and others, was a member of what Tom Brokaw has called "The Greatest Generation". He enlisted in the Army Air Corps and served as a pilot flying night fighters in the North African and Italian campaigns. He left military service in 1944 and practiced law with his father and Mr. Agee until 1946, when he was elected prosecuting attorney for the 15th Judicial Circuit, which consisted of Crawford, Franklin, Logan, and Scott Counties. He served in this position through 1950, when he chose not to run again in deference to Jack Yates of Ozark who wished to serve. He once again returned to private practice in the firm with his father. In 1966, he was elected to the state senate and served one term through 1970. In that year he was elected circuit judge for the 15th Judicial Circuit. He served in that position until 1979, when Crawford County was placed in the 12th Judicial District along with Sebastian County. As earlier stated, he was elected, unopposed, to the newly created judgeship for the 12th District. He served in that position until his retirement in 1986.

Judge Partain was married to Norma Lee Matthews, a native of Tahlequah, Oklahoma, on December 11, 1954. She had been working in Fort Smith for OG&E and was introduced to David by a mutual friend. They had one child, Paige Partain Zelikow, who was born on January 6, 1956. She is married to Philip Zelikow, the director of the School of Foreign Affairs of the University of Virginia in Charlottesville. He served on the 9-11 Commission investigating the terrorist attack on the World Trade Center and Pentagon. They have two children: Alexander and Carolyn. Judge Partain passed away May 21, 2002, at age 82.

A case heard by Judge Partain, then later appealed to the Arkansas Supreme Court, is *Alvin Lee Myers vs. State of Arkansas*, 271 Ark. 886, 611 S. W. 2d 514 (1981). This was a criminal case of attempted rape and third-degree battery. It is not the criminal offense for which this case was appealed or noted here but the effect of Amendment 55 on the divided justice system of Sebastian County. The defendant had challenged the jury panel. The defendant moved to quash the jury panel on the ground that the jury was not drawn from the entire population of the county. The fact that the jury was drawn merely from the population of the Fort Smith district was contended to be illegal and unfair.

The court noted that Article 3, Section 5, of the Arkansas Constitution provides that Sebastian County may have two districts and two county seats. Enabling legislation established the districts as Fort Smith and Greenwood, the dividing line being the city limits of Fort Smith. The boundaries of the districts change as the City of Fort Smith changes through annexation. Each district maintains its own jury panel with persons residing in the district selected from voter registration rolls, separately maintained.

JUDGE DAVID O. PARTAIN
CIRCUIT JUDGE
1979-1986
PHOTO COURTESY OF CRAWFORD COUNTY

In the motion to quash at trial level, the defendant did not address the issue of Amendment 55. This was, instead, raised for the first time on appeal and the Supreme Court did not address the effects of that Amendment. The case does recognize the distinction between the two unique judicial districts in a single county.

The question of the effect of Amendment 55 was addressed in a case heard by Judge John Holland and appealed to the Supreme Court. This case was *Morgan vs. State*, 273 Ark. 252, 618 S. W. 2d 161 (1981). In this criminal case, the issue of Amendment 55's effect on the jury pool of Sebastian County was raised and ruled upon at the trial court level. Judge Holland denied the motion to quash the jury panel, based on the assertion that they were drawn only from the Fort Smith District of the county. The court cited Article 13, Section 5 of the Constitution of Arkansas of 1874: "*Sebastian County may have two districts and two county seats, at which county, probate and circuit courts shall be held as may be provided by law....*" The court also cited Ark. Stat. Ann. Sec. 39-205 (Supp. 1979) which provides that "*...prospective jurors...shall be selected among the current list of registered voters of the applicable district or county....*" The court supplied the added emphasis. The justices noted that the case of *Robinson vs. Greenwood District*, 258 Ark. 798, 528 S. W. 2d 930 (1975) only concerned whether the separate quorum court provision of Article 13 Sec. 5 of the 1874 Constitution had been repealed by Amendment 55. It ruled that it had. But in this case, it ruled that the distinction of the two districts of Sebastian County as concerns the judiciary remained intact.

The case load in the 12th Judicial District continued to grow. There was a need for help for both the chancellors and the circuit judges. This need was met by the Legislature, in the form of Act 38 of the 1st Extraordinary Session of 1981. This created a hybrid circuit/chancery judgeship in the district. This position had both legal and equitable jurisdiction and foreshadowed the unification of the court system. The position became effective on January 1, 1982. The person selected to fill the position by Governor Frank White was Sebastian County Judge Robert Boyer.

Judge Boyer was born December 18, 1927. He is the son of Tom and Leona Boyer. He has a brother, Tom Boyer, and a sister, Jacqueline Carey. Judge Boyer is a native of Fort Smith. He graduated from Fort Smith Senior High School in 1945. He enlisted in the Navy V-5 aviator training program and served in World War II. Following his discharge he enrolled at the University of Arkansas. He graduated with a law degree in 1950.

When the Korean War started in June of 1950, he entered the Army and served in the Judge Advocate General's Corps with the 11th Airborne Division. During a break in his military service, he served on the staff of Congressman

James W. Trimble and as a Special Agent for the FBI. He returned to Army active duty in 1955 and served a total of 21 years. He went in as a First Lieutenant and retired as a Colonel. During the period from 1966 until 1969, he served in the Secretary of the Army's Legislative Liaison Office. He then served in Vietnam from 1969-70, as staff judge advocate of the First Logistical Command. At the time of his retirement from the military in 1973, he served as the Senior Circuit Judge at Fort Knox, Kentucky.

He is a graduate of the Judge Advocate General's Career Course at the University of Virginia, the Army Command and General Staff College at Fort Leavenworth, Kansas, and the Army War College at Carlisle, Pennsylvania. He is also an Army graduate of the National College of the State Judiciary at the University of Nevada.

During his military service he was twice awarded the Legion of Merit for exceptional and outstanding performance of duties while serving in difficult assignments. He was also awarded the Bronze Star, two awards of the Army Commendation Medal, General Staff Identification Badge, Vietnam Service Medal, Vietnam Campaign Medal, Meritorious Unit Medal, National Defense Service Medal, World War II Victory Medal and the Parachutist Badge.

Following his military retirement, he returned to Fort Smith and served on the staff of Prosecuting Attorney Charles Karr for two years. He was elected Sebastian County Judge in 1978, defeating incumbent Glenn Thames. He was reelected in 1980 but resigned to accept appointment as circuit/chancery judge in late 1981. He served in this position until replaced by the elected circuit/chancery judge, Don Langston, on January 1, 1983. In 1986, Judge David Partain announced his retirement and Judge Boyer sought that judgeship, running as an independent against Van Buren Municipal Judge Floyd Rogers. Crawford County voted overwhelmingly for their native son and Judge Boyer was defeated.

Judge Boyer is admitted to practice before the Arkansas Supreme Court, the United States District Court for the Western District of Arkansas, the United States Court of Military Appeals, and the United States Supreme Court. He was active in many community and civic, charitable and veteran's organizations. He has been on the boards of and has served as officer for many of them. In 1991, he received The Americanism Award from American Legion Post 31. A member of the Fort Smith Exchange Club, he served as its president in 1991-92 and was selected as "Exchangite of the Year" for 1989 by the Arkansas-Louisiana District.

In 1991, he volunteered to lead the fight against what he considered to be excessive legal fees in a class action lawsuit involving state income tax refunds for approximately 33,000 military and federal civilian retirees at the fee hearing in the Pulaski County Chancery Court. He was successful in getting the requested

Judge Robert E. Boyer
Circuit Judge
1982
PHOTO COURTESY OF ROBERT BOYER

fee reduced from $11.25 million (25% of the retirees' award) to $6.75 million (15% of the award); he saved the retirees $4.5 million in the face of strong opposition from several Arkansas law firms and ten out-of-state attorneys called as witnesses to support the fee request. Local veteran's organizations awarded him various commendations for his efforts and Mayor Ray Baker of Fort Smith proclaimed December 3, 1993 as "Bob Boyer Day."

In 1995, Judge Boyer was active in the fight to keep Fort Chaffee from being totally closed and disposed of by the Base Realignment and Closure Commission (BRAC). He served as one of the speakers making arguments at the regional BRAC hearing in Dallas. They considered their mission very important due to the fear that, if Fort Chaffee were totally closed, the area might also lose the 188th Fighter Wing of the Arkansas National Guard, since the bombing range used by the Wing was on Fort Chaffee's reservation. The arguments were mainly successful: Only 7,000 acres of the 73,000-acre base were declared surplus land. The remainder, including the bombing range, was converted into an Arkansas National Guard Training Base where Guard and visiting active- duty units could train.

Boyer was married to the former Jo Bowerman. They were the parents of two daughters. Susan Rosenthal is a schoolteacher and homemaker in Little Rock and the mother of Molly and Grant. Joan Boyer is a police officer in Colorado Springs, Colorado. Judge Boyer passed away October 28, 2008 and is buried in the Fort Smith National Cemetery.

A case that was heard by Judge Boyer and later appealed to the Arkansas Supreme Court is that of Marion Albert Pruett, a serial killer known as "Mad Dog Pruett.". The facts of this case, *Marion Albert Pruett vs. State of Arkansas*, 282 Ark. 304, 669 S. W. 2d 186 (1984), are that Pruett had been a hit man for a motorcycle gang. He was in the witness protection program in New Mexico. There, he was charged with the gruesome killing of his wife, a crime which he denied to the grave. He committed several killings including a bank clerk in Mississippi and two convenience store employees in Colorado. In Fort Smith, he abducted and killed Bobbie Jean Robertson, a clerk in a convenience store near Phoenix Ave., I-540, and Old Greenwood Road. He took her to a wooded tract adjoining of Leigh Avenue and killed her. He disposed of some trash from his car around the body, including gasoline and motel receipts with his name on them.

He was captured in Texas during a stop for speeding. It was determined he had no driver's license, and the police noticed a gun holster under the seat and drug paraphernalia in the open glove compartment. He was tried in Mississippi, Colorado, New Mexico and Arkansas for capital murder. He received the death sentence in Mississippi and Arkansas and life sentences in Colorado and New

Mexico. The Mississippi sentence was reversed and Arkansas ended up executing him many years after his conviction.

One of the issues in the appeal in Arkansas was that a second change of venue should have been granted. The law in Arkansas allows for a change of venue when a defendant cannot obtain a fair trial due to prejudice against him. The problem is that it can only be changed to an adjoining county within the judicial district. A change had been granted from Sebastian to Crawford County. Judge George Howard, of the United States District Court, had this question on appeal for two years before deciding in favor of the defendant and vacating the conviction and sentence. His decision was later reversed by the 8th United States Circuit Court of Appeals. The Arkansas Supreme Court addressed the issue by determining that he was not denied an impartial trial because a jury was seated, none of whom were excused for cause.

Another issue was the denial of motions for continuance due to the defense wanting more time to prepare. The murder was committed on October 12, 1981. The trial began on August 30, 1982. The other issues concerned whether electrocution was cruel and unusual punishment, the voluntariness of a custodial statement made by Pruett, the search and seizure of the gun and bullets, the claim that the memory of a witness had been "hypnotically refreshed", and a jury instruction regarding the defendant's mental abilities at the time of the crime due to self-induced intoxication from drugs. The fact that he emptied his car of incriminating papers at the crime scene was claimed to indicate that he was "hopped up" at the time. These arguments, however, were rejected by the court.

The person elected to the circuit/chancery judgeship to which Judge Boyer had been appointed was Don Langston. He served as circuit/chancery judge and then as circuit judge, after the designation of the office was changed by the legislature, from 1983 through 1998. Judge Langston was a native of Coal Hill, Arkansas. He was born December 12, 1937, the son of Porter W. and Marie Stallings Langston. He graduated from Coal Hill High School in 1955 and attended the College of the Ozarks in Clarksville for two years before transferring to the University of Arkansas School of Law in Fayetteville. He graduated with an LLB degree in 1961 and ranked at the top of his class academically. His LLB was converted later, as were all others, to a Juris Doctor degree.

From December 1961 until January 1967, he served as staff trial counsel for the Arkansas Highway Commission mainly handling condemnation cases to obtain land for the construction of the interstate highway system. From January 1967 until March 1970 he served as a deputy attorney general for Arkansas Attorney General Joe Purcell in the litigation division. He handled a great many criminal appeals and some civil appellate work as well. He did the litigation for the state in the Federal Courts and argued many cases before the Eighth

JUDGE DON LANGSTON
CIRCUIT JUDGE
1983-1998
PHOTO COURTESY OF DON LANGSTON

Circuit Court of Appeals. He argued two criminal cases before the United States Supreme Court. From March,1970 through January 1971 he served as a deputy prosecuting attorney for Pulaski County under Richard Atkinson. From January 1971 until December of that year he served as a deputy prosecutor for Sebastian County under Bill Thompson.

During this period of service with the state he was permitted and did maintain a private practice in general civil law. All during his career he was a member of the Army Reserve in the Judge Advocate General's Corps. He rose to the rank of Colonel and had over 20 years' service. For eight years he was the commander of the 32nd JAG Detachment in Little Rock, Arkansas, and served as the commander of the 29th JAG Detachment in Tulsa, Oklahoma. He completed the JAG Career Course in 1973, and the Command and General Staff College in 1978, finishing in the top 20% of his class. He completed the Military Judge Course at the Judge Advocate General's School in 1979.

In December 1971 he was appointed Public Defender for Sebastian County. It was the first public defender position in Arkansas. He served in this position for nine years. He established and administered the office which had one deputy, two secretaries, and a legal intern. Judge Langston prepared and tried misdemeanor and felony cases in the Municipal and Circuit Courts of the county including four capital murder cases. The most notable of these was the trial of John Edward Swindler for the murder of Fort Smith policeman Randy Basnett.

In 1981, he was appointed Municipal Judge for Fort Smith by the city board of directors to serve the unexpired term of Judge Lawson Cloninger who had been elected to the Arkansas Court of Appeals. In 1982 he was elected circuit/chancery judge. In that election he defeated Harry Foltz who was later elected chancery judge. In 1991, his position was changed to that of circuit judge by the legislature. He was defeated for reelection in 1998 by J. Michael Fitzhugh.

This uncommon challenge and defeat of Judge Langston followed a series of stories in the *Southwest Times Record* in which it was pointed out that he regularly drank and dined on the tab of his friend and local attorney Bob Blatt. Although he produced checks contemporaneously reimbursing Blatt for the charges, this complaint, along with the influence of some defense attorneys who felt that he was too liberal in his rulings for the plaintiff's bar, defeated him. It is also notable that Fitzhugh ran as a Republican in a changing political demographic. Fitzhugh is the first judge elected as a Republican in Sebastian County.

Following his defeat, Judge Langston practiced law with the firm of Sexton and Fields and then Fields, Tabor and Shue. When Steve Tabor was elected prosecuting attorney in 2002, he began a solo practice and officed with Joel

Price. Judge Langston suffered a stroke and passed away on August 8, 2005. He is buried in the Fort Smith National Cemetery.

A case that was heard by Judge Langston and appealed to the Arkansas Supreme Court was brought by the person who later defeated Judge Langston for reelection: J. Michael Fitzhugh. The case is *Little Rock Newspapers, Inc. vs. J. Michael Fitzhugh*, 330 Ark. 561, 954 S. W. 2d 914 (1997).

Mike Fitzhugh sued the company that publishes The Arkansas Democrat-Gazette, a statewide daily newspaper. Fitzhugh had been the United States Attorney for the Western District of Arkansas. On Monday, June 20, 1994, the paper printed an article on the front page of the ARKANSAS section entitled, WHITEWATER COUNSEL KICKS OFF FIRST PROSECUTION. There were two photographs included in the article; one of which was of J. Michael Fitzhugh, the former U. S. Attorney. The caption underneath the picture said "Fitzhugh". The article discussed Eugene Fitzhugh and his indictment along with Charles Matthews and former Pulaski County Municipal Judge David Hale for conspiring to defraud the Small Business Administration of $900,000 through Hale's federally licensed lending company, Capital Management Services, Inc. The article mentioned "Fitzhugh" as being a Little Rock lawyer who represented a Shreveport family used by Hale in his deceit.

After the paper received calls from Mike Fitzhugh, it printed a correction the following day. It was in the left lower corner of the front page of the paper in the ARKANSAS section under the heading, GETTING IT STRAIGHT. It had a picture of the correct "Fitzhugh" and read: *"On Monday on the front of the Arkansas section a photo of J. Michael Fitzhugh was run in place of a photo of Eugene Fitzhugh. The correct photo of Eugene Fitzhugh is shown.."*

Mike Fitzhugh filed a complaint stating that running the incorrect photo with the story was defamatory *per se* and the result of gross carelessness on the part of the paper. The paper answered that, since Mike Fitzhugh was a public figure (former U.S. Attorney), it was necessary for him to prove that the paper acted with actual malice in misplacing his photograph in a story concerning the indictment of a similarly named person. The jury ruled in Fitzhugh's favor and awarded him monetary damages.

On appeal, the paper contended that Judge Langston erred in not granting a directed verdict in favor of the defendant. In its decision, the court noted the elements of an action for defamation: 1. defamatory nature of the statement of fact, 2. identification and reference to the plaintiff, 3. publication of the statement, 4. the defendant's fault in the publication, 5. the statements falsity, and 6. damages. The court reviewed the evidence on each of these elements and concluded that there was a jury question on each and that the denial of the directed verdict was not error.

The court noted that this case was a first for Arkansas, i.e. the erroneous publication of a photo of an innocent person in a story concerning criminal activity. The court reviewed cases from other jurisdictions and concluded that there was sufficient evidence to submit to the jury the issue of whether the article could be construed as being a false statement of and concerning Mike Fitzhugh.

The court then discussed damage to one's reputation. They concluded that actual injury is not limited to out-of-pocket loss. The more customary types of actual harm inflicted by defamatory falsehood include impairment of reputation and standing in the community, personal humiliation, and mental anguish and suffering. There need be no evidence which assigns an actual dollar value to the injury. There does need to be proof of reputational injury. It is a fundamental concept of the law of defamation. It turns on whether the communication of the publication tends or is reasonably calculated to cause harm to another's reputation. The proof necessary may include: 1. that people believed the plaintiff to be guilty of the conduct asserted; or, 2. that people thought less of the plaintiff as a result of the publication. There must be proof of injury to reputation beyond mental suffering or anguish. In this case, proof must be from witnesses who read the article and initially believed that the plaintiff was the subject of the stated Whitewater investigation. The court reviewed the testimony and concluded that the proof was sufficient. The judgment in favor of future Judge Fitzhugh was affirmed.

The next person to serve Sebastian County and the 12th Judicial District as circuit judge was Floyd R. "Pete" Rogers. He was elected to replace the retired David Partain. He was born at home near Natural Dam, Arkansas, on October 31, 1935. He was the seventh child of ten who lived through childhood. His parents were William Edward and Agnes Fain Rogers. His father was a member of a pioneer Crawford County family which had immigrated to the Cane Hill area in Washington County from near Shelbyville, Tennessee, in 1834. They later moved to northern Crawford County. As many in the depression era, the Rogers family found life hard and money scarce in the Ozarks. He moved with his family in 1940, to Portland, Oregon. There his father found work in the shipyards. A relative suggested a move to Washington state shortly thereafter as there was work in the orchards which better suited Mr. Rogers. When Floyd was 12 years old, the family returned to Crawford County. Young Floyd soon returned to Washington where he lived with an older brother and attended school.

After graduation he attended Gonzaga University in Spokane, Washington for two years. He worked to pay his way. He then returned to Crawford County and obtained a provisional teaching certificate. He became a coach and teacher

JUDGE FLOYD R. "PETE" ROGERS
CIRCUIT JUDGE
1987-1996

PHOTO COURTESY OF FLOYD ROGERS

at Cedarville teaching seventh and eighth grade English. While there he met Hazel Hopkins, a senior in the high school.

He soon realized that teaching was not his desired profession. He went to Tulsa, Oklahoma, and began law school while working as a janitor and later a policeman. Hazel followed him to Tulsa and they were married on July 5, 1957. They had two children, Lenora and Edward.

Upon graduation he returned to Van Buren and began the practice of law with Cotton Robinson who later became chancery judge. Judge Rogers also owned and operated the Crawford County Abstract Company for several years. In 1966, he was elected prosecuting attorney for the 15th Judicial Circuit which consisted of Crawford, Logan, Scott, and Franklin Counties. He served in this position from 1967 through 1974. In 1974, he was elected Van Buren municipal judge. He served in this position through 1986. In that year he was elected circuit judge for the 12th Judicial District defeating former Circuit/Chancery Judge Bob Boyer. He served in that capacity until Crawford County was designated the 21st Judicial District in 1997. His judgeship was also converted to a circuit/chancery position in the change. He continued to serve the 21st Judicial District until his retirement at the end of 2002. He is now enjoying retirement engaging in his favorite pastimes, hunting and gardening.

A case that was heard by Judge Rogers and appealed to the Arkansas Supreme Court is *Doris Mikel vs. Hubbard and Hubbard Marine Services, Inc.*, 317 Ark. 125, 876 S. W. 2d 558 (1994). This case is interesting as it refers back to the creation of the Indian Nations and the state of Arkansas. One Doris Mikel brought suit for ejectment against the defendants. Both had color of title. The background of the case involved the Indian treaties of Doak's Stand, Washington, D.C., and Dancing Rabbit Creek ratified by Congress in 1820, 1825, and 1830, respectively. These treaties placed title to land that was west of the western boundary of Arkansas in the Choctaw Nation. At the time of statehood, in 1836, the western boundary of Arkansas was east of the Poteau River. In 1904, the area between the western boundary of Arkansas and the Poteau River was platted and subdivided as part of West Fort Smith, Choctaw Nation, Indian Territory. In 1905, Congress extended the western boundary of Arkansas to the thread of the Poteau River and, by moving the boundary west, placed the land in dispute in Arkansas. In 1908, the Choctaw Indian Nation began selling its platted lots in West Fort Smith, Arkansas. In 1909, the area was annexed into the city of Fort Smith, Arkansas.

In 1918, William Ray purchased unallotted Indian land tracts 510 and 526 and subsequently wrote a letter of complaint to the Commissioner of the Five Civilized Tribes that the lots "were badly damaged by the river." Part of these two tracts was later acquired by plaintiff Mikel as Lot 7 of West Fort Smith,

Arkansas. In 1981, Hubbard Marine purchased lots 10 and 11, which are part of lot 7, and constructed a concrete driveway and dock that extended into the river. Mikel claimed title to the driveway and dock.

The jury ruled in favor of Hubbard Marine. The opinion of the Supreme Court dealt with the fact that the plaintiff, Mikel, had to prove her case on the superiority of her title not on the weakness of the defendant's claim. She was barred from raising the sufficiency of the evidence as she had not moved for a directed verdict at the conclusion of her case and the case of the defendant. There were other procedural deficiencies that prevented the court from considering the appeal in its entirety.

In the same year that Judge Rogers was elected circuit judge Judge Bernice Kizer opted to retire and was replaced by Judge Harry Albers Foltz. Judge Foltz took office January 1, 1987, after winning contested elections in both the Democratic primary and the general election. Judge Foltz was born in Fort Smith on April 19, 1939. He is the son of Dr. Thomas Price Foltz and Eleanor Albers Foltz. Both sides of his family were pioneers in Fort Smith, coming to the city in the 1880's. His paternal grandfather was Dr. James Arthur Foltz, one of the first surgeons in Fort Smith and his maternal grandfather, Harry King Albers, became one of the first insurance agents in Fort Smith after joining the agency founded in 1897 by Judge Foltz's great uncle, Allan Kennedy. Judge Foltz attended Fort Smith schools through the ninth grade and graduated from Middlesex School in Concord, Massachusetts in 1958 after having been elected valedictorian of his class. He graduated from Washington and Lee University in 1962, with a bachelor's degree in English and from The University of Arkansas School of Law in 1965 with his Juris Doctor. He married Eleanor Shoemaker in 1966. They have two children, Henry and Embry.

After graduating from law school, Foltz joined the firm of Warner, Warner, Ragon and Smith where he had worked for several summers during law school. After a year of practice in a corporate law firm he decided corporate law was not his preference and left the firm to go into business. After a period with Rector-Phillips-Morse Real Estate Co. in Little Rock and several years with Arkansas Best Freight in Fort Smith he decided to go back into law. In 1971, he was hired as an Arkansas Legal Aid attorney with Arkansas Social Services, a post in which he served both as an attorney for the indigent and represented Arkansas Social Services in abuse and neglect cases. In 1973, he was asked by Judge Paul Wolfe to investigate the possibility of founding a county funded legal aid office, and in 1973, he was hired by Sebastian County as Sebastian County Legal Aid Attorney.

JUDGE HARRY ALBERS FOLTZ
CHANCERY JUDGE 1987-2001
CIRCUIT JUDGE 2001-2010
PHOTO COURTESY OF HARRY FOLTZ

He served in that capacity until 1978 when he was hired by the National Legal Services Corporation as Executive Director of Western Arkansas Legal Services, a new entity which was to be organized and staffed by him and which was to serve six counties in western Arkansas with a branch office in Russellville. This was the first comprehensive legal aid program in western Arkansas. Judge Foltz remained at Western Arkansas Legal Services until 1983 when he took office as Fort Smith Municipal Judge after having been elected the previous November. While municipal judge, Judge Foltz caused the municipal court business office's accounting system to be completely reorganized and computerized, an event which resulted in a more efficient office with much tighter accounting controls. At the time he served as municipal judge, Judge Foltz was the only municipal judge in Fort Smith and presided over the highest municipal caseload in the state with an annual load of over 39,000 cases.

In 1986, Judge Foltz was elected Chancellor of Division II of the 12th Judicial District, replacing the retired Judge Bernice Kizer. This position, as with all former chancery positions, was designated a circuit judge position by Amendment 80 to the Arkansas Constitution. Judge Foltz retired at the end of 2010, due to reaching the mandatory retirement age of seventy. He is a member of the Sebastian County, Arkansas and American Bar Associations. He served as President of the Sebastian County Bar Association in 1980-81. He is a former member of the United Way Board of Directors, was a founding member of the board of the Lincoln Day Care Center and past chairman of the Crawford-Sebastian Community Development Council. He is a member of St. John's Episcopal Church.

A case heard by Judge Foltz that was appealed to the Arkansas Supreme Court is *Campbell vs. Campbell*, 336 Ark. 379, 985 S. W. 2d 724 (1999). This was a change of custody case. In the original divorce case in 1993, the father was awarded custody of children Natasha and Michael and the mother was awarded visitation and ordered to pay child support. Each parent was prohibited from having overnight guests of the opposite sex when the children were present. In 1996 the mother filed a motion seeking a change of custody based on a change of conditions. Judge Foltz awarded the change after a two-day hearing. The father appealed to the court of appeals that affirmed Judge Foltz on a tie vote. The father then petitioned for review by the Supreme Court; the high court reversed Judge Foltz.

The Supreme Court's opinion refers to the Court of Appeals opinion that had earlier reviewed the facts of the case and mentioned that the original custody decision was based on mental problems from which the mother suffered resulting from the divorce and custody fight. The mother's mental and personal welfare had greatly improved by the time of the second hearing. The children, aged 8 and 10 at the time the petition for change of custody was filed, suffered from emotional anxiety but were doing well in school and exhibited no physical health problems. Each parent had a good and loving relationship with the children. The parent's relationship with each other, however, was described as acrimonious and contemptuous, even in the presence of the children. Both parents, moreover, had violated the prohibition of having persons of the opposite sex over for the night in the presence of the children. In addition, the father had some anger problems.

The key to the case, from the chancellor's point of view, was the younger child, Michael. Judge Foltz had complimented the father on his accomplishments in raising the children but the emotional fragility of the younger child became apparent in the original court proceedings. What "turned" the case was the emotional condition of the young boy. This was noticed by Dr. Phil Barling, a clinical psychologist. While being interviewed by Dr. Barling and Judge Foltz, the child became tearful. The child climbed up in Dr. Barling's lap and begged, "Don't tell my father." He exhibited the same behavior with Judge Foltz, expressing an overwhelming desire to live with his mother. Dr. Barling could not explain it. Judge Foltz noted, "...a tearful, stressed, almost frightened little boy who desperately needs to be with his mother..." and when the chancellor reminded Michael of how hard his father had tried to be a good father, the boy started crying and said, "He's not going to let us go to Mom." Foltz concluded that "...This little boy wants and needs his mother for whatever reason and I am...convinced not to grant this desire would be emotionally damaging, if not devastating, to him.

The Supreme Court, however, opined that the desires of the child were insufficient to justify a change of custody. They were concerned about testimony that the mother had implanted some of the child's concerns and the fact that she was living with a man to whom she was not married. Notwithstanding the child's concerns and the anger problems of the father, the court found that Judge Foltz' decision should be reversed. This case points out the difficulty of applying legal rules and equitable principles when it comes to the emotional well-being of children caught up in domestic situations not of their making.

The Arkansas Supreme Court made a ruling in *Walker vs. Arkansas Department of Human Services*, 291 Ark. 43, 722 S.W.2 558 (1987), that changed the judiciary in Arkansas. When the courts of Arkansas were established in 1874, there was no such thing as a juvenile court. The legal system did not differentiate on the basis of age; laws applied to old and young equally, for good and ill. When, in time, society embraced the idea that young offenders should be dealt with separately from adults, that job was delegated by the Arkansas legislature to the county judges under the provision that juvenile justice was a "local matter". Therefore, in any Arkansas county the designated juvenile judge was the county judge. Many county judges in later years delegated this authority to individuals designated as "Juvenile Referees". Most of these persons were not attorneys. In response to the Walker case, which held this arrangement to be unconstitutional, the legislature adopted Act 14 of 1987. This measure set up a juvenile court system within the judicial branch. It stipulated that the juvenile judge be an attorney. This new law was, at least initially, "honored in the breach" in Sebastian County: the acting juvenile referee, one Audit Kincannon, a former court reporter, was allowed to continue in office, "grandfathered in," so to speak. Act 949 of 1989 ended such continuations of the old habit, set up the Arkansas Juvenile Code and established a judgeship to handle juvenile matters. This person was a full-fledged judge who had circuit and chancery authority. This was necessary as the job dealt with child custody, injunctions and adjudication of delinquents requiring incarceration. The juvenile judge could also act in other judicial matters as well. This person had to have the qualifications required for a trial judge in the state of Arkansas because that was what he/she was.

The first occupants of these positions were appointed by the governor. For the 12th Judicial District and Sebastian County the person appointed by Governor Bill Clinton was Sherri Cunningham Karber. She took office in 1988 and served through 1990.

Sherri Cunningham was born March 17, 1954, in San Francisco, California. She is the daughter of Ed and LaRue Cunningham who resided in Jonesboro. She attended public schools around the country as her father was frequently transferred in his position as an FBI agent. She graduated from Jonesboro High School in Craighead County in 1972. She attended Southern Methodist University and the University of Arkansas at Fayetteville from which she graduated with her undergraduate degree in 1975. She obtained her law degree from the University of Arkansas School of Law in Fayetteville in 1978.

She was employed as a staff attorney for the Legislative Bureau of the Arkansas General Assembly for the 1981 session. She was then employed by the Western Arkansas Legal Services as a staff attorney. The director of that program at the time was Harry Foltz, later a circuit judge. In 1987, she was appointed as juvenile referee for Crawford and Sebastian Counties and then as circuit/chancery judge for the 12th judicial district assigned to hear juvenile cases. She served in this position until Mark Hewett took office on January 1, 1991.

Judge Karber, being an appointee, was unable to run for the office. She was engaged in the private practice of law and full-time motherhood from 1991 until 1995, at which time she went to work for the Department of Finance and

JUDGE SHERRI CUNNINGHAM KARBER
JUVENILE JUDGE
1988-1990
PHOTO COURTESY OF SHERRI KARBER

Administration / Office of Child Support Enforcement. She was holding that job at the time of this writing. She has one son, Gregory Karber Jr. who was born February 20, 1987; he is a screenwriter living in Los Angeles. Judge Karber is involved in many activities. In 1994, she was elected the first woman President of the Sebastian County Bar Association and she was named a Woman of Distinction by the Magazine Mountain Council of the Girls Scouts of America in 2003.

During her tenure as juvenile judge there were no appeals from any of her cases.

✦ ✦ ✦

Judge Karber's successor was Judge Mark Hewett. He was born in Amarillo, Texas, on July 20, 1943. His parents were the late Herman Newell Hewett and Opal Dunn Hewett. Judge Hewett graduated from Fort Smith Senior High School in 1961. Judge Hewett enjoyed a legal heritage: an uncle, Roy S. Dunn, served as a chancery judge in the chancery circuit that included Logan County and his cousin James M. Dunn was a Fort Smith attorney.

He married Judy Jay of Fort Smith, then a recent high school graduate, on Friday, January 28, 1966. He was to graduate from the University of Arkansas the very next day but due to an eight-inch snowfall, he was unable to attend; considerately, the University mailed his diploma to him. The following day the young couple set out for Houston, Texas, pulling a U-Haul trailer containing all their belongings. They resided there until 1969. During this time he was employed by Foley's Department Store as a buyer. In 1969 the Hewetts returned to Fort Smith and started a retail clothing business; later, they operated several Subway sandwich shops in the Fort Smith area. Tammy, their first child, was born February 1, 1968. The second child, Heather, was born November 11, 1970. The third and final child, Scott was born July 5, 1973. They are now proud grandparents.

Judge Hewett decided to go to law school in 1974. He graduated from the University of Arkansas with a Juris Doctor in 1976. He then began a private law practice with his friend and classmate Ron Harrison under the firm name of Harrison and Hewett. He continued his practice until he was elected to the position of circuit/chancery judge for the juvenile division of the 12th Judicial District in 1990 replacing Sherri Karber who, as previously indicated, was not eligible for election. Judge Hewett retired at the end of 2014, having reached the mandatory retirement age of seventy.

In 2002, Judge Hewett was recognized as the Juvenile Judge of the Year in the state of Arkansas. Judge Hewett is a past member of the Arkansas Trial Lawyers

Association and was on the board of governors for six years. He is presently a member of the Sebastian County Bar Association, the Arkansas Bar Association and the American Bar Association.

For many years Judge Hewett heard chancery, civil, and criminal cases as well as juvenile. Later he exclusively heard juvenile cases. A case presided over by Judge Hewett that was later considered by the Arkansas Court of Appeals is *Donna Snow Burks and Larry Burks vs. Arkansas Department of Human Services*, 76 Ark. App. 71, 61 S. W. 3d 184 (2001). This was a case involving the termination of parental rights pursuant to A.C.A. Sec. 9-27-341(b)(3).

On September 20,1996, the state's Department of Human Services (DHS) took custody of Joseph Burks, age 9 months. He had a broken leg and the story explaining the injury given by the mother was not consistent with the injury itself. DHS also took custody of Joseph's elder brother Larry Ray Burks, age 21 months. There emerged allegations of abuse by the father, Larry Burks. An agreed order was entered November 18, 1996, which found the children to be dependent and neglected, pursuant to Arkansas law. A case plan was instituted with the goal being reunification of the children with the family. As part of the plan, the parents were to do certain things. These included a psychological evaluation, completion of parenting classes, visiting regularly with the children and cooperating with the case worker. A review order was entered August 12, 1997 that returned the children to the parents but kept open a protective service case. A review order was entered in February, 1998 which found the parties had complied with the case plan.

On June 16, 1998, the mother reported that Mr. Burks had whipped the boys with a belt leaving bruises and that she had left Mr. Burks. A review hearing was held on June 30, 1998. Custody was continued with Mrs. Burks and she was ordered to have no contact with the father. Mr. Burks did not appear but was ordered to attend counseling for anger management and domestic violence issues.

A review hearing was held on December 1, 1998. Neither parent appeared. A warrant was issued for Mrs. Burk's arrest. She was picked up on January 28, 1999. The children were placed into the custody of DHS. At this time the couple's youngest child, William Burks age 1, was taken into custody as well. Review hearings were held throughout 1999, and Mrs. Burks was told not to have any contact with Mr. Burks and to report if she learned his whereabouts or talked to him. The last such order was January 6, 2000.

On February 15, 2000, DHS petitioned for termination of parental rights of both Mr. and Mrs. Burks. The children had been in DHS custody for over one year. A.C.A. section 9-27-341(b)(3)(i)(a) provides that parental rights can be

JUDGE MARK HEWETT
CIRCUIT JUDGE
1991-2014

PHOTO COURTESY OF MARK HEWETT

terminated where a juvenile has been adjudicated to be dependent-neglected and has continued out of the home for 12 months, despite a meaningful effort by the department to rehabilitate the home and correct the conditions which caused removal, and those conditions had not been remedied. There was no question but that this was the case.

The appeal was based on the fact that the children could claim Native American descent through the father. This meant that provisions of the federal Indian Child Welfare Act of 1978, a measure that governs the removal and out-of-home placement of American Indian children applied. This act requires a greater standard of proof as regards removal of the children and termination of the rights of the Indian parent. The decree was attacked on sufficiency of the evidence on behalf of the mother as well.

The decision reviewed the fact that the father had not complied with the last requirements of the court, i.e. that he undergo anger management and domestic violence counseling, had not visited with the children and had subsequently beaten the two older boys with a belt. Mrs. Burks, despite being ordered not to have contact with Mr. Burks, had maintained daily contact with him. She had been ordered to report to the court his whereabouts if she had contact with him. This she did not do. Mrs. Burks stated at the hearing that if DHS would get out of her life that she would reunite with Mr. Burks and return the children to the home. Based on this, the court affirmed Judge Hewett.

The significance of the issue of the Indian Child Welfare Act had to do with the degree of expertise held by the witnesses for the state. The act required that the testimony be from a witness having substantial experience in the delivery of child and family services to Indians, or a professional person having substantial education and experience in his or her specialty.

The expert witnesses were an occupational therapist and a counselor in domestic violence. The court allowed them to testify and ruled that their expertise was sufficient.

There was, however, a dissent, joined by one other appeals judge. The dissent was on the grounds that the witnesses were in truth not qualified under the act. The judges were also concerned that the state had been rushed to terminate by the terms of the act and DHS regulations concerning a child being in DHS care in excess of one year.

The next change in the judiciary of Sebastian County came about by Act 97 of 1991. This added a new chancery judgeship and converted the circuit/

chancery judgeship held by Judge Don Langston to a conventional circuit judge's position. This new position was filled by appointment by Governor Bill Clinton; John Van Winkle was the appointee. He was a Fort Smith attorney who had served as Sebastian County Democratic Chairman during Governor Clinton's 1990 reelection Campaign. For the first time, Clinton carried Sebastian County. He had memorably promised that if he carried the county, he would dance in the middle of Garrison Avenue. He did so, along with Hillary and John and Cathy Van Winkle. In July of 1991, John Van Winkle became chancery judge in the newly created Division III.

The addition of a new chancery judgeship created a problem of space. The Crawford County Courthouse had but one court room and the Sebastian County Courthouse had one chancery and one circuit along with the courtroom that was designed for the grand jury on the third floor that was being used by the juvenile court and the municipal court room on the second floor that was situated adjacent to the circuit court on the second floor. The courtroom in Greenwood was unavailable, since it was already shared by chancery, circuit and municipal courts. There were now seven judges sharing the trial court courtrooms. This was untenable. Sebastian and Crawford Counties entered into an agreement and space was rented for the new court at 200 Garrison Avenue in a newly renovated space that had been a hardware wholesale business known as Speer Hardware. There was a suite of offices for the new judge and a chancery and a circuit courtroom. The other judges used the court space as needed.

John Van Winkle was born December 18, 1951, at Fort Knox, Kentucky. He was the son of John L. and Kate Van Winkle. His father was a career military man. His parents divorced in 1953, when young John was two years old. His mother was employed by the Arkansas Forestry Commission until her retirement in 1985. He was raised in Conway and graduated from Conway High School in 1969. He attended The State College of Arkansas, now known as The University of Central Arkansas, and graduated in 1974 with a degree in sociology. He went to work for the Arkansas Mental Retardation-Developmental Disability Services from its Fort Smith office, as a case worker in a region covering six counties in western Arkansas. He decided to attend law school and did so from 1977 through 1980 when he obtained his Juris Doctor.

He began the practice of law in Fort Smith as a deputy prosecuting attorney for the 12th Judicial District. He entered private practice with Charles R. Garner, who was to succeed him as chancery judge, in 1981. He was in a partnership with Gary Person under the name of Person and Van Winkle from 1983 through 1986, and then in the firm of Sexton, Kirkpatrick, Nolan, Van Winkle and Caddell from 1986 through 1989. He was then in the firm of Hewett, Shock and Van Winkle from 1989 until his appointment as chancellor. The "Hewett"

JUDGE JOHN VAN WINKLE
CHANCERY JUDGE
1991-1992
PHOTO COURTESY OF SEBASTIAN COUNTY

in the last firm is Judge Mark Hewett, the now retired juvenile division circuit judge.

Judge Van Winkle resigned from the bench in 1992 to seek the congressional seat vacated by Congressman John Paul Hammerschmidt. He was unsuccessful in this attempt, defeated by Tim Hutchinson. Following the election he moved to Little Rock and practiced law with John Wesley Hall from 1992 through 1993. He then moved to Fayetteville and practiced with Jim Rose as Rose and Van Winkle through 2000. He practiced in Fayetteville until shortly before his death in 2021. Judge Van Winkle was listed in Who's Who of American Law; America and the World.

A case heard by Judge Van Winkle that was appealed to the Arkansas Supreme Court is *Sonya Howard and Morgan Cole vs. City of Fort Smith, Arkansas*, 311 Ark. 505, 845 S. W. 2d 497 (1993). This was a case testing the occupation tax collected by the city. The city had a policy of collecting the occupation tax and prorating it if the tax were paid for the first time in the second half of the year. In no case was the tax to be less than one-fourth of the annual license fee. The plaintiffs contended that the policy violated due process and equal protection and was unconstitutional.

Judge Van Winkle granted summary judgment for the city. The Supreme Court affirmed. They noted that the "rational basis" test was applicable. That is a basis for review of tax legislation. The appellate court must presume that the legislation is constitutional and that the tax is rationally related to achieving a legitimate governmental objective. It is the burden of those challenging the tax to overcome that presumption. The court also noted that the United States Supreme Court has held that the power to discriminate is inherent in the power to tax, and that courts should defer to legislative determinations. Governing bodies have always been given wide discretion in selecting the subjects of taxation. The court also held that for a tax classification to be struck down it must be shown that the classification was purely arbitrary and the discrimination invidious. In the present case all taxpayers paying the tax on the same day were treated the same. The reasons given by the city for prorating taxes paid in the latter half of the year but not those paid in the first half were uniformity and efficiency.

The court noted that the test for due process and equal protection were the same and did not discuss them separately. It noted also that a person attacking a tax on these grounds must disprove every conceivable basis which might support the tax. This they did not do and the policy of the city was upheld.

When Judge Van Winkle resigned to run for Congress in 1992, Governor Jim Guy Tucker appointed a retired lawyer from Fort Smith to succeed him. This was Charles R. Garner Sr. Charles Garner was born in Pine Bluff, Arkansas on January 21, 1921. He attended school there and graduated from high school in 1942. In April of that year he enlisted in the Army Air Corps and became a fighter pilot. He served in the Pacific Theater as a member of the Fifth Air Force, 82d Fighter Reconnaissance Squadron, 71st Reconnaissance Group, flying a Bell P-39 Airacobra. He was shot down and spent a year in the hospital in the Pacific. He earned the Purple Heart and the Air Medal. He was discharged from the service in 1950, with the rank of 1st Lieutenant.

Judge Garner attended the University of Arkansas School of Law on the GI Bill. While in school he served on the Law Review; he graduated in 1950. His first job following graduation was as a law clerk for Dr. Robert A. Leflar, one of his law professors, who at the time was serving as an associate justice on the Arkansas Supreme Court. Dr. Leflar was later dean emeritus of the law school and a recognized authority on tort law, conflicts of law, and taught appellate judges throughout the country.

Judge Garner then went into private practice and served as deputy prosecuting attorney for the judicial district covering Polk, Howard, Pike, Little River and Sevier Counties. In 1952, he moved to Fort Smith and went into practice with Hugh Hardin in the firm of Hardin, Jesson and Barton. He left the firm after eight years and set up his own practice in which he trained several young lawyers. In 1969, he served as a delegate to the Constitutional Convention under his old mentor Dr. Robert A. Leflar who chaired the convention. He was also selected as an outstanding alumnus of the University of Arkansas School of Law. He retired in 1982.

One of the lawyers he mentored was Eddie N. Christian Jr. Christian recalled at the time of Judge Garner's death that the Judge had once told him, "If you tell someone you're going to be there at noon with a dollar, you be there at 11:30 with two dollars." He was a person who really enjoyed the practice of law. Former Chancellor Warren Kimbrough said of him, "He could do it in a pleasant and jovial way. He could keep people's attention when presenting a case." Eddie Christian recalled a defense argument in a capital murder case: "His closing argument was beyond a doubt the best argument I've ever heard urging someone to exercise mercy and compassion for someone that had no mercy or compassion. He was just one hell of an advocate."

Judge Garner loved to hunt, fish and spend time with his family. He had two sons, Charles R. "Bud" Garner Jr. who was a lawyer in Fort Smith, and Chip. Judge Garner was married more than once, but his wife Sandy was the love of his life. They were a close and devoted couple. Judge Garner was proud to be able to serve as chancery judge following Judge Van Winkle's resignation. According to Eddie Christian, "He sort of felt he was giving something back to the profession that had been so good to him." He once more served the profession by filling in

Judge Charles R. Garner
Chancery Judge
1992
PHOTO COURTESY OF SANDY GARNER

for his successor, Judge Jim Spears, while Judge Spears was undergoing chemotherapy in 1994.

Judge Garner died on July 2, 1995, in Hot Springs, Arkansas, of a heart attack. He is buried in the Fort Smith National Cemetery.

A case heard by Judge Garner that was appealed to Arkansas Supreme Court is *Arkansas Department of Human Services vs. Robert Hardy*, 316 Ark. 119, 871 S. W. 2 352 (1994). The facts of this case are that Robert Hardy, at the time the commander of the Fort Smith Air National Guard unit, fathered a child by one Brenda Elliot who at the time was married to another man. She maintained that her husband was the father of the child born on February 8, 1986. She was then divorced and her husband was found not to be the father of the child. No action was filed seeking to hold Mr. Hardy to be the father until September 24, 1991. The child was by then five years old.

The case garnered a great deal of interest by the local newspaper due to Mr. Hardy's prominent position in the community. Judge Garner attempted to bar the press from the proceedings and sealed the final order. In that order he set child support at $300 per month rather than the amount mandated by the Supreme Court guidelines of $824 per month. He justified the deviation by stating that the child qualified for Medicaid, dental and hospital insurance, the mother had only requested $300 per month and that the father-son relationship would never exist between the man and boy. Judge Garner also did not allow any back child support (the case was decided by the trial court in 1993, and the child would by this time have been entitled to seven years of back child support).

The court first discussed the sealing of the final order. This it found to be erroneous. The court mentioned the difficulty that this had caused the court in determining if the order was final and appealable. The court said there was no authority for doing what Judge Garner did. It stated:

> "One of the basic principles of a democracy is the people have a right to know what is done in their courts. Correlative of this principle is the vital function of the press to subject the judicial process to extensive public scrutiny and comment. Secret orders could defeat this synergy of the people's right and the press's function, especially in cases in which the state is a party, as in this case......"

The court went on to state that there are exceptions such as adoption records and protective orders concerning trade secrets but that none of those applied here. Obviously, Judge Garner had sought to spare Colonel Hardy the embarrassment of the publicity the newspaper wanted to give him.

The court then discussed the amount of child support set by Judge Garner. They reversed on this issue and said that the amount called for in the child support chart could only be deviated from for the reasons stated in the court's *per curiam* order. It also disputed the finding by Judge Garner that the mother had only requested $300 per month. She had requested this amount for back child support but asked for $824, the amount called for in the chart, for future support. The reasoning of Judge Garner was also disputed in his determination that the child support should be lessened due to the child receiving Medicaid: "It would be incongruous to hold that a father is relieved of child support because his child is receiving public assistance as a result of the father's failure to pay the full amount of child support." The court did, however, affirm Judge Garner in his determination that no back child support should be awarded. It concluded that the circumstances of the case could not be said to warrant that the findings of the chancellor were against the preponderance of the evidence. The court also ordered the support to be paid by means of income withholding and ordered the father to provide health insurance.

At this point, the author begs the indulgence of readers. He has reached the place in this chronicle of the split jurisdictions of Sebastian County where he himself enters the narrative. Rather than reveal all he knows about the subject of this section, he has instead opted to skim lightly over his personal biography, preferring to focus on his time on the bench and what led up to that service. More detailed biographical information may be found in the author's profile at the end of this book; he hopes that you will rejoin him there.

In 1992, Jim D. Spears was elected to the Division III chancery court position; he took office January 1, 1993. Spears was born March 5, 1946, in Fayetteville, Arkansas, grew up in Fort Smith and attended Fort Smith Junior College and Arkansas Polytechnic, graduating with a dual major in History and Political Science. In 1970, he enrolled in the University of Arkansas School of Law, graduating in 1973. He spent several years in private practice until, in late 1980, he was named a Special Assistant Federal Public Defender for the Cuban refugees at Fort Chaffee. In 1982 he returned to private practice before being named Administrative Law Judge for the Arkansas Worker's Compensation Commission in May 1983. He held this position until January 1, 1993 when he was sworn in as chancery judge, division III, of the 12th Judicial District.

JUDGE JIM SPEARS
CHANCERY JUDGE 1993-2001
CIRCUIT JUDGE 2001-2016
PHOTO COURTESY OF JIM SPEARS

Judge Spear's term of service on the chancery bench was punctuated by another in the series of mishaps befalling the county's seats of justice. On the night of Sunday, April 21, 1996, the court complex at 200 Garrison Avenue came to an unexpected demise. Like the courthouse in Greenwood in 1968, it was struck by a tornado. Judge Spears was soundly sleeping following a day's work in the yard; he knew nothing of the storm when he awoke on Monday morning. He noticed when he rose that the television cable was out and the newspaper had not been delivered. The radio, however, told the tale: KUAF, the University of Arkansas public radio station, reported that a killer tornado had hit Fort Smith the night before. A subsequent telephone call from his mother announced to the judge that his sister was out of surgery: Her house in Van Buren had been destroyed and she had been critically injured after having been thrown through the air into a neighbor's back yard.

As the shock of the events was absorbed, Spears made his way to downtown Fort Smith. The city looked as if it had been bombed. There was much damage from peripheral storms along the way. Fallen trees and tree limbs littered Free Ferry Road. The downtown near the west end was devastated. The 200 Garrison complex suffered extensive damage to the third floor and the building at the corner of Third and Garrison had extensive damage as did the building next door. Bricks littered the street and a van that had been parked in front of 200 Garrison was crushed under fallen bricks. The court complex was intact on the second floor but the sprinkler system was running and ran for many hours before it could be disconnected, rendering the court room, chambers and offices unusable. Without a place to hold court, Judge Spears and his staff were given space by Willard Smith, a lawyer who owned an office building across Parker Street from the courthouse.

The 3rd division court remained without a permanent courtroom until July 1997, when the county refurbished the 5th floor of the Garrison Building at 523 Garrison Avenue (previously known as the Ward Hotel) and leased this space for the courts. The courtroom fixtures that had been at 200 Garrison were placed there after much repair work due to the water damage from the tornado. Ultimately, in 2008 Judge Spears, along with the other circuit judges, moved to the new Sebastian County Courts Building. He served there until the end of 2016 when he retired, having reached the mandatory retirement age of seventy.

A case heard and decided by Judge Spears that was later appealed to the Arkansas Supreme Court was *Linder vs. Linder*, 348 Ark. 322, 72 S. W. 3d 841 (2002). This was and remains the leading case in Arkansas jurisprudence concerning grandparental visitation rights in light of the United States Supreme Court's ruling in *Troxel vs. Granville*, 530 U.S. 57 (2000).

The facts of this case are as follow: The father of a minor, one Brandon Linder, died in a four-wheeler accident while hunting. The mother, Lea Ann, lived with the deceased and their child Brandon in a family compound-like community in Crawford County. Shortly after her husband's death Lea Ann Linder moved from the family compound to Fort Smith. After this relocation, she began to resist requests made by her father-in law, Bill Linder, to visit with Brandon, his grandson, always with stated justification or pretext. Frustrated, Bill Linder brought an action seeking court-ordered grandparental visitation. This relief was granted and some visits occurred, but they became the pretext for a battle of wills between the mother and the grandfather. When visits occurred, Lea Ann interfered by calling at all hours, spying on the grandfather when he took Brandon to the fair and continued to find excuses for cancelling or blocking requested grandparental visits. On occasion, police involvement was needed for the visits to happen. This led to several court appearances. At no time was evidence presented that contact with the grandparent was not in the best interest of the child (the standard set out in the Arkansas grandparent visitation statute).

Following one court appearance Lea Ann Linder, the family unit—Brandon, Lea Ann, her mother and her sister—all disappeared. The Fort Smith house was sold, and the mother left no forwarding contact information; in short, she had evidently "done a runner." Judge Spears issued an *ex parte* order changing custody of the child to the grandfather on a temporary basis. This allowed the grandfather to seek a warrant for the mother, grandmother and aunt on the charge of interference with custody and a Federal charge of interstate flight.

The Sebastian County Sheriff's Department and the FBI conducted an intense investigation seeking the whereabouts of the family. They nevertheless remained on the run for 18 months. The grandmother and aunt eventually returned to Fort Smith and were arrested. A petition was filed in the chancery court and the grandmother and aunt were granted immunity from the criminal charges, both state and Federal. Initially they refused, however, to reveal the whereabouts of Lea Ann and Brandon. They were then placed in jail and decided, overnight, to talk. Acting upon their information, the FBI took custody of Brandon and Lea Ann in Ohio. They had been on a cross-country odyssey to avoid the court order for grandparental visitation; Lea Ann had remarried and had changed the child's name to her maiden name.

When they were returned the court ordered intensive psychological investigation of the situation. Lea Ann claimed that her late husband had warned her to not let his father have anything to do with the child in the event anything ever happened to him. She was focused on this to the point of irrationality, in the opinion of the court. She also attacked the constitutionality of the act under which the grandparent's visitation had been awarded (it is worth noting that the

Troxel decision had been issued by the U.S. Supreme Court during the time she was evading Arkansas authorities; this ruling affirmed that there exists, under the Fourteenth Amendment, a fundamental right of a parent to oversee the care, custody and control of his or her child). The trial court ultimately returned custody of the child to the mother since she had taken good care of the child and was a good mother except for her irrationality concerning the grandfather. The court-ordered visitation was continued and the Troxel case distinguished from the one at bar. Unsurprisingly, this finding was appealed.

On appeal the state Supreme Court did not find the distinctions found by the trial court to be persuasive. They cited the Troxel decision and recited those findings. The court found that such Arkansas law as applied as applied constituted an intrusion on the parent-child relationship. The interest of parents in the care, custody, and control of their children was perhaps the oldest of fundamental liberty interests recognized by the court. "Liberty," protected by the Due Process clause, includes the right of parents to establish a home, bring up their children, and to control their education. This also includes deciding with whom the children shall visit. This even includes grandparents. Once a parent has been determined "fit," any decisions made by the parent are presumed to be proper. Arkansas's grandparent visitation law, much like the Washington statute questioned in the Troxel case, made no provision for presuming the decisions of the parent to be in the child's best interest. The decision of Judge Spears was reversed and dismissed and the statute held unconstitutional in part and as applied in this case. The Arkansas General Assembly later enacted a new law to allow grandparent visitation that they hoped would comply with both the Linder and Troxel decisions.

Act 900 of 1995
Twelfth Judicial Circuit
Sebastian County

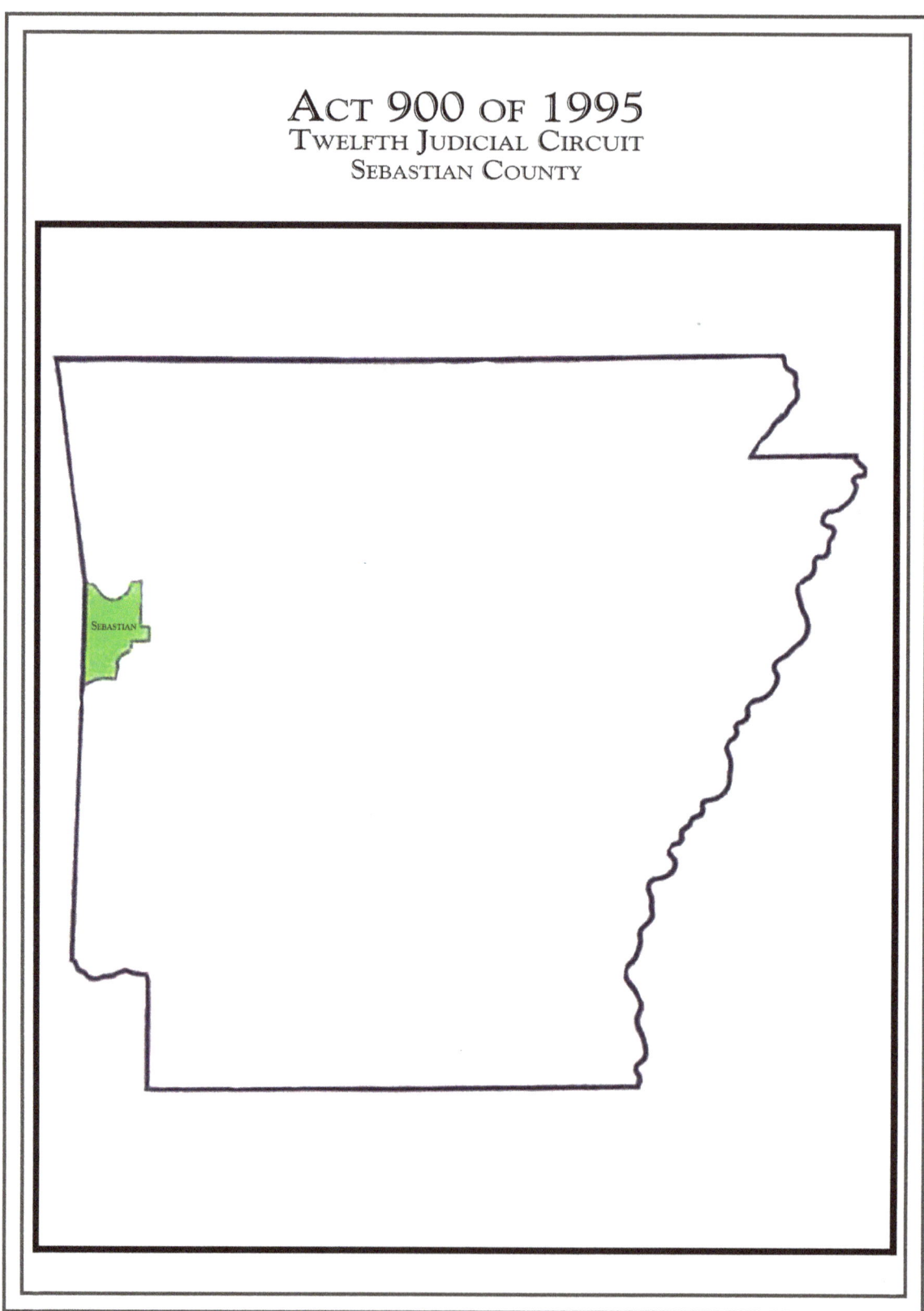

CHAPTER NINE

New Faces, a New District and a New Judicial Article

Some in Crawford County had not been happy when the 10th Chancery Circuit and the 12th Judicial Circuit were combined into the 12th Judicial District. The boundaries of that district were determined to be those of Sebastian and Crawford Counties. In the past Crawford County had always been the dominant county in the circuit of which they were part. That meant that usually, the circuit judge and prosecuting attorney were Crawford County residents. That was no longer the case after the new district was established in 1977. Parochialism reigned, as well as a fear of loss of "identity." The lawyers of Crawford County also feared that they would be at a disadvantage in any election for judicial office due to the disparity in population between the two counties. This was proven baseless by the election, unopposed, of Judge David Partain who had been the sitting circuit judge of the former 15th Judicial District and, subsequently, of Floyd "Pete" Rogers over Bob Boyer, a popular Sebastian County Judge and appointed trial judge, to the position following Judge Partain's retirement.

An earlier, unsuccessful attempt was made to separate Crawford from the 12th Judicial District. However, after Arkansas adopted term limits, it left Crawford with a very able and successful state senator, Morril Harriman. Sebastian County had no comparable legislator to counter this power. As a favor to his attorney constituents, Harriman pushed through Act 900 of 1995. This established the 21st Judicial District, composed of a single county: Crawford! The 12th Judicial District was once again, also composed of a single county: Sebastian. Judge Floyd "Pete" Rogers was designated a circuit/chancery judge and served as the sole judge in the 21st District for some time.

The 12th Judicial District, following the creation of the 21st District, had six judges: Judge Holland, and Judge Langston, circuit judges; Judge Hewett, juvenile judge, and Judges Kimbrough, Foltz and Spears, chancellors. Electoral change and retirement were soon to take their toll. At the end of 1996, Judge Warren Kimbrough reached the age of mandatory retirement. That was the only way he would have left office absent death or electoral defeat. He adored being a judge and was miserable in his retirement.

The person elected to be his replacement in Division I of chancery court was Norman Wilkinson, who took office as of January 1, 1997. Judge Wilkinson was born May 30, 1955. He is the son of the late Norman Means Wilkinson and Betty Wilkinson of Greenwood, Arkansas. He has three siblings, Stanhope, Susan and Edward. The family has been in the banking business since his grandfather, William Norman Wilkinson, founded The Farmers Bank in 1907. His grandmother was the former Myrtle Means. Judge Wilkinson was educated in the Greenwood Public Schools and was the salutatorian of his graduating class. He received his BS/BA in accounting from the University of Arkansas in 1976, graduating with high honors. Following his graduation he passed the entire CPA examination on his first attempt and worked for a multinational accounting firm in Tulsa, Oklahoma for two years. While working full time, he attended law school at night at The University of Tulsa until he transferred to The University of Arkansas at Fayetteville for his final year. He earned his law degree from that institution in 1980. He established a law practice in Fort Smith following his graduation from law school.

Judge Wilkinson enjoyed a heritage in the lawn as his father was admitted to the bar in 1931 (this was before his career in publishing, banking, and service in the state legislature). The senior Mr. Wilkinson was a state representative from 1931-41. He served as the speaker of the Arkansas House of Representatives in 1941 prior to his service in the Navy in World War II. Judge Wilkinson's brother Edward carried on the family tradition of legislative service to the state having served in the Arkansas House of Representatives and the Arkansas Senate. Ed is now president of the bank and Judge Wilkinson's brother Stanhope is the CEO. His mother Betty is the chairman of the board. His mother is a former schoolteacher in the Hartford and Greenwood school districts. The bank received a statewide award from Governor Mike Huckabee and the Department of Volunteerism in 2000. This recognized the bank and the Wilkinson family for their years of serving others and enhancing the quality of life for the citizens of the state.

Judge Wilkinson is the father of three children, Christine, Jeffrey and Jenny. He is the grandfather of five, Callie Davis, Casey Davis, Cooper Davis, Hunter Wilkinson and Hayley Wilkinson. His hobby at one time was running.

Judge Norman Wilkinson
Chancery Judge 1997-2001
Circuit Judge 2001-2007
photo courtesy of Norman Wilkinson

He competed three times in the Boston Marathon. At his age, this required him to complete the 26.2 miles in 3 hours and 30 minutes to even qualify. In January 2007 Judge Wilkinson announced that he would leave the bench effective February 1, 2007 in order to join the family banking business full time.

A case that was heard and decided by Judge Wilkinson and later appealed to the Arkansas Supreme Court is *Linda Chapman vs. Elnora Bevilacqua, et. al*, 344 Ark. 262, 42 S. W. 3d 378 (2001).

The facts of the case are as follow: The city of Fort Smith, in the years 1997 and 1998, received from the federal government Community Block Grants and Home Funds for the rehabilitation of urban dwellings owned by qualifying individuals who applied for the grants. The city, as the implementing agency, carried out the housing rehabilitation programs pursuant to federal and state laws, allowing municipalities, counties or established housing authorities to redevelop urban or rural areas suffering from unsafe, unsanitary, or blighted conditions as determined by federal guidelines. Under the program, when granted money was used, the property was subject to a recorded guarantee that the rehabilitated housing unit would be used for income-eligible occupants for five years. The city conducted the disbursement of the federal funds so that none of the money involved would be paid directly to the homeowner or to the repair contractor, whose names were both included on the grant checks. This policy allowed the beneficiary of the funds to be the dwelling itself and thus the community, guaranteeing that the repairs and renovations were made. The contractor would submit his bill to the program supervisor who, in turn, would request a drawdown of funds from the United States Department of Housing and Urban Development. The program supervisor was paid with federal monies as well. The funds would be placed in dedicated accounts and checks issued to the contractor and homeowner jointly.

One Linda Chapman, represented by Fort Smith attorney Oscar Stilley, filed suit against 32 private homeowners seeking to recover from them the value of repairs or rehabilitations of their private property that had been accomplished through these federally funded programs. Specifically, she sought as a taxpayer to recover for the city those monies paid to the defendants for rehabilitation of their homes because, she implied, the money had been unlawfully expended from the city's general fund and the county treasury, alleging a violation of Article 12, section 5 of the Arkansas Constitution. She asserted that the payment of these funds constituted an illegal exaction (expenditure of public money) and that the defendants should be required to repay the monies.

The City of Fort Smith intervened in the suit and after much discovery filed a motion for summary judgment; Chapman filed a cross-motion for summary judgment. Summary judgment was granted in favor of the defendants and the city.

In his ruling on summary judgment, Judge Wilkinson ruled that Chapman did not have standing to bring the suit. The Supreme Court agreed. It ruled that to bring such a suit it must be shown that she had a financial interest in the funds. These were, however, dedicated federal funds, not co-mingled with other funds. They also noted that she had not shown that the funds, if misapplied, would have to be repaid from public funds. Judge Wilkinson also ruled that the small amount of city funds used in administration did not give Chapman standing. The funds expended on this project were merely the salaries paid to city staff for the time spent writing the checks. This was said to be 30 minutes to 2 hours per week. Judge Wilkinson ruled that this was *de minimus* (that is, too little to be of concern). The Supreme Court disagreed, stating that there was not a *de minimus* exception to an illegal exaction. However, the opinion held, this was not to be taken to mean that there had been in this case an illegal exaction.

Chapman's challenge to the expenditure of general funds to write the checks was based on Article 12 section 5 of the Arkansas Constitution which states, *"No county, city, town or other municipal corporation shall become a stockholder in any company, association or corporation; or obtain or appropriate money for, or loan its credit to, any corporation, association, institution or individual."* The court in response cited precedent and the statute authorizing urban redevelopment programs and plans, pointing out that the plans had already been designated as public purposes for which public monies might lawfully be expended. This type of expenditure was for the public welfare and not for individual enrichment and therefore did not violate the constitutional prohibition. There was, therefore, no illegal exaction and the ruling of Judge Wilkinson was affirmed.

At the end of 1998, Judge John Holland retired after 23 years of service. His successor was James Robert Marschewski. Judge Marschewski was born in Helena, Arkansas, on August 14, 1946. He graduated from Central High School in Helena in 1964. He first attended college at Arkansas State University at Jonesboro, where he played football, from 1964 through 1965. He left school to join the U.S. Army at the height of the Vietnam War because he felt a responsibility to serve; he was in uniform from 1966 through 1969 and served in Vietnam from 1967 to 1969.

And serve he did: As a 21-year-old lieutenant during the Tet Offensive, he was leading a depleted platoon of about 20 soldiers on a sweep in an area recently hit by the North Vietnamese. They came under attack and shrapnel from a rocket

Judge James R. Marschewski
Circuit Judge
1999-2006
photo courtesy of James Marschewski

tore through his left arm and shoulder. In shock and operating on adrenaline, he didn't realize that he had been hit until he saw the grotesque wound which required 10 surgeries over the next 25 years. Despite his injuries, Marschewski and another soldier were able to call in an artillery strike to suppress the enemy fire so the platoon could be evacuated. This came shortly after he had written his soon-to-be wife not to worry because he knew what he was doing! As a result of his service he was awarded the Silver Star, the Bronze Star with V for Valor, the Purple Heart, the Vietnam Service Medal, the Vietnam Campaign Medal and the Combat Infantryman's Badge. The Silver Star is the third highest award given by the Army for heroism. He and his fiancé Judy Jensen of Little Rock were married on August 24, 1968.

Following his military service, he completed his education on the GI Bill. He attended the University of Arkansas in Fayetteville and graduated with a BSBA in accounting in 1971. He obtained a Juris Doctorate from the John Marshall Law School in Chicago, Illinois in 1974. Marschewski first practiced law in Chicago from 1974 through 1978, then in Russellville, Arkansas, through 1986. As part of his practice he was a deputy prosecuting attorney from 1980 through 1984 and chief deputy prosecutor from 1984 until 1986. He became the Public Defender for Sebastian County in 1987 and served until his election as circuit judge in 1998. He served in that capacity from January 1, 1999. Judge and Mrs. Marschewski have four sons, Joe, Jeff, Jess and Chad. Mrs. Marschewski was an eighth-grade teacher in the Greenwood schools. In June of 2006, Judge Marschewski was selected to serve as the Magistrate of the United States District Court for the Western District of Arkansas. He assumed those duties January 3, 2007.

A case heard in Judge Marschewski's court and later appealed to the Arkansas Supreme Court was *Oscar Stilley vs. Margaret James, et.al*, 345 Ark. 362, 48 S. W. 3d 521 (2001). This was a case wherein Fort Smith attorney Oscar Stilley was himself the defendant; this was the same Oscar Stilley who, with Linda Chapman, had earlier sued the recipients of federal block grant funds administered by the city, which Stilley had attempted to style as illegal exactions. In this case, Judge Marschewski granted a summary judgment against Stilley because of an indemnity agreement he signed with a client who was a co-defendant in a malicious prosecution case. Prior to the Supreme Court hearing this case, it was forced to rule on a motion brought by Stilley asking that the entire Supreme Court recuse itself; this they refused to do.

The case started with a suit filed by Stilley on behalf of one John Speed, who had been fired by the Western Arkansas Chapter of the American Red Cross. Speed's suit was for non-payment of vacation pay and other compensatory time. The Red Cross counterclaimed alleging that Speed had made personal purchases on Red Cross credit cards. Stilley asserted that the claims against Speed were without merit and orally promised that he would pay any judgment taken against Speed. Speed lost on his suit and on the counterclaim. A $4000 judgment was entered against Speed and Stilley paid it.

The individual defendants in Speed's counterclaim then filed suit for malicious prosecution against Speed and Stilley. Although Stilley had a conflict of interest, he continued to represent himself and Speed. About a month before the matter was set for trial, Speed became concerned about the conflict and consulted an attorney, Mike Spades. Speed considered hiring his own lawyer. When advised of this potential course of action, Stilley agreed to indemnify Speed for any judgment if he would allow Stilley to continue representing him and that Speed would forego requesting a continuance. Spades prepared an indemnity agreement and Stilley signed it. The indemnity agreement specifically referenced the malicious prosecution lawsuit and stated that Stilley received "$10 and other good and valuable consideration." Stilley agreed to "indemnify and hold harmless the defendant, John Speed, for any damages assessed, apportioned, or otherwise charged to the co-defendant John Speed whether such damages are assessed, apportioned, or charged individually, or jointly and severally against John Speed and the co-defendant Oscar Stilley." Stilley also agreed to pay any such judgment in a timely manner, to protect Speed's credit rating and dignity.

At trial the suit was terminated, insofar as Stilley was concerned, by summary judgment. However, a judgment was returned by the jury against Speed for $200,000. Speed accordingly made demand on Stilley to pay the judgment; Stilley refused. The judgment creditors learned of the indemnity agreement and they too made demand on Stilley for payment. Again, Stilley refused. They then filed an action for declaratory judgment against Stilley. In light of the language of the written contract, and the undisputed facts of a judgment, with no surety bond having been posted, they moved for summary judgment. Stilley also filed a motion for summary judgment, claiming that there was no consideration for the indemnity agreement.

Judge Marschewski granted summary judgment against Stilley. He determined that Speed's decision to allow Stilley to represent both co-defendants, and thereby control the litigation, constituted consideration. Speed had filed no appeal. The court noted that there was no legal requirement for Speed to do so. It was not required by the indemnity agreement. The Supreme Court noted that Stilley could have done so on his own behalf since he had a pecuniary interest in the lawsuit due to the agreement. Judge Marschewski also ruled that the judgment creditors could bring the suit for collection of the judgment against Stilley since they were third-party beneficiaries of the indemnity agreement.

The Supreme Court affirmed Judge Marschewski in all respects and referred the matter of Oscar Stilley to the Arkansas Judiciary's Committee on Professional Conduct for any appropriate action.

The election year of 1998 brought about a rare contested judicial election involving an incumbent judge. Judge Don Langston had become the subject of a series of articles in *The Southwest Times Record* concerning his using the Town Club membership of a local lawyer and favorable rulings concerning that lawyer. He had also incurred the wrath of some of the defense bar concerning some of his rulings. Opposing him in the election was J. Michael Fitzhugh, the former Republican United States Attorney. Fitzhugh was victorious and became the first Republican elected circuit judge in Sebastian County since Reconstruction. He also was the last Republican so elected as Amendment 80 to the Arkansas Constitution of 1874 was adopted in 2000, making the office of circuit judge a non-partisan position. On January 1, 1999, Sebastian County and the 12th Judicial District had two newly elected circuit judges, Judge Jim Marschewski and Judge Mike Fitzhugh.

Judge Fitzhugh was born August 5, 1947, in Little Rock, Arkansas. He is the son of Vernon and Clara Fitzhugh. He was raised in Fayetteville and graduated from Fayetteville High School in 1965. He attended the University of Arkansas and graduated in 1969 with a BA. He attended the University of Arkansas School of Law and earned his Juris Doctorate in December 1972. In May 1973 he became law clerk for Senior United States District Judge of the Eastern District of Arkansas, J. Smith Henley. In May 1974 he became an Assistant United States Attorney for the Western District of Arkansas and moved to Fort Smith. He served in this position until November 1985 when he was appointed United States Attorney for the Western District of Arkansas to replace Asa Hutchinson who had resigned to run for the United States Senate against Dale Bumpers. He served in this position until August 1993 when President Bill Clinton appointed P. K. Holmes as United States Attorney in the new administration. Fitzhugh then entered private practice with the firm of Bethell, Callaway, Robertson, Beasley and Cowan as a partner. In 1998, he was elected circuit judge. Judge Fitzhugh is married to Ann, who was, until her retirement, a teacher and coach in the Fort Smith School District. They have three children, Jason, Ashley, and Alex. Judge Fitzhugh reached mandatory retirement age and left office at the end of 2020. He was replaced by Judge Gunner Delay.

A case heard by Judge Fitzhugh that was later appealed to the Arkansas Supreme Court is *James Richard Halford vs. State of Arkansas*, 342 Ark. 80,

Judge J. Michael Fitzhugh
Circuit Judge
1999-2020

photo courtesy of J Michael Fitzhugh

27 S. W. 3d 346 (2000). Halford was convicted of aggravated robbery and sentenced to life in prison as a habitual criminal with five previous felony convictions in Texas.

On April 15, 1998, one Everett Tolton, age 58, pulled into the driveway of his residence in Fort Smith for lunch and found a red Ford Escort station wagon parked there. He thought it might be his sister-in-law's car. He walked to the front door of his house and found it locked. He unlocked the door and went inside. After he said, "Hello, is anyone here?", he heard a voice behind him say, "Hit the floor." He turned and saw a person behind him who said, "Hit the floor I said, I will kill you." The intruder was wielding a knife. Tolton fell to the floor and the intruder, who was later identified as Halford, tied his hands behind his back. After taking the money from Tolton's wallet and a gold ring, Halford told Tolton that he had to kill him. He turned Tolton over and began stabbing him in the face and ears. He next tried to choke him saying, "Give it up old man, you can't fight me." He added, "Goodbye." Tolton freed his hands and grabbed Halford in the groin. He then grabbed the knife and backed Halford up into the entrance way of the house, at which time Halford began kicking him. Tolton fled the house, but while in the yard, Halford hit him on the head with an iron skillet. Tolton passed out for a few minutes. When he came to, Halford had fled. Tolton then called 911.

On appeal, Halford raised the issue of photographs that had been introduced depicting blood stains on the carpet and of Mr. Tolton after the attack. The admission of multiple photographs, he contended, was to "get more blood in front of the jury." They were excessive, he maintained, and the unfair prejudicial nature of the photographs outweighed their probative value. The Supreme Court disagreed. They stated that the photographs were all at a different angle, either of the scene or of Tolton, and therefore not cumulative and excessive. They also noted that the judge considered each of the photos and their possible effect on the jury; he had not simply admitted them *carte blanche*. This was deemed permissible since the photographs served a valid evidentiary purpose rather than simply inflaming the jury.

The next issue for appeal was the court's refusal to allow the defendant's counsel to question Patricia Payne, a witness for the state, regarding her husband's incarceration and warrants out for her brother. Judge Fitzhugh ruled it not relevant. He did permit counsel to question concerning any promises made to the witness for her testimony. This, counsel did not do. Judge Fitzhugh was affirmed.

As one of his last appointments, Governor Mike Huckabee named Sebastian County Prosecutor Steve Tabor circuit judge to replace Judge Marschewski who was, as noted earlier named Federal Magistrate (the Hon. Gunner Delay, who now serves as circuit judge, was picked to replace Tabor as prosecutor). Soon after Tabor took office, Judge Norman Wilkinson announced that he was leaving the judiciary to work for Farmers Bank. Newly elected Governor Mike Beebe then appointed James O. Cox to replace Wilkinson. These appointments were effective until the next general election. While neither could run to succeed himself, each could run for the other position—and this they successfully did. Judge Tabor is currently the administrative judge; Judge Cox reached mandatory retirement age and retired at the end of 2020.

Stephen Merrill Tabor was born May 3, 1956, at Sparks Hospital in Fort Smith Arkansas. He is the youngest of four children and has two brothers and a sister. His father, Merrill Tabor, served in World War II as a machine gunner in the army and was wounded in the shoulder and hand during operations on Okinawa. His mother, Maxine Myers Tabor, was the youngest of six children raised on a farm deep in the Ozarks in Madison County Arkansas near Marble. Maxine's mother died when Maxine was eight and the young girl became responsible for cooking the meals for the family and the farm hands working the fields.

Judge Tabor attended Fort Smith Public Schools including Belle Pointe and Fairview Elementary, Ramsey Junior High and Southside High School graduating in 1974. He next attended Arkansas State University in Jonesboro. He graduated in 1978 with honors. His degree is in history. Judge Tabor then pursued a law degree at the University of Arkansas School of Law in Fayetteville and obtained his Juris Doctor in 1981. Following his admission to the bar, he was interested in but one job and that was with the office of the prosecuting attorney in the 12th Judicial District. He began work there in August of that year. He remained in that position for fifteen and a half years. He rose to the position of chief deputy and only left after his boss, Prosecuting Attorney Ron Fields, was defeated for re-election. Following Field's defeat Tabor practiced law with him and other former deputies for six years. When the office of prosecutor became vacant, he ran and was elected to the job he had wanted for many years getting 61% of the vote. He was re-elected without opposition in 2006 but was appointed circuit judge before the commencement of that term. As earlier discussed he ran for the circuit judge position to which James Cox had been appointed and was elected.

Judge Tabor has two children, Stephen Andrew and Sarah Elizabeth. He is married to Becky Tabor who is the administrator of the Sebastian County drug court. He has been active in civic affairs including volunteer work at the Fort Smith Boys and Girls Club since age six. In his adult years he has served as a board member. He is a graduate of the Leadership Fort Smith class of 1997 and

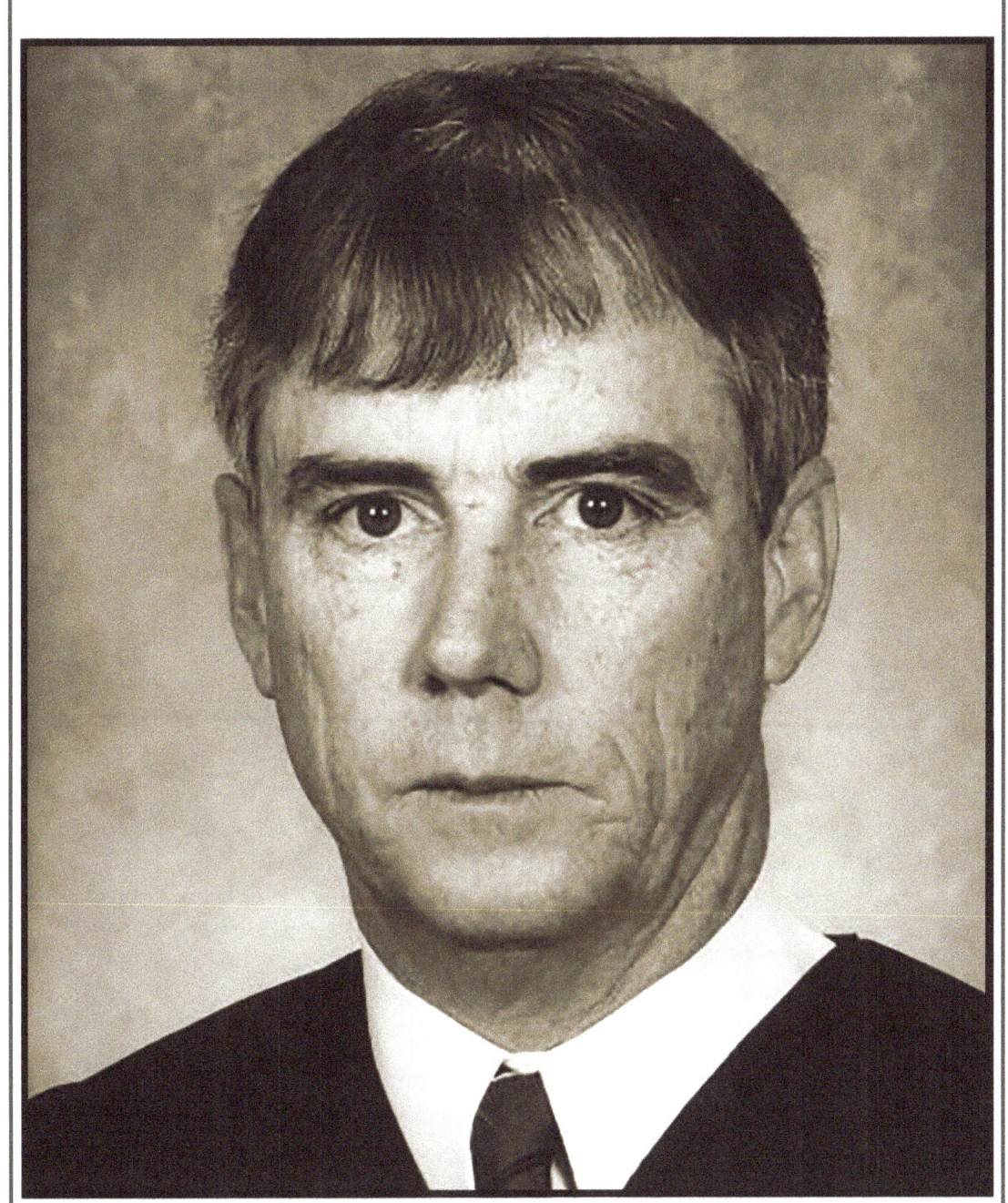

JUDGE STEPHEN MERRILL TABOR
CIRCUIT JUDGE
2007-PRESENT
PHOTO COURTESY OF STEPHEN TABOR

has served as a lecturer and presenter for that group as well. He has served as a Scout leader and is active as a board member and Sunday school teacher at his church, Cavanaugh Free Will Baptist. Judge Tabor is very family-oriented and enjoys golf, fishing and reading.

James Oldham Cox was born at St. Edward Hospital in Fort Smith, Arkansas, on July 20, 1950. He is the son of James B. and Josephine Markham Cox. His parents met when his father was a student at Oklahoma City University, attending on the G.I. Bill, and his mother was a professor. Both had been in the Navy during World War II: James B. had been an aviation instructor at Pensacola until the war started winding down, then was transferred to Portland, Oregon, assigned him to the Shore Patrol. This caused him to lose interest in his military career and, following his discharge, returned to his hometown of Waldron in Scott County Arkansas along with his wife and young daughter.

James B. began work at the *Advance Reporter*, a family-owned newspaper. Following his divorce from his first wife, Cox then used his GI Bill benefits as earlier noted. He returned to Waldron with the new Mrs. Cox and he and his brothers ran the paper and he raised Angus cattle. Judge Cox's mother began teaching at the Waldron High School and had a career there that stretched over twenty years. In the 1960s the Cox family sold the paper in Waldron to Ferrell Faubus, son of Governor Orval Faubus, and Mr. Cox went into the real estate business.

Judge Cox is a product of the Waldron school system, graduating in 1968. He was a good student. A member of the Beta Club, he played in the band and attended Boys State. Following high school he attended Hendrix College in Conway. When he was about to graduate from Hendrix he received his draft notice: His number in the lottery was 23. Although he had been accepted into The University of Arkansas School of Law in Fayetteville, he joined the U.S. Army instead with a contract to attend Officer Candidate School. The day he graduated from basic training at Fort Jackson, South Carolina, The Paris Peace Accords were signed. The Army evidently decided they had enough second lieutenants and his OCS class was cancelled. He was discharged honorably at the convenience of the government.

He was dating a Fort Smith girl, Patti Shields, at the time. Shields was a student at Hendrix. Cox was given the option of attending law school in Little Rock and he took it to be closer to her. He attended the University of Arkansas School of Law in Little Rock from 1973-77. He was on the Law Review and worked for Wright, Lindsay and Jennings, serving as Bill Haught's assistant for the last two years. In 1975, while a law student, he married Patti Shields. Her father ran the Albers Feed & Farm Supply and her mother worked at the Boston Store. Following the marriage, while Judge Cox was going to law school, she worked for

Judge James Oldham Cox
Circuit Judge
2007-2020
photo courtesy of James O. Cox

the *Arkansas Democrat*. She later worked for the *Southwest Times Record* when the young couple returned to Fort Smith.

Judge Cox began his legal career in 1977, practicing in Greenwood with Bill Walters. His was a very general practice, meaning that it deals with "anything that came in the door." Over the years he also served as city attorney for all the cities in the Greenwood District except for Central City and Barling. When Walters was elected to the state Senate in 1982, Cox, along with Hal Davis (another associate of Walters) started their own firm under the shingle of Davis and Cox. They practiced together for eighteen years in two different locations in Fort Smith. In 1984 Greenwood Municipal Judge Wayland Parker passed away and Cox was appointed to succeed him. This story is told in a later chapter. In 1998 Cox was a candidate for circuit judge in the election to replace Judge John Holland. He lost that election to Judge Jim Marschewski by ninety-four votes. In 2000 the firm of Davis & Cox split up and Cox went into a firm along with Eddie Walker, David Harp and Randy Shock.

In 2005 he bought out the law office of Wayland Parker Jr., the son of the Municipal Judge he had been appointed to replace. Judge Parker "the younger" had become the full time District Judge for the Greenwood District and thus was no longer permitted to maintain a private practice. It was while Cox was working in this office that he was appointed to replace the retiring Norman Wilkinson. As noted earlier, Judge Cox could not run for re-election to a position to which he had been appointed and he and Judge Tabor simply ran for the seat to which the other had been appointed!

Judge Cox served on the Greenwood School Board for eighteen years, on the Arkansas Judicial Discipline and Disability Commission for five years, as a special appointed justice on The Arkansas Supreme Court, as a member of the Sebastian County Election Commission, and was named as the Arkansas Bar Association/Bar Foundation Lawyer Citizen of the Year in 1994. He also notes that he was the head coach of the Davis & Cox "Litigators" soccer team for three years and during that time they lost only three games.

He and Patti have two children: Ben, who graduated from UA Fayetteville and resides there with his wife and young son and Katie, who is a graduate of Hendrix College (*cum laude* with distinction). Katie lives in Portland, OR with her husband and young son and is a chef. The Coxes are members of First Methodist Church in Fort Smith. Judge Cox is a Mason and a member of the Rotary Club of Fort Smith. He is a past president of the Greenwood Chamber of Commerce and former member of the 4-H Foundation for Sebastian County. He presently serves on the Board of Visitors for the University of Arkansas Fort Smith. Patti retired as the development director for the University of Arkansas School of Law in Fayetteville. He retired at the end of 2020 and is living the good life.

◈ ◈ ◈

In November 2000, the voters of Arkansas approved Amendment 80 to the Arkansas Constitution of 1874. This was a new judicial article. It totally revamped the way that the justice system in the state was handled. Arkansas was one of very few states that had retained separate courts of law and equity. In its early decades, our state did not have separate courts of equity (commonly called "chancery courts"). The circuit judge heard cases of equity as well. The style before the court would be "Judge John Doe, setting in Equity or Chancery." The separate courts of chancery began appearing, pursuant to constitutional permission, in 1860. In 1903, as noted previously, a statewide system of separate courts of chancery was established. In the 1930's probate court was removed from the county court and placed under the jurisdiction of the chancery judges sitting in probate. There also existed a mishmash of city courts, police courts, courts of common pleas and municipal courts throughout the state. Amendment 80 was designed to make efficient and simplify the system, and to prevent the necessity of transferring cases whenever equitable claims and defenses were asserted in an ongoing case at law. Another purpose was to remove the judiciary from partisan politics.

Circuit judges had previously served a four-year term and chancellors a six-year term. Amendment 80 made all trial judges into circuit judges and the term was extended to six years. The distinction between courts of law and equity was abolished, so trial courts might now hear both equitable and legal claims in the same case. Probate had always been considered a court of limited jurisdiction; form this point forward it would be merged as well with equity and law.

Amendment 80 provided that the judicial power would be vested in the Judicial Department of the state government, consisting of a Supreme Court and other courts established by the Constitution. There was no change in the nature or powers of the Supreme Court or its governance. One change stipulated that the Supreme Court could hold its sessions "pursuant to rules adopted by it." By reason of this, the Court has held sessions at the law school in Fayetteville, at the University of Arkansas - Fort Smith, Jonesboro and other locations around the state (it previously was required to hold its sessions in Little Rock). The Supreme Court continued to have superintending control of the inferior courts and of the practice of law.

The Court of Appeals was carried forward in Amendment 80. The judges of that court must have the same qualifications as a justice of the Supreme Court. The Court of Appeals would enjoy such appellate jurisdiction as was granted by the Supreme Court.

Circuit courts were deemed the trial courts of original jurisdiction for all justiciable matters not otherwise assigned by the Constitution. There were no longer to be courts of chancery or probate. The judges of the circuit might divide the caseload into subject matter divisions, and any judge could sit in any division, subject to the superintending control of the Supreme Court. This innovation brought about, as innovations often do, some friction between the Supreme Court and the various circuit judges in the state. To the consternation of some, the Supreme Court handed down Administrative Order 14. This came out right before Amendment 80 went into effect. It required that each judicial district submit a plan for caseload distribution. It provided that there could be five divisions; criminal, civil, domestic relations, probate and juvenile.

Not all districts were cooperative, at least initially, with the new system, and the plans of several districts were rejected. The judges of these districts were, apparently, content in continuing to handle the types of cases they always had handled. The Supreme Court opined, however, that each judge should now hear all types of cases. This was not popular with old chancellors who had not been involved in jury trials in many years on the bench or old circuit judges who could think of no more cruel punishment for long years of service than to decide the fate of children in custody cases. The plan eventually approved for the 12th district had the old chancellors, Judges Spears and Foltz, hearing all the cases in the probate and domestic relations divisions. The other judges divided up the remainder excluding the Juvenile Division. Judge Hewett retained all the juvenile cases. It also meant that all equity cases formerly heard by the chancery court that not dealing with domestic relations would now be heard by judges Wilkinson, Fitzhugh and Marschewski.

Further changes were in the works. In early 2003, the Supreme Court issued a new order. This emerged after much complaining from the judges that the court would even exercise their supervisory role. Most trial judges preferred that the judges in each circuit handle the case load division in that circuit without interference, so long as the cases were all fairly and expeditiously handled. The new plan required the judges from each district to elect from their members one who would serve as the administrative judge. The first judge so selected from the 12th District was Harry Foltz, the longest-serving judge in the district. The duties of the administrative judge are to meet and make reports and submit a new case assignment plan yearly with input from the other judges in the district. This aids the Supreme Court in their supervisory capacity over the trial courts. With this modification, the dispute has largely gone away. With a few exceptions, the districts are left to their own devices, within reason. The addition of two new circuit judges in 2007 did not necessitate a new court plan. Judges Tabor and Cox agreed to the case division as it existed and took over the case assignments of Judges Marschewski and Wilkinson. Retirements and new judges coming on board will probably necessitate changes in the future.

There was also created in Amendment 80 a new judicial entity called the District Court. This supplanted the old Municipal Courts. This is a court of limited jurisdiction as to amount and subject matter. This subject matter and amount in controversy jurisdiction would now be Supreme Court rulings and not by legislation, as was done previously. The District Courts have criminal jurisdiction in misdemeanors. The amendment authorized at least one District Court in each county and, if there were only one, that court should have countywide jurisdiction. District judges can exchange districts temporarily and can be assigned by the Supreme Court to another district with their permission.

The goal of this innovation was the elimination of part-time judges of inferior courts. A "city judge" hired by a municipality is often a judge one day a week and a lawyer the remaining six. This creates an inherent conflict of interest. There really is no place for part-time justice. Each judge needs to be a full-time judge. Amendment 80's solution was effective but not instantaneous in its effect: City courts were allowed to continue until changed by the legislature. This suggests acknowledgement of a practical consideration: Such courts did—and do—have their political patrons!

The experiential qualifications for the various judicial offices were specified in the amendment: Supreme Court-eight years' practice, Court of Appeals-eight years' practice, Circuit Court-six years' practice and District Court- four years' practice. The terms of office are the same as the required years of practice for qualification. This marked a change for the circuit judges, whose previous terms of office had been but four years. Chancellors' terms had always been six years and municipal judges' terms had been a mere two years long. The election of all judicial officers, as noted earlier, was made non-partisan as well. This was meant to remove the elected judiciary as much as possible from the slings and arrows of partisan politics. This has, however, not worked quite as planned. One other change brought about by Amendment 80 was the lengthening of the term of the prosecuting attorney from two to four years.

Before this writer took office in 1993, there was talk concerning the need for a new county building. It is not referred to as a courthouse since the non-judicial functions of county government would be the focus of the new building. The third division of chancery, now circuit court, could not be housed in the courthouse along with all the administrative offices. In anticipation of the new facility and for general efficiency, the voters of Sebastian County, pursuant to Amendment 55, reassigned duties between the county clerk and the circuit clerk. The county clerk had been the repository for files dealing with probate cases and the circuit clerk had maintained the real estate filings. This was historic as the county judge had been the probate judge up until the 1930s. Under the change, unique to Sebastian County, all court filings, including probate, would be with the circuit clerk and the real estate filings would be with the county clerk. This would enable the circuit clerk, now the clerk for all the courts, to remain in the courthouse where all court business is conducted exclusively.

Originally, as indicated, it was proposed to use the existing building as the courts building and to build a new administration facility. Security concerns and lack of usable space caused this plan to be abandoned on the recommendation of the architects. The downside was that the magnificent old court rooms in that building can be used for little else. The plan then became to build a building exclusively for the use of the courts, circuit clerk and prosecutor. Land was secured next to the Sebastian County Detention Center and following agreement with the City of Fort Smith, the new facility (as was the case with the old one) is a joint city-county facility as the district courts are located there and the city contributed to the construction costs.

The jail had been in the 1937 courthouse on the top two floors until 1994 when a new and expanded jail was opened on Wheeler Avenue, on property formerly occupied by the Fort Smith Boy's Club and donated to the county by George Hernrich. The jail, originally opened in 1994, is still inadequate even following expansion. The saying "if you build it they will come" certainly applies to jail space. The undersized jail presented problems in the construction of the new courts building. Money originally available for the court complex had to be diverted to the jail. Additional funds also had to be diverted to this use when the bids for the jail expansion came in over estimate.

Additionally, a dispute arose between the trial judges and some of the quorum court over the jail prior to the decision to add to the jail. The dispute arose over the question of whose prisoners should be housed in the jail. The Sebastian County jail houses Federal prisoners but is not required to do so. When the present jail was planned, monies from the U.S. Marshals Service were not sought as this would have obligated the jail to take Federal prisoners. Incentive existed, however, to accept these "guests": The Feds paid—and pay—very timely and well for housing their charges. They also provide the sheriff with many in-kind benefits. On the other hand, had it not been for the Federal prisoners the jail would not have had to be expanded and the money designated for courts building would not have been diverted.

The circuit judges ordered that the jail refuse Federal prisoners to keep the population low. This created a firestorm from Sheriff Atkinson, the Marshals and Justice of the Peace Jake Patterson, a former United States Marshal for the Western District of Arkansas. The order was rescinded. This episode totally alienated Patterson from the trial judges on the issue of the courts building. It was ultimately negotiated that the Marshals Service would provide $500,000 toward the construction of the jail expansion to ensure a place to keep Federal prisoners. This is proper, considering the unique relationship in history that Fort Smith and the United States Marshals Service enjoy.

The need for the court complex was undeniable. At that time, the county located Judge Spears in rented space at 523 Garrison Avenue. In 1996 Spears and his staff were in renovated space at 200 Garrison. This location was damaged and later demolished following a tornado. For a little more than a year that court was in an office building across the street from the courthouse and court was held around a conference table. It was later moved to the 5th floor of the Garrison Building at 523 Garrison; the space consisted of the entire 5th floor of that building with a circuit and chancery courtroom. Litigants and witnesses were easily confused as to where they should go for court. This added to the confusion generated by the fact that historically, there were and had been two courthouses in Sebastian County; there were now three possibilities for the location of a trial! There was, moreover, also no security to speak of in any of the courts. There were courtroom bailiffs, but access to the courts and to the judge's chambers was not monitored. An incident happened in Judge Spears' court in 2005 when a mentally incompetent man managed to get a gun from the holster of a deputy. The gun discharged and the bullet ricocheted from the floor, nearly striking a young lady from the prosecutor's office before cutting a gouge in the edge of a door. This situation was simply not acceptable.

The city, at that time, also rented space in the State Office Building for District Court and there was a District Court in the courthouse as well. Again, confusion reigned as to where one should appear for court! In the courthouse itself there were four courtrooms and seven judges, counting two district judges. In the 523 Garrison complex there were two courtrooms. Only one had jury facilities. There were no facilities for prisoner detention or witness or jury isolation in the rented space. Amendment 80 raised the possibility that all courtrooms might someday need facilities for juries, including jury boxes, in the courtrooms and deliberation rooms. The 1936 facility was also old and not suited for the technological needs of the day.

Predictably, conflicts between political entities and individuals plagued the courts building project. One problem developed between the city and the county. The county had assumed, based on informal talks with the previous city administrator Strib Boynton and County Judge David Hudson, that the city would be a participant in the new courts building. Nothing was done officially. When it came time to consider the plans, the city had a new administrator along with new city directors. The city's desire was to build a city hall rather than a courts building. The judges believed the district courts should be included. The justices of the peace were angry at the city and the city was angry with the county because of their assumptions and lack in communication and planning. This author appeared before the city board of directors along with the county judge and District Judge David Saxon to appeal to them to participate. This was not received well but Judge Saxon along with Justice of the Peace Tom Craft continued to work the idea and the city was persuaded in early 2005 to become a partner in the project.

Almost fifteen years from the inception of the plan and original talks with architects *The Southwest Times Record* reported on June 1, 2005: COUNTY VOTE PUTS PROJECT ON AGENDA, COMMITTEE DISCUSSES REVISED PLANS FOR COURTS BUILDING CONSTRUCTION, The story reported that the Quorum Court voted 9-4 to proceed with the plan and place it on the agenda for approval in the next meeting. The vote was taken in a "committee of the whole" planning session. The four members to vote against the plan were Shawn Looper, Warren Holcombe, Jake Patterson, and John Van Gorder. Each of these members represented the Greenwood district (one of the results of Amendment 55 has been to give the Greenwood District a say in what the county does in the Fort Smith District and vice versa). This was the first time since the adoption of that amendment that the county had been faced with building a court building and, maybe predictably, that old rivalry going back to the county's creation raised its head. The justices from the Greenwood District initially voted against the court building except one. He was then defeated in the next election and replaced by Justice Van Gorder who fell into line and voted against the court building.

The plans were finally approved by all and the building became a reality. The district courts are located on the first floor of the building along with the juvenile court. On the second floor are the circuit clerk's office, the prosecutor's office and five circuit courtrooms. Public access to the judge's chambers is restricted and security is provided as never before. All administrative offices remain in the old courthouse as well as the non-court functions of the county. On June 22, 2005, *The Southwest Times Record* headlines proclaimed, COUNTY INKS COURTS DEAL WITH CITY. The story went on to explain that the city would consider the agreement formally on July 5. The cost was reported to be $13 million. The vote was 9-4 with Justices of the Peace Shawn Looper, Warren Holcombe, Jake Patterson and John Van Gorder voting against it. All the opposing justices, as noted, lived in the Greenwood district of the county. The story went on to say:

Under the terms of the agreement, the two bodies will cooperate in the construction of a 71,000 square-foot building that will house juvenile, circuit and district court operations...in one building and will provide additional security that is lacking in existing facilities....The building will be located on South A Street south of the Fort Smith Police Department. The agreement calls for the county to provide $10,865,432 toward the project and the city to contribute $2,058,759, with an additional allocation of $225,000 from the city to the county for a county-owned parking lot at South Fourth Street and Garland Avenue. The agreement also calls for the city to forgive the balance of $181,532 the county owes for title to the existing courthouse, fully satisfying the $645,000 purchase price for the building.

It was noted also that the two entities would share the cost of the architectural work. Design for the building was hoped to be completed by October and construction complete by August 2007.

Problems continued. The consulting architect from Kansas City was fired by the local architect. The plans were revised to get them within available funds following the high bids for the jail. The inflationary economy continued to boost the costs of materials as did Hurricane Katrina. On March 18, 2006, *The Southwest Times Record* headlined: COURTS COSTS WITHIN BUDGET, HUDSON SAYS. The revised plans came in at an estimated $9.85 million. *"The proof will be in the bids,"* County Judge David Hudson was quoted as saying. The bids were to be submitted in April 2006 and opened in May.

Ultimately, the jail expansion was completed in 2007 and the courthouse in Spring of 2008. The funds for the two projects had been set aside starting in the late 1980s, from the one cent county sales tax. The projects did not require a new tax and there was little bonded indebtedness. In July 2007 the expanded jail was completed and the courts building was well under way. Court operations moved into the new building on September 8, 2008 and the dedication ceremony, with Governor Beebe in attendance, was held on October 10, 2008. No provision had been made for growth, however, so it was probably inevitable that a new District Court position came along, followed by a new circuit court position in 2019. Office space had to be created on the first floor of the new courts building in the area originally designated as a break room for appointed judge Gunner DeLay.

Since occupying the new building in 2008, five new circuit judges have been elected, including a newly created position. Following a trend, all but two have been women. The first of these was Judge Annie Powell Hendricks. With the election of Judge Hendricks Sebastian County had two judges that have Native

Judge Rachael Anne Hendricks
Circuit Judge
2011-Present

photo courtesy of Archives

American heritage: Hendricks is a member of the Absentee Shawnee Tribe of Oklahoma and Judge James Cox is a member of the Cherokee Nation. Judge Hendricks was elected in 2012 to replace retiring Judge Harry Foltz.

Judge Hendricks was born Rachael Anne Powell in St. Louis, MO to Robert Morgan Powell and Sara "Sally" Shipley Powell (later Bowers) on August 10, 1960. She was the third of three girls including Carolyn and Maud Powell. Her father was a terminal manager for Arkansas Best Freight in East St. Louis; her mother was from a pioneer Fort Smith family that owned Shipley Baking Company. Her mother's best friend was Marilyn Young Speed whose father, Robert Young Sr., founded Arkansas Best. It was through that connection that Bob Powell went to work for Arkansas Best. They had met in North Carolina where they were in school. After graduation Bob went into the Navy where he served with distinction. When young Annie was two Bob was recalled into the Navy and they lived in Seattle, WA until he was released and they moved back to St. Louis. They were there from 1966-67. During this period both Bob and Sally lost their parents and Sally called on her friend Marilyn once again to get Bob transferred to Fort Smith. Annie was in the second grade at the time and finished school at Ballman. They lived in the Shipley family home on South 25th Street. About this time her parents divorced and Annie's mother remarried; she lived with her mother and new stepfather Don Bowers, attending Chaffin Jr. High where she played basketball and ran track. She graduated from Southside High School and then the University of Arkansas where she was a member of the Pi Phi sorority, majoring in History with an English minor. She graduated in 1982 and worked for Senator David Pryor (who referred to her as "Little Annie") in his Little Rock office for a year. She then attended and graduated in 1986 from the UALR School of Law; upon graduation, she went to work for Fort Smith attorney Eddie N. Christian. Eddie Christian provided her with tough-minded mentorship: He impressed on her the need to "always be thirty minutes early" and to be prepared—by which he meant to both know the file and know the law, every time. He discouraged her from joining things that would take up her time or distract her from her work, such as the Junior League and Leadership Fort Smith. She did, however, serve on some boards, such as Head Start, that overlapped with her specialty, family law and domestic relations. She worked with Eddie and his son (usually referred to as "Little Eddie", which he hated) for eleven years. In 1997 she opened her own office, remaining in private practice until Judge Foltz retired in 2010. She was elected and took office in 2011.

She was married to Andy Hendricks, an executive at Weldon, Williams and Lick printers on October 3, 1987. They have three children: Emma who is an optometrist now living in Fayetteville, Rachael, a graduate of UAFS in psychology and Andrew, a graduate of the University of Arkansas. Emma and her husband recently made Judge Hendricks a very proud grandmother Judge Hendricks is a member of the Sebastian County Bar Association and the Immaculate Conception School Board. She has been a member of the Sparks Regional Medical Center Advisory Board and involved with the United Way for many years. She serves also on the Junior League of Fort Smith's Aging Out Foster Care Task Force. She is very proud of the fact that she was a member of 5West, a committee made up of five persons including beside herself Sheriff Bill Hollenbeck, Prosecuting Attorney Dan Shue, County Judge David Hudson and Jim West the then director of the Western Arkansas Guidance and Counseling Center. They travelled to Washington D.C. to get training to set up a mental health court in Sebastian County. This diversion program is now up and working with the first shelter of its kind in the state. This is due to the work of the people on this committee. Judge Hendricks supervises the operation.

A case that has been taken up on appeal that was initially decided by Judge Hendricks is *Erin M. Fischer vs. Damon L. Smith*, 2012 Ark. App. 342 (May 16, 2012). The case dealt with the removal of a child from the jurisdiction of the court. In this case, the removal was to the U.S. Virgin Islands. Smith, the father, and Fischer, the mother, had the male child before marriage. They later married and, in their divorce a year later, acknowledged the boy's paternity. The mother was granted custody and the father had visitation. He was ordered to pay $62.00 per week child support. At the custody hearing it was revealed that the father over $1000.00 behind in his child support, out of work and living with his mother. Moreover, he had a drug problem: His drug of choice was oxycontin and he had recently gotten out of rehab. The parents' relationship was rocky but she had allowed him to move in with her for a while; Smith maintained they had rekindled their intimate relationship but Fischer denied this.

The mother, Fischer, was a teacher of American Sign Language and wanted to further her career in the Virgin Islands, where her father owned a resort. Her father was quite wealthy: In addition to his property in the Virgin Islands, he also owned homes in Canada and Oklahoma and was a pilot with a plane which was available to transport the child for purposes of visitation. Fischer's siblings, it was noted, visited the Virgin Islands a couple of times each year. In gte face of this, however, Judge Hendricks denied the petition to relocate, stating that Fischer's purpose in moving was simply to get away from Fort Smith and the child's father; it would not be in the child's interest to relocate.

Judge Hendricks's decision rested on precedent set in *Hollandsworth vs. Knyzewski*, 353 Ark.470, 109 S.W.3d 653 (2003). In that case, the court set forth five factors to be considered in such cases to overcome a presumption in favor of the relocation: the reason for the relocation; education, health and leisure opportunities; visitation and communication for the non-custodial parent;

effect of the move on extended family relationships; and the preference of the child. The proof was that, indeed, the relationships with the extended family of the father would be adversely affected; the child would have more contact with Fischer's family due to their visits and the grandfather's presence nine months out of the year. The educational opportunities were about equal and phone contact and visits facilitated by the grandfather was adequate. The child's preference was not considered due to the age of the child. Judge Hendricks ruled that it had not been shown to be in the child's best interest. The Arkansas Supreme Court, however, ruled that Hendricks had flipped the burden of proof and put it on Fischer, the mother, to show the move would be in the best interest of the child. To overcome a presumption the father must prove it would not be in the child's best interest and the proof at best was it was equal and that is not the law. The court reversed and remanded the case for an order consistent with the court's ruling.

The next judge to be elected was Judge Leigh Tompkins Zuerker. In 2014, she was elected to replace Judge Mark Hewett, who had reached the judicial retirement age of seventy. Judge Zuerker was born in Jackson, Mississippi on August 22, 1969, the daughter of Paula and Dr. William C. Tompkins. Both of her parents were raised in Greenville, Mississippi next door to one another. Her maternal great-grandfather, Dominick Signa, was aa Sicilian immigrant, who met his future wife, Mamie, while both were on a ship bound for Ellis Island. The Signas went originally to Chicago where they operated a fruit stand before opening a grocery in Greenville in 1903. Here they found a place to settle and prosper: They had fifteen children, twelve of whom survived to adulthood, and they lived in a house adjacent to the family business. The grocery prospered until the great flood of 1927; the grocery survived but was to recover from his losses, "Doe" Signa temporarily diversified into bootlegging to help support the family. After a while he sold his forty-gallon still for $300 and a Model T Ford. Around that time his wife Mamie got a recipe for tamales, started making them and selling them. They proved so popular that they closed the grocery, as the food business was more profitable. Doe Signa ran a honky-tonk in the front of the former grocery, serving African Americans, while selling tamales out the back door to whites in a reverse of the usual pattern of segregation. A local doctor started coming by for a steak in the back between calls and this helped the business grow into what became Doe's Eat Place. "Big Doe" Signa retired in 1974 and turned the business over to his sons Charles and "Little Doe." Mamie passed away in 1955 and "Big Doe" in 1987. The tradition and original building along with the family atmosphere continues; Judge Zuerker's grandmother still works at Doe's and is one of the few that know the original tamale recipe. Franchised outposts of the original Doe's operate in Fort Smith and Little Rock; the Doe's franchise in Little Rock on Markham Street, a block from the local Salvation

Judge Leigh Zuerker
Circuit Judge
2015-Present

photo courtesy of Leigh Zuerker

Army, was the gathering place for politicos and journalists during Bill Clinton's 1992 campaign for president.

Judge Zuerker's parents married in 1966. Her father became a general and peripheral vascular surgeon. They moved to Texarkana, Texas in 1974 when young Leigh was in kindergarten. She has one brother. Upon her graduation from Texarkana High School she attended Ole Miss for one year, then transferred to the University of Arkansas in Fayetteville. She graduated in 1991 with a degree in accounting and attended law school at the University of Arkansas. While in line to get her law student ID, she met fellow law student Scott Zuerker, who would become her husband. Judge Zuerker relates that they were "just friends" and did not date for a while. This changed in July 1993: They were engaged by August and got married in September 1994. Upon Scott passing the bar, he took a position with the Eddie Walker law firm in Fort Smith, while Leigh worked for JMC Exploration until she could take the bar in the spring. In September 1995 Leigh Zuerker she went to work in the Sebastian County Public Defender's Office under later Circuit Judge and US Magistrate Jim Marschewski. She also did *ad litem* work for DHS under another contract. She ended up doing primarily juvenile court work and this prepared her very well for the juvenile division of circuit court when this position became vacant upon Judge Hewett's retirement.

She is a member of the Sebastian County Bar Association and the Arkansas Bar Association. She is a 2014 graduate of Leadership Fort Smith and a member of The Junior League of Fort Smith. She served on the Junior League "Children Aging Out of Foster Care Task Force' and was recognized by the Junior League as Sustainer of the Year in 2014. She currently serves on the Sebastian County Juvenile Justice Prevention Coalition. She has been active in the PTO and PTA of her children's schools. She also serves on the Pi Beta Phi Alumnae Board.

Judge Zuerker and Scott, who now works at the Ledbetter Firm in Fort Smith, have three children. Mary Claire a graduate of UA Fort Smith with a major in organizational leadership. Their son Will is a student at UA Fayetteville and like his dad is an avid hunter and fisherman. Cooper, the youngest is into baseball, hunting and fishing like his dad and brother.

The next judge to assume the bench was Shannon Blatt, elected in 2016 to replace Judge Jim Spears, your writer, who reached the mandatory retirement age of seventy. Judge Blatt was born March 12, 1973, in Fort Smith, the daughter of Bob and Marcene Blatt. Her father was the manager of Levine's General Store in Fort Smith and her mother was an employee at McCrory's Five and Dime on Garrison Ave; Bob always said he "Found My Million Dollar Baby in a 5 and 10 Cent Store," as in the old song. Marcene was a single mother of three children at the time and living at Heartsill Ragon Homes (a public housing development) on North 6th Street. They both decided to better themselves by furthering their education. Marcene attended nursing school at the Saint Edward School of Nursing at St. Edwards Hospital. At the time each local hospital had its own nursing school. She graduated in March of 1968 and passed her state boards in March of that year. Bob decided he wanted to get out of the retail business and started law school at The University of Arkansas School of Law in 1969. Marcene worked at Washington Regional Medical Center and the V. A. Hospital in Fayetteville to support her, Bob and the three children. Bob worked as well in the law school library and elsewhere to keep food on the table while he studied law. He graduated in 1972, and they moved back to Fort Smith. He went to work as a deputy prosecuting attorney for Bill Thompson. In those days in Sebastian County a deputy prosecutor could also have a private practice on the side. Working with the police gave him a steady stream of business handling their divorces and other problems as well as those he came in contact within the day-to-day business of the prosecutor's office. When the other deputy, Charles Karr, became prosecutor upon Bill Thompson deciding to go into private practice things changed. A change in the law upgraded the office. Deputy prosecutors could no longer have a private practice. Bob was furious. He resigned and moved his stuff out in a very short time. He opened his own office on Court Street in 1975. Bob was later joined in his law practice by Steve Sharum. This began a very productive collaboration/competition that lasted until Bob's death on June 21, 2009.

It was into this house—surrounded by the law, lawyers and judges—that Shannon Leigh was born in 1973. As a young girl she would often accompany her father to court or to the jail or on trips to the prison. One time she went with him to Judge Kimbrough's court. Judge Kimbrough was a stickler for courtroom decorum and dress. He had a thing about people wearing shorts in court. One day a little Shannon was with her dad and he had her stay behind the bench in the massive chancery courtroom. Judge Kimbrough saw her and threw a fit. He had her removed from the courtroom. She remembers that to this day. After Shannon got out of law school and purchased a wardrobe for court her father had her return one outfit as it was a pantsuit; Judge Kimbrough did not approve of ladies wearing pantsuits to court. He also did not like for ladies to wear the color red! He was one of the last of the old "southern gentlemen" in the Arkansas judiciary.

Judge Blatt graduated from Southside High School in Fort Smith and did her undergraduate work at Tulane. She attended and graduated from St. Mary's School of Law in San Antonio, TX in December 1997. After passing the bar in the fall of 1998, she opened a law office on Court Street in property owned by her father and Mr. Sharum. This was no free ride: she paid rent and her share of the phone bill! At the time there was no room for her in their office but later,

Judge Shannon L. Blatt
Circuit Judge
2017-Present

photo courtesy of Archives

when one of the lawyers working there left, they let her have the opportunity to join them on condition she was now responsible for her share of the total office expenses. She did quite well and established an outstanding legal practice. Judge Blatt served for several years on the Fort Smith School Board and served as president in 2010. She is a graduate of Leadership Fort Smith and a member of the Junior League of Fort Smith. She is a member of the Sebastian County Bar Association, The Arkansas Bar Association and the Arkansas Bar Foundation. Her honors and contributions to the community are numerous. She is very proud of the fact that her first jury trial was a criminal case where her client was found with a pound of cocaine, and she obtained an acquittal. Another case that she successfully defended was a murder case. A wife had killed her husband. She in effect argued to the jury that the deceased "needed killin'." In 2016 she decided to run for Judge Spears's soon-to-be-vacated seat and did so successfully.

In 2019 the Arkansas legislature created a new judgeship in the 12th Judicial District. This was Division VII. Appointed to this position was Gunner Delay. Judge Delay had earlier been appointed by Governor Hutchison to be a District Judge replacing Judge Ben Beland who retired prior to the expiration of his term of office. There were no facilities for Judge Delay to occupy upon his appointment to the new circuit judgeship; when the government builds a new building it is designed for present needs and no thought of future growth is contemplated... and this was no exception. A new office was created from the break room on the first floor as the space was rarely used. This did not cure the problem of one more judge needing a courtroom. Division VII does not have a designated courtroom as do the other six circuit judges. Courtroom usage is now scheduled by the court administrator.

R. Gunner Delay was born in Sparks Hospital on June 14, 1963. His father, Robert Delay was a dentist that practiced in Fort Smith for 40 years. His mother was the former Anna Louise Rodgers. She trained as a dental hygienist. She met her husband at Baylor Dental School. Dr. Delay's father, Dr. Warren D. Delay, was a small-town doctor who owned a hospital in Sulphur, OK. His wife, Zelma Lee Delay, was the hospital administrator. Judge Delay's maternal grandfather, Woody Rodgers was a bus driver in the city of Fort Smith until he started his own transfer and storage business.

Judge Delay attended Echols Elementary, Chaffin Jr. High and Southside High School in Fort Smith, graduating in 1981. He attended the University of Arkansas where he was a member of Phi Gamma Delta Fraternity and was active in the student senate. He graduated from the University of Arkansas in 1985 with a degree in marketing. He then attended law school at the University of Arkansas Little Rock obtaining his Juris Doctor in 1988.

Judge R. Gunner Delay
Circuit Judge
2019-Present
photo courtesy of Archives

He married Robin Ross on May 25, 1988. She is the daughter of Dr. Wendell Ross who for many years was a general practice physician in Van Buren. He and Robin have four children: Taylor, Gunner Jr, Caroline and Suzanna. All the children are graduates of the University of Arkansas. There are two grandchildren: Robert Gunner Delay III (Tripp) and Tatum Jayne Delay.

Judge Delay started his legal career in August 1988 at the firm of Shaw, Ledbetter, Hornberger, Cogbill & Arnold. He was charged with workers compensation defense and appellate work. In 1991 he started his own law firm and then joined the firm of Rush, Rush and Cook. Upon his becoming a partner it became the best-named law firm anywhere around: Rush, Rush and Delay! That gained a great deal of notoriety. There, Delay handled a general practice representing mainly plaintiffs.

In 1994 Delay ran for the Arkansas General Assembly from the Fourteenth District and defeated a 16-year incumbent, Buddy Blair. A Republican, Delay was swept into office as a part of the Republican "Contract With America" movement. In 1996 Delay decided not to seek reelection as serving in the legislature was a drain on him financially but circumstances overtook his avowed intent. Mac McGehee, a popular businessman, had made plans to run for the office as a Democrat. Asa Hutchison, a lawyer practicing in Fort Smith planned to run for the seat as a Republican. A lively race between two plausible, popular candidates seemed likely...and then dominos began to fall. Tim Hutchison, the Third District Congressman (and brother to Asa) decided to vacate his office to run for the U.S. Senate. Asa then decided to not run for the General Assembly but to instead run to replace his brother in Congress. Don Hutchins, a local pastor, then became the Republican candidate and was defeated by Mac McGehee. While this was going on, long-time incumbent 12th District Democratic Representative B. G. Hendrix was being challenged by a political neophyte who had no history of ever voting, had formerly worked as a male dancer, and had child support difficulties. When these complications became public knowledge, he dropped out of the race. Delay, his financial fortunes improved came to the rescue for the party and jumped into that race. Delay, a consummate campaigner, prevailed. He had now unseated two long time incumbents. While serving in the House, Delay was a member of the Judiciary committee, the committee on Aging and Legislative Affairs, the Transportation committee and was chair of the subcommittee on nursing home abuse.

In 1998 there was an open seat in the Arkansas Senate. Delay put his hat in the ring and was elected, defeating long time Whirlpool executive Sandy Sanders by a landslide of some 200 votes! Sanders later served as director of the Fort Smith Chamber of Commerce, Executive Director of the Fort Chaffee Redevelopment Authority and Mayor of Fort Smith. Delay served in the State

Senate from 1999 to 2003. While there he served on the Judiciary committee, Senate Rules committee, the Budget committee and the Committee on City, County and Local Government. In 2001 he was the recipient of the Arkansas Medical Society's "Legislator of the Year Award".

In 2007 Governor Mike Huckabee appointed Delay to serve out the remaining two years of the term of Prosecuting Attorney Steve Tabor. Tabor, you will recall, had been appointed to the circuit court bench vacated by Judge Marschewski when he became the Federal Magistrate. Judge Delay "did his time," then returned to Rush, Rush and Delay following that tenure. In 2009 Delay ventured into financial and estate planning, apart from his former firm. He obtained his insurance license as well as other licensures so he could offer a full range of estate planning services. In 2018 he was appointed by Governor Asa Hutchison as District Judge in Fort Smith, replacing Judge Ben Beland who retired. In 2019, as earlier mentioned, he was appointed as circuit judge for the newly created Circuit Court Division VII. In 2020 he then ran unopposed for the Circuit Court Division V position vacated by the mandatory retirement at age 70 of Judge Mike Fitzhugh. This is the office he currently holds but how long is in question. He is a great campaigner and has announced as of this writing, as a candidate for the Arkansas Supreme Court against an incumbent justice, Karen Baker. In this he was not successful.

The person elected in 2020 to the new circuit position, Division VII, to which Judge Delay was previously appointed is Judge Dianna Hewitt Ladd. She is a native of Southern California, having lived a block or so from Knott's Berry Farm in Buena Park. Her father, David Hewitt, was from the Charleston, AR area; His parents were Ralph and Nora Hewitt, who lived in the family farm on Potato "Tater" Hill. The Hewitt family migrated to California during the "Dust Bowl" of the depression in the 1930' and the farm was incorporated into Camp Chaffee in 1941; today, it serves as the artillery target area for Fort Chaffee. Ladd's mother, Patricia Boylan Hewitt, is from Long Island, NY. The story in her family is that they moved to California because her grandfather, Victor Boylan, was a die-hard Brooklyn Dodgers fan. When the Dodgers moved to Los Angeles so did he. It's a good story and thus one worth repeating...unfortunately, as with many other good stories, it's not demonstrably true! It was told to this writer as the truth by Judge Hewitt, because her mother had never denied it before! As it turns out, Victor and Harrietta Boylan may well have arrived in L.A. well in advance of the Dodgers, but this is nitpicking; never should we allow the truth in interfere with a good and cherished family story!

Judge Dianna Hewitt Ladd
Circuit Judge
2021-Present
photo courtesy of Archives

The Hewitts moved back to Charleston after selling the house in California for a nice profit. Dianna was in the sixth grade at the time of the move. After high school, she attended John Brown University in Siloam Springs. She made a few "unfortunate decisions" which led to her not completing her course of study there. She attended classes at Westark College in Fort Smith and eventually graduated from John Brown through the remote campus in Fort Smith. It took her ten years to complete college. During that time she met her husband, Jeff Ladd, while waiting tables at Greenladd's Restaurant (and yes, the business name is significant—Jeff was one of the owners). She also was involved with the scholarship pageant system. She was first runner-up in the Ms. Arkansas pageant! She went on to complete law school, earning her Juris Doctor from the University of Arkansas School of Law in 2000.

Her first legal position was with the Bill Walters Law Firm in Greenwood. Her brother-in-law, John Verkamp, was already in that firm. Later she and John started their own firm, Verkamp and Ladd. They had a very successful firm and she first ventured into judicial politics upon the retirement of Judge Jim Spears in 2016 but was unsuccessful in that race against Shannon Blatt. When the new circuit judgeship was created she decided to get into that race and was successful. She took office January 1, 2021. Judge Ladd and her husband are the proud parents of two boys; Reece who is 13 and Knox who is 10 as of this writing.

In 2020 Judge Jamie Cox was also required to retire due to reaching age 70. The person selected to replace him is Judge Greg Magness. Greg Magness was born on September 1, 1964. His parents are Dr. Jack L. Magness Jr. and Carolyn R. Magness. Dr. Magness first practiced in Fort Smith as a pediatrician and later as a dermatologist with Cooper Clinic. His sister Cara is married to Fort Smith lawyer David Gean. Judge Magness's wife is Van F. Magness and they have two children, John and Anna.

Judge Magness is a product of the Fort Smith Public Schools. He graduated from Southside High School in 1982 and then attended the University of Arkansas, where he was a member of the swim team and was an All-Southwest Conference performer. In 1987 he was recipient of the Dr. Lon Farrell Award. This award is given by the Razorback Letterman's Club for outstanding achievements in athletics and academics. In 2008 he was inducted into the Arkansas Swimming Hall of Fame. He majored in chemistry at the U of A and was a member of Phi Beta Kappa. Judge Magness intended to follow his father into the practice of medicine. He was admitted into medical school at UAMS and attended the fall semester in 1987. That lasted four days! Judge Magness had struggled with the desire to break from his long-standing plan to be a doctor in undergraduate school but could never make the tough "final decision." Medicine to him was a noble profession but he was more interested in the law. When he

JUDGE GREG MAGNESS
CIRCUIT JUDGE
2021-PRESENT
PHOTO COURTESY OF ARCHIVES

found himself in medical school he realized the decision could no longer be delayed. On his way to anatomy class one morning, he veered off toward the Dean's office and withdrew from medical school.

Judge Magness then enrolled at the University of Texas School of Law in Austin, where he excelled. He served as the associate editor of the law review and was awarded the Outstanding Constitutional Law Note Award by the Texas Law Review Association. After graduating with honors, Magness began his legal career at the Fort Smith law firm of Hardin, Jesson and Terry where he practiced for 26 years concentrating on civil litigation, banking and commercial law. The judgeship is not his first experience in public service. He was elected to the Fort Smith School Board in 2016 and served in that capacity until he resigned to enter the judicial race in 2020.

The trial court judiciary as of this writing in 2021 consists of seven divisions: Division 1, Judge Steve Tabor; Division 2, Judge Annie Powell Hendricks, Division 3, Judge Shannon Blatt, Division 4, Judge Leigh Zuerker, Division 5, Judge Gunner Delay, Division 6, Judge Greg Magness and Division 7, Judge Dianna Hewitt Ladd.

CONCLUSION

With Amendment 80, a new courthouse and the partial unification of the county by Amendment 55, the situation remains in Sebastian County as it has since 1851: justice is divided. The smallest county in the state has two independent judicial districts sharing elected officials within that one small county. Improvements have been made. All county business can be completed in either courthouse now thanks to computers. One no longer must assess property or pay taxes in the separate courthouses on property located in different districts for instance.

But...Greenwood is very possessive of "their courthouse." A mention of any change can change the outcome of an election as it did in 1984. Long time Greenwood Municipal Judge Wayland "Lefty" Parker had died. Governor Clinton had appointed attorney (and later, circuit judge) James O. Cox to replace him. He was then a candidate for the position against attorneys Jack Skinner and David Rogers. Cox was expected to win easily. Skinner ran ads attacking Cox over coming to the aid of Fort Smith Municipal Judge (and, later, circuit judge) Harry Foltz due to his excessive caseload. Skinner charged that area legislators were intending to shut down the Greenwood courthouse and consolidate the two districts into one. On October 24, 1984, *The Southwest Times Record* headlined above the fold, Lawmakers say claim unfounded:

> *"This comes as a complete shock to me," said Rep. Ralph "Buddy" Blair of Fort Smith. "If there's a plot going on, I don't know anything about it." State Rep. Carolyn Pollan of Fort Smith said, "It's a bunch of baloney, I haven't heard anything like that come up. I don't know of any such plans." Rep. B.G. Hendrix of Fort Smith said, "I am certainly not going to make any deals on it and I don't know anybody who would...I haven't heard anything about it and have no intentions of introducing legislation along that line."*

Hendrix was quoted as saying that the last time he heard rumors about the Greenwood courthouse being closed and moved to Fort Smith had been after the Greenwood tornado in 1968. State Senator Travis Miles of Fort Smith opined that the matter was "better left alone right now." He said he would have heard about it if any concrete efforts were underway to strip the Greenwood District of its jurisdiction or close the Greenwood courthouse and averred that he would not be the one to introduce any legislation for that type of action. Sen. Bill Walters of Greenwood, however, claimed that he had heard such rumors. He said that the action would be met with "vicious" opposition from South Sebastian County... shades of *Patterson vs. Temple*! Both Cox, who was tainted with the prospect of being complicit in the rumored closure of the courthouse, and Skinner, who was tainted with spreading unsubstantiated rumors, were defeated and David Rogers (who had been given no chance of winning going into the race) was elected. Unsubstantiated fear of losing the treasured courthouse had decided the contest.

This fear is still present. This author was questioned in Greenwood as to the effect of the new court building on the Greenwood courthouse. The answer was obvious: there is no effect. The districts stand. This is not to say, though, that the situation is immune from questioning. Does it make sense to draw two separate jury pools in the state's smallest county? Does it make sense to have two separate case numbering systems in the state's smallest county? (Now corrected I believe). Does it make sense for the courtrooms in Greenwood to remain unavailable when courtroom space is scarce, merely because a case was filed in the Fort Smith District? Alas, we shall continue to be a county where justice is divided. Fort Smith is wet. Greenwood is dry. (The Supreme Court ruled the districts were as separate counties, at least for purposes of a wet/dry election) Fort Smith is urban. Greenwood is rural. This distinction, this division is cultural. It is emotional. It is historical. It is not reasonable. It is parochialism and paranoia, leading to even a rumor becoming "fightin' words." It is, however, as Tevye the dairyman sang in *Fiddler on the Roof*, "TRADITION!" And so it is likely to stay.

SOURCES LIST

In this section I have attempted to list the main sources for each chapter, roughly in the order in which they were used. This is by no means a complete roster of sources from which I have benefited. Readers may notice that in the latter chapters, I have relied on interviews and personal communications. I am grateful to the individuals who kindly shard their memories and opinions with me.

CHAPTER ONE: THE BEGINNING

Dougan, Michael. *Arkansas Odyssey: The Saga of Arkansas From Prehistoric Times to Present.* Rose Publishing Co. 1994, p.82

Arkansas Constitution of 1836, Article VI

Arkansas Constitution of 1836, Amendment of November 17, 1848.

Arkansas Constitution of 1836, Amendment of November 24, 1848

The Goodspeed Histories of Sebastian County, Arkansas. Woodward and Stinson Printing Co. 1977, pp.696-722.

Wilkinson, Means. *Greenwood, Sebastian County, Arkansas, 110 Years a County Seat.* Farmers Bank of Greenwood, 1961.

Hempstead, Fay. *A Pictorial History of Arkansas From the Earliest Times to the Year 1890.* N. D. Thompson Publishing Co., 1890. p.1037.

Shropshire vs. State, 12 Ark. 190 (1851).

Felix Batson letter, February 12, 1854, to his wife; courtesy Liz Powers

Rogers vs. Sebastian County, 21 Ark. 440 (1860)

Tucker vs. Bond, 23 Ark. 268 (1862)

Omey vs. State, 23 Ark. 281 (1861)

CHAPTER TWO: DIVISION, DESTRUCTION AND REBIRTH

Stafford, L. Scott. "The Arkansas Supreme Court and the Civil War." *Journal of Southern Legal History* vol.vii, numbers 1 & 2, pp. 46-47.

Clark County Past and Present, p. 731, Taylor Publishing Co., 1992.

Pollan, Carolyn. "Fort Smith Under Union Military Rule." *The Journal of the Fort Smith Historical Society*, vol.6, no.1(April 1982), p.7.

CHAPTER THREE: TOWARD A NEW STATE

Williams, T. Harry. *The Life History of the United States*, vol. 6. Time Inc. 1974. pp.110-111.

Dougan, *Arkansas Odyssey*, p.239.

Batson letter, March 24, 1867, appendix

Harper v. State, 25 Ark. 83 (1867)

Arkansas Gazette, May 7, 1867

Reynolds, J.H. and Thomas, David. *History of the University of Arkansas* University of Arkansas, 1910.

Herndon, Dallas. *Centennial History of Arkansas*. Clarke Publishing Co.,1936. pp. 302, 553, 668, 997.

King v. Carnall, 26 Ark. 36, (1870).

Bailey, Thomas and Kennedy, David. *The American Pageant, A History of the Republic*, 10th edition. D.C. Heath and Company, 1994. p. 497.

Batson letter, March 29, 1867, *Clark County Past and Present*. Taylor Publishing Co., 1992.

Kanaga, Tillie and Wallace, W.F. *History of Napa County, comprising an account of its topography, geology and early settlements*. Enquirer Printing, 1901.

The New Era, Jan. 9. 1869.

Arkansas Gazette, Jan. 26, 1869.

The New Era, Jan. 26, 1871.

Patterson v. Temple, 27 Ark. 202 (1871).

The Goodspeed Histories of Sebastian County, Arkansas, p.700.

The New Era, April 7, 1871.

The New Era, Sept. 8, 1871.

The New Era, Sept.- Oct. 187

Fort Smith Herald, Jan. 20, 1874

The Arkansas Historical Quarterly, vol. 25 ,p.236; vol. 8, p. 75; vol. 30,p.331; vol.6,p.430; vol. 31,pp. 156-153.

CHAPTER FOUR: RETURN OF THE DEMOCRATS

Arkansas Constitution of 1874, Article 7, section 1.

Arkansas Constitution of 1874, Article 18.

Fort Smith Herald, January 13, 1875.

Hempstead, *A Pictorial History of Arkansas*, p. 1041

Barlow vs. Lowder, 35 Ark. 492 (May 1880).

Fort Smith Herald, November 6, 1875.

Hempstead, *Historical Review of Arkansas*, p.463

Hicks vs. Brown, 38 Ark. 469 (May 1882).

The Fort Smith New Era, March 2, 1881.

Arkansas Gazette, August 4, 1881.

The Fort Smith New Era, March 1, 1883.

The Arkansas Gazette, June 20, 1883.

The Goodspeed Biographical and Historical Memoirs of Northwest Arkansas. Goodspeed Publishing Co., 1889.

Author interview with Fadjo Cravens.

State of Arkansas vs. Parker, 39 Ark. 174 (1882).

Griffith & Another vs. Sebastian County, 49 Ark. 24, 3 S.W. 886 (1887).

The New Era, October 2, 1884.

The Fort Smith Elevator, July 30, 1886.

CHAPTER FIVE: A NATIVE TAKES OVER

Whayne, Jeanne, DeBlack, Thomas, Sabo, George and Arnold, Morris. *Arkansas, a Narrative History*. University of Arkansas Press, 2002.

The Fort Smith Elevator, November 26, 1886.

Little, Freed. "John Sebastian Little, The Great Commoner.", *Fort Smith Historical Journal*. v.21, No. 2, (1997). Pp.2-8.

Echols vs. Tate, 53 Ark. 12, 13 S.W. 253 (1890).

The Goodspeed Histories of Sebastian County.

The Fort Smith Elevator, January 22, 1888.

Acts of Arkansas, Act 31 of 1889.

The Fort Smith Elevator, December 26, 1890.

Railway Company vs. State, 55 Ark. 200 (1891).

Goodspeed, supra, p. 1380.

Priest, Sharon. *Historical Report of the Secretary of State*. 199).

Wallace vs. Bernheim, 63 Ark. 108 (1896).

Goodspeed, supra, p. 1361-62; Hempstead, H*istorical Review of Arkansas*, vol. 2 p. 889.

The Southwest American, June 3, 1913.

Kansas & Texas Coal Co. vs. Gabsky, 70 Ark. 434, 66 S.W. 915 (1902).

CHAPTER SIX: A NEW CENTURY AND A NEW COURT

Act 166 of 1903, *Acts of Arkansas*

Herndon, *A Centennial History of Arkansas*, vol. 2, p. 273,-4

Pace, B.F. *Bench and Bar of Arkansas*, 1935

Southern Crawford Road Improvement District vs. Brown, 156 Ark. 267, 245 S.W. 821 (1922).

Lyric Theater vs. State, 98 Ark. 437, 136 S.W. 174 (1911).

Information provided by Powell Woods, grandson of Judge Hon.

Blair, Diane, and Barth, Jay. *Arkansas Politics and Government*, 2d Edition. University of Nebraska Press, 2005. p.p. 281-282.

The Southwest American, various issues, 1910-1916.

Jennings vs. Fort Smith District of Sebastian Co., 115 Ark. 130, 171 S.W. 920 (1914)

The Greenwood Democrat, March 26, 1997.

Aetna Life Insurance Co. vs. Little, 146 Ark. 70, 225 S.W. 298, (1920).

Conversations with Franklin Wilder.

Little, Freed. "The Governor John S. Little Family." *The Journal of the Fort Smith Historical Society*, vol. 22, no. 1, p. 26 (April 1998).

Bourland vs. Baker, 141 Ark. 280, 216 S.W. 707, (1919).

The Southwest American, August 17, 1913.; Herndon, op. cit. vol. 2, p. 914.

Information provided by Michael Gilleland, St. Paul, MN. As forwarded to the author by David Dunagin.

Kujawa, Stan. *Garrison Avenue, Fort Smith, Arkansas; Arkansas Memories and Photographs*. Privately published, 2001. pp. 27,122.

Fenolio vs. Sebastian Bridge District, 133 Ark. 380, 200 S.W. 501, (1917).

Information provided by Cindy Joyce-Griggs; other materials derived from funeral Records, Fentress Funeral Home.

The Southwest American, February 9, 1955.

Aetna Life vs. Little, supra.

Information provided by Franklin Wilder.

70. Little, Freed. "John Eaton Tatum." *The Key, South Sebastian County Historical Journal*. vol. 31, p.55.

Bevers vs. Bradstreet, 170 Ark. 650, 280 S.W. 667 (1926).

Arkansas Constitution of 1874, Amendment Nine.

Act 205 of 1925, *Acts of Arkansas*.

Article written by Judge Wood, provided by his son J.S. Wood, Jr.

Memorial Service, Sebastian Co. Bar Association, September 10, 1976.

Ballentine vs. State, 198 Ark. 1037, 132 S.W.2 384 (1939).

Pace, *Bench and Bar of Arkansas*.

Pruitt vs. Sebastian County Coal and Mining, 215 Ark. 673, 222 S.W.2 50, (1949).

CHAPTER SEVEN: A NEW COURTHOUSE AND A NEW ERA

Amendment 7; Arkansas Constitution of 1874

Jewett vs. Norris, 170 Ark. 71. 278 S.W. 652 (1926)

The Southwest American, various issues, 1936-1937

Amendment 11; Constitution of Arkansas, 1874

Information supplied by Cynthia Wolfe

Rush vs. State, 238 Ark. 149, 379 S.W.2 29 (1964)

Rush vs. State, 239 Ark. 149, 395 S.W.2 3 (1965)

Information supplied by Bernice Wilder

Southwest Times Record, September 5, 1995

Jones vs. OZ-ARK-VAL Poultry Co., 228 Ark.76, 306 S.W.2 111 (1957)

Southwest American, various issues, 1960-1963

Fentress Funeral Home Records

Interview with Bill Wiggins, Judge Bland's law clerk, October 12, 2000.

Ark. Highway Commission vs. Scott, 288 Ark. 883, 385 S.W.2 636 (1966)

Memorial Service, Sebastian Co. Bar Association, May 23,1980 given by Judge H. Zed Gant.

Plastics Research and Development vs. Bill Norman et. al. 243 Ark. 780, 422 S.W.2 121 (1967).

Acts of Arkansas; Act 304 of 1967

Information provided by Judge Warren O. Kimbrough

Korolko vs. Korolko, 33 Ark App. 194, 803 S.W.2 448 (1991)

CHAPTER EIGHT: THE WINDS OF CHANGE

The Southwest American, April, 20, 1968.

County Court Record Book "R"-p.p. 106-376.

Blueprints for Greenwood Courthouse, Nelson, Laser & Cheyne.

Supra, county record books.

The Southwest American, March, 14, 1970.

Act 34 of 1973, *Acts of Arkansas*

Information supplied by Judge Zed & Imogene Gant along with personal observations by the author.

James R. McWilliams & Dottie Ann Kimes vs. Marjorie Tinder, executrix of the Estate of Velpoe Petty McWilliams, deceased, 256 Ark. 994, 511 S.W.2 480 (1974).

Information provided by Judge Bernice Kizer and her daughter Karolyn Bond, along with personal observations by the author.

Deborah Faye Rapp vs. Judge Bernice Kizer, 260 Ark. 656, 543 S.W.2 458 (1976).

Information supplied by Judge John Holland and several acquaintances along with personal observations by the author.

H. Clay Robinson vs. Greenwood District, Sebastian County Quorum Court, 258 Ark. 798, 528 S.W.2 930 (1975).

Act 432 of 1977, *Acts of Arkansas*

Amendment 58, Arkansas Constitution of 1874

Information supplied by Judge David and Norma Partain along with personal observations by the author.

Alvin Lee Myers vs. State of Arkansas, 271 Ark. 886, 611 S.W.2 514 (1981)

Morgan vs. State, 273 Ark. 252, 618 S.W.2 161 (1981)

Act 38 of the 1st Extraordinary Session of 1981, *Acts of Arkansas*

Information supplied by Judge Bob Boyer.

Marion Albert Pruitt vs. State, 282 Ark.304, 669 S.W.2 186 (1984)

Information supplied by Judge Don Langston along with personal observations by the author.

Little Rock Newspapers, Inc. vs. J. Michael Fitzhugh, 330 Ark. 561, 954 S.W.2 914 (1994)

Information supplied by Judge Floyd "Pete" Rogers

Mikel vs. Hubbard & Hubbard Marine Services, 317 Ark. 125, 876 S.W.2 558 (1994)

Information provided by Judge Harry Foltz

Campbell vs. Campbell, 336 Ark. 379, 985 S.W.2 724 (1999)

Walker vs. Arkansas Dept. of Human Services, 291 Ark. 43, 722 S.W.2 558 (1987)

Act 14 of 1987, *Acts of Arkansas*

Act 949 of 1989, *Acts of Arkansas*

Information supplied by Sherri Karber

Information supplied by Judge Mark Hewett

Donna Snow Burks and Larry Burks vs. Arkansas Dept. of Human Services, 76 Ark. App. 71, 61 S.W.3 184 (2001)

Act 97 of 1991, *Acts of Arkansas*

Sebastian County Court Order Book

Information supplied by John Van Winkle

Sonja Howard & Morgan Cole vs. City of Fort Smith, Ark., 311 Ark. 525, 845 S.W.2 497 (1993)

Obituary, *Arkansas Democrat-Gazette*, Sandra Cox, July 3, 1995, and eulogy at Sebastian County Bar Assn. by Eddie Christian.

Arkansas Dept. of Human Services vs. Robert Hardy, 316 Ark. 119, 871 S.W.2 352 (1994)

Linder vs. Linder, 348 Ark. 322, 72 S.W.3 841 (2002)

CHAPTER NINE: NEW FACES, A NEW DISTRICT AND A NEW JUDICIAL ARTICLE

Act 900 of 1995, *Acts of Arkansas*

Information provided by Judge Norman Wilkinson

Linda Chapman vs. Elnora Bevilacqua et al. 344 Ark. 262, 42 S.W.3 378 (2001)

Information provided by Judge Jim Marschewski

Oscar Stilley vs. Margaret James, et al. 345 Ark. 362, 48 S.W.3 378 (2001)

Information provided by Judge Mike Fitzhugh

James Richard Halford vs. State of Arkansas, 342 Ark. 80, 27 S.W.3 521 (2000)

Information supplied by Judge Stephen Tabor

Information supplied by Judge James Cox

Amendment 80, Arkansas Constitution of 1874

Southwest Times Record, June 1, 2005; June 22 2005; March 18 2006.

Interview with Judge Annie Hendricks

Erin M. Fischer vs. Damon Smith, 2012 Ark. App. 342,(May 16, 2012)

Doe's website

Interview with Judge Leigh Zuerker

Interview with Judge Shannon Blatt

Conclusion

Southwest Times Record, October 24, 1984

Scaramuzza vs. McLeod, Commissioner of Revenues, 207 Ark. 855

ILLUSTRATIONS

1. Map, Dec. 29, 1848. 4th Judicial Circuit..3
2. Map, Act of Jan. 10, 1851..5
3. Alfred B. Greenwood (1851-1852)...7
4. Felix I. Batson (1853-1858)..12
5. John M. Wilson (1859-1860)...14
6. Joseph J. Green (1860-1861)...16
7. Map, Act 107 of 1861..17
8. Sebastian County and Surrounding Area..18
9. Elhanan J. Searle (1867-1868)..30
10. Map, Act 7 of 1868..35
11. Elijah D. Ham (1868-1874)..37
12. Map, Act 53 of 1873..53
13. Benton Brown (1874)...54
14. Map, Ark Constitution of 1874..56
15. William Walker Mansfield (1874-1876)...61
16. Map, Act 41 of 1877..63
17. John H. Rogers (1877-1882)..65
18. Greenwood Courthouse, Dedicated 1882..67
19. Robert Beall Rutherford (1883-1886)..70
20. John Sebastian Little (1887-1890)...74
21. Ft. Smith Courthouse, Dedicated 1887..78
22. Map, Act 31 of 1889..80
23. T.C. Humphrey (1890)...82
24. Edgar E. Bryant (1890-1898)...84
25. Styles T. Rowe (1899-1906)...88

26. Map, Act 166 of 1903..92
27. James V. Bourland (1903-1912 & 1919-1930).............................94
28. Daniel Hon (1907-1914)...99
29. Painting, Down by the Courthouse. John Bell...........................110
30. Photo (of same courthouse)...110
31. Newspaper ad "Some Court House History"............................116
32. Greenwood District Courthouse, Dedicated 1916....................117
33. The 1916 Greenwood Courthouse Under Construction...........117
34. Paul Little (1915-1919)...120
35. William A. Falconer (1913-1918)...124
36. John Brizzolara (1919-1922)...127
37. John Eaton Tatum (1923-1926)..130
38. Map, Act 18 of 1928...133
39. John Sam Wood (1927-1954)...134
40. C.M. Wofford (1931-1954)..138
41. "Time's March Overtakes Old Sebastian Landmark"...............146
42. Fort Smith Courthouse, Dedicated 1937..................................149
43. Paul Wolfe (1955-1974)..151
44. Franklin Wilder (1955-1960)..155
45. Hugh M. Bland (1961-1966)..163
46. Ralph "Cotton" Robinson (1966)...166
47. Map, Act 304 of 1967...169
48. Warren O. Kimbrough (1967-1996)...171
49. Greenwood Courthouse Damaged by 1968 Tornado................177
50. Greenwood Courthouse, Dedicated 1970.................................177
51. Horace Zed Gant (1973-1974)..179
52. Bernice Lichty Kizer (1975-1986)..183
53. John G. Holland (1975-1998)...187
54. Map, Act 432 of 1977...189
55. David O. Partain (1979-1986...191
56. Robert E. Boyer (1982)...194

57. Don Langsgton (1983-1998) 197
58. Floyd R. "Pete" Rogers (1987-1996) 201
59. Harry Albers Foltz (1987-2001) 204
60. Sherri Cunningham Karber (1988-1990) 208
61. Mark Hewett (1991-2014) 211
62. John Van Winkle (1991-1992) 214
63. Charles R. Garner (1992) 217
64. Jim D. Spears (2001-2016) 220
65. Map, Act 900 of 1995 224
66. Norman Wilkinson (2001-2007) 227
67. James R. Marschewski (1999-2006) 230
68. J. Michael Fitzhugh (1999-2020) 234
69. Stephen Merrill Tabor (2007-Present) 236
70. James Oldham Cox (2007-2020) 239
71. Rachael Ann "Annie" Powell Hendricks (2011-Present) 248
72. Leigh Zuerker (2015-Present) 252
73. Shannon L. Blatt (2017-Present) 255
74. R. Gunner Delay (2019-2020) 257
75. Dianna Hewitt Ladd (2021-Present) 260
76. Greg Magness (2021-Present) 262
77. Sebastian County Courts (2022) 264

JUDGES WHO HAVE SERVED SEBASTIAN COUNTY

1. Alfred Burton Greenwood, 1851-1853
2. Felix Batson 1853-1858
3. John M. Wilson, 1859=1860
4. Joseph J. Green, 1860-1862
5. Henry Bolling Stuart, 1862-1865 (Confederate) no photo available
6. Augustus H. Hargrove, 1864-1867 no photo available
7. Elhanan John Searle, 1867-1868
8. Elijah B. Ham, 1868-1874
9. Benton Brown, Oct. 1874
10. William Walker Mansfield, 1874-1876
11. John H. Rogers, 1877-1882
12. William Walker, 1882-1883, no photo available
13. Robert Beall Rutherford, 1883-1886
14. John Sebastian Little, 1887-1900
15. T. C. Humphrey, 1890
16. Edgar E. Bryant, 1890-1898
17. Styles T. Rowe, 1899-1906
18. James V. Bourland, (chancellor) 1903-1913 and 1917-1930
19. Daniel Hon, 1907-1914
20. Paul Little, 1915-1919
21. William A. Falconer, (chancellor) 1913-1918
22. John Brizzolara, 1919-1922
23. John Tatum, 1923-1926
24. J. Sam Wood, 1927-1954
25. C. M. Wofford, (chancellor) 1931-1954
26. Paul Wolfe, 1954-1974
27. Franklin Wilder, (chancellor) 1955-1960
28. Hugh Bland, (chancellor) 1960-1966
29. Ralph "Cotton" Robinson, (chancellor) 1966

30. Warren O. Kimbrough, (chancellor) 1967-1996

31. H. Zed Gant, (chancellor) 1973-1974

32. Bernice Lichty Kizer, (chancellor) 1975-1986

33. John G. Holland, 1975-1998

34. David O. Partain, 1979-1986

35. Robert Boyer, (circuit/chancellor) 1981-1982

36. Don Langston, (circuit/chancellor)1983-1998

37. Floyd R. "Pete" Rogers, 1987-1997

38. Harry A. Foltz, (chancellor converted to circuit by Amendment 80) 1987-2010

39. Sherri Cunningham Karber, (juvenile division) 1988-1990

40. Mark Hewett, (juvenile division) 1991-2014

41. John Van Winkle, (chancellor) 1991-1992

42. Charles R. Garner,(chancellor) 1992

43. Jim D. Spears, (chancellor converted to circuit by Amendment 80) 1993-2016

44. Norman Wilkinson, (chancellor) 1997-2007

45. James Robert Marschewski, 1999-2006

46. J. Michael Fitzhugh, 1999-2018

47. Steve Merrill Tabor, 2007-Present

48. James O. Cox, 2008-2020

49. Annie Powell Hendricks, 2011-Present

50. Leigh Tompkins Zuerker, (juvenile division) 2015-Present

51. Shannon Blatt, 2017-Present

52. R. Gunner Delay, 2019-2020

53. Greg Magness, 2021-Present

54. Dianna Hewitt Ladd, 2021-Present

About the Author

BIOGRAPHICAL SKETCH OF THE AUTHOR BY FORMER CAPITOL HISTORIAN AND CURRENT STATE HISTORIAN, DAVID WARE

A FEW WORDS ARE NEEDED IN order to properly introduce the author of this volume, retired Circuit Judge Jim Spears. He was born Jimmie Dennis Thomas on March 5, 1946, in Fayetteville, Arkansas, the son of Wilberta Ferris and Wayne Wilson Thomas. The Kings, his maternal grandmother's family, were Washington and Madison County pioneers. His great-great-great grandfather, Frederick King, immigrated to Madison County in 1837, from Lauderdale County, Alabama. His great-great grandfather, John Wesley King, was born that same year in Arkansas. John Wesley King was a soldier in the Confederate Army serving in Company I of the 16th Arkansas Volunteer Infantry. He was taken prisoner at Port Hudson, Louisiana, in 1863, and paroled. Spears's biological father was a native of Saint Paul, Arkansas and came from pioneer stock: His great-great grandfather on the paternal side served in the 1st Arkansas Infantry

Regiment on the Union side and at one time was stationed at Fort Smith during the Civil War.

When the future Judge Spears reached the age of 18 months, his mother left him in the care of his grandparents, Howell and Cora Belle Ferris while she attended nursing school in Fort Smith at Sparks Memorial Hospital. While there, she met Davis C. Spears Jr., a U.S. Navy veteran of World War II. They were married in 1950. He soon after adopted the young boy, who grew to be Judge Spears.

Jim Spears attended the Fort Smith public schools and graduated from Northside High School in 1964. During his high school years he lived with his grandmother, Cora Ferris. He then attended Fort Smith Junior College (which became a state-supported school known as Westark Junior College while he was a student; today its cognomen is U of A Fort Smith). While at the junior college, he was active in student government and was student body president in the fall of 1965. He also served as business manager of the yearbook. He continued his education at Arkansas Polytechnic (today's Arkansas Tech) in Russellville, graduating in 1968 with a degree in History and Political Science.

After graduation, Spears was employed by the Westark Area Council of the Boy Scouts of America as a district executive, serving four counties in the Russellville area. In the winter of 1969, however, he made a fateful choice: he decided on the law as a profession and career. He resigned from the Scouts position and took up a one-semester teaching position in Fort Smith with the Bost School for Limited Children. The Bost School, founded by a Fort Smith pediatrician, had been started in 1959 in a church basement with the simple goal of assisting children with special needs not met in the public school system. Spears admits that he had no qualifications to teach learning-disabled children but, he says today, he "learned on the job." He entered the University of Arkansas School of Law in the fall of 1970. While in law school he was once again active in student government and served as president of the Student Bar Association in 1972-73.

Upon graduation and admittance to the bar he took employment as an associate in the firm of Sam Sexton and Associates in Fort Smith. He remained in that position until the summer of 1978. In 1974, he ran unsuccessfully for a seat in the Arkansas House of Representatives and in 1978 he ran, again unsuccessfully, for prosecuting attorney for the 12th Judicial District.

After establishing his own law practice he took over the office of Sebastian Legal Aid with attorney Harry Foltz, who was setting up the federally funded Western Arkansas Legal Services office. He remained in his private practice until late 1980, when he was employed by the federal government as an Assistant

Federal Public Defender. This was a special office, created to serve the Cuban refugees being detained at Fort Chaffee during the Cuban Relocation Program; the position terminated in February 1982. He once again returned to private practice until May of 1983, when he was named as an Administrative Law Judge for the Arkansas Workers Compensation Commission. He held this position until January 1 1993 when he was sworn in as chancery judge, Division III, 12th Judicial District.

Judge Spears's time on the bench has been punctuated with drama and crisis, both external and personal. In March 1994, a little more than a year after taking his seat on the chancery bench, he was diagnosed with lymphoma and underwent a course of chemotherapy and radiation treatments. In April 1996, as related in Chapter 8, a cyclone wrought havoc on Fort Smith. Not only were Judge Spears' courtroom and office destroyed, but the twister hit close to home: his sister's house in Van Buren was demolished and she was thrown two houses away, into a neighbor's back yard. Her left arm was torn off, left dangling by some skin. Happily, thanks to heroic medical work and deft surgeries by Dr. Robert Bebout and others, her arm was reattached; after a long convalescence, she regained almost total use of her arm and hand. A few days later, while conducting a trial in the chancery courtroom of the courthouse, Judge Spears was alerted yet another disaster: the Eads Furniture Store, a four-story building, and a fort Smith landmark since the late 1800s, was burning out of control. This store was about two blocks from the courthouse on Garrison Avenue. The downtown was perfect pandemonium, in sore need of cool heads. Judge Spears rose to the occasion, directing traffic at the intersection of 6th Street and Rogers Avenue in front of the courthouse (presumably not in his judge's robe, but I haven't had the heart to ask him) to prevent emergency vehicles and civilians from colliding in their haste! The *annus clades* was not over, however: In October, Spears's cancer recurred, and he underwent a stem cell transplant at the University of Nebraska Medical Center in Omaha, Nebraska. He has been in remission since. Jim Spears was married to Dixie Bean, a native of Rogers, on August 2, 1975. They have two children: John David who was born February 21,1977 and Julia Diane, who was born October 13,1981. John is a graduate of the University of Arkansas and holds a master's degree from the Fletcher School of Law and Diplomacy of Tufts University. He was an employee of the United States Department of State for a time and graduated as a member of the inaugural class of the Clinton School of Public Service of the University of Arkansas in December 2006. He presently is serving as a foreign service officer with USAID in Amman, Jordan. Julie is an honors graduate of the University of Arkansas, Eleanor Mann School of Nursing and UAMS with a masters degree and is an Advanced Practice Nurse in pediatrics and practices in Bentonville. Judge Spears has four grandchildren; Nathan Adams, Colin Adams, Michael Spears and Laura Spears.

Jim Spears has been active in many civic activities. He served for many years on the Fort Smith Convention Center Commission. He is the recipient of the District Award of Merit from the Boy Scouts as well as The Silver Beaver Award, the highest award a "Scouter" can be awarded at the council level. He is a graduate of Leadership Fort Smith and was awarded the Jack White Community Leadership Award by the Leadership Fort Smith Alumni Association in 1998. He is also the recipient of the Grady Secrest Humanitarian Award presented by the Fort Smith Jaycees in 1996. He was named the Lawyer/Citizen of the year in 2004 by the Arkansas Bar Association and Arkansas Bar Foundation and was presented the Community Service award by the Arkansas Judicial Council in 2004 as well. He is a past president of the Fort Smith Rotary Club and a Paul Harris Fellow of Rotary International. He is also a James E. West Fellow of The Boy Scouts of America. Finally, or nearly so, he has long been a member and board member of the Arkansas Supreme Court Historical Society, in which context I made his acquaintance, discovering him to be a good conversationalist, a thoughtful jurist and someone who can tell a wicked good story.

About the Editor

David Ware has served as state historian and director of the Arkansas State Archives since January 2021. Before this, he spent over 18 years as historian of the Arkansas State Capitol. He is a native of Washington DC, grew up in Nebraska and earned his Ph.D. in American history from Arizona State University. His career has included both academic and public history, as well as busking, rough carpentry, and an extended stretch in the oil patch. He lives in Little Rock with his librarian-turned-archivist-turned-librarian wife, daughter (when she is home from college) and their elderly Airedale in a small house filled with model trains, musical instruments, old cameras, clocks and many books.

www.ingramcontent.com/pod-product-compliance
Lightning Source LLC
Chambersburg PA
CBHW041238240426
43661CB00067B/2909